Manhood Lost

PUBLISHING FOR THE WORLD
125 Years

THE JOHNS HOPKINS UNIVERSITY PRESS

New Studies in American Intellectual and Cultural History
Dorothy Ross, series editor

Manhood Lost

Fallen Drunkards and Redeeming Women
in the Nineteenth-Century United States

Elaine Frantz Parsons

The Johns Hopkins University Press
Baltimore and London

© 2003 The Johns Hopkins University Press
All rights reserved. Published 2003
Printed in the United States of America on acid-free paper
9 8 7 6 5 4 3 2 1

The Johns Hopkins University Press
2715 North Charles Street
Baltimore, Maryland 21218-4363
www.press.jhu.edu

Library of Congress Cataloging-in-Publication Data
Parsons, Elaine Frantz, 1970–
    Manhood lost : fallen drunkards and redeeming women in the
nineteenth-century United States / Elaine Frantz Parsons.
        p. cm. — (New studies in American intellectual and cultural
history)
    Includes bibliographical references and index.
    ISBN 0-8018-7166-2 (hardcover : alk. paper)
    1. Alcoholism—United States—History—19th century.
2. Drinking of alcoholic beverages—United States—History—19th
century. 3. Sex role—United States—History—19th century.
I. Title. II. Series.
    HV5292 .P37 2003
    363.4′1′097309034—dc21   2002007590

A catalog record for this book is available from the British Library.

To Jotham

Contents

Acknowledgments

The eight years that I have spent working on this book have been enormously fulfilling, thanks largely to the many people who have given me advice and support throughout the research and writing process. In all stages, I have benefited from the help, generosity, and insight of a wonderful group of colleagues, friends, and family.

First, it is fitting to thank my thesis advisor, Ronald Walters. The many students who have had the opportunity to work with Ron well know his excellence as teacher, mentor, and editor. When I came to study with him I had little training in history and little confidence in my ideas. I expected Ron to paternalistically guide and evaluate my training and work. In this respect, Ron refused to give me what I wanted and instead gave me what I needed, insisting that I go off in my own directions and believe in my own work. He has always been scrupulously careful to leave me space to develop my own intellectual agendas. At the same time, I have become increasingly aware of how formative his intellectual influence has been on my work. While helping me through the thesis process, he has combined a sometimes-heroic level of patience with an equal amount of encouragement.

I also have been extremely fortunate in the advice and support of other faculty members. Dorothy Ross, my second reader and one of the editors of this series, has been an ideal counterpart to Ron Walters, inspiring me in new intellectual directions and giving me much-needed and always solid criticism. Joanne Brown, John Higham, Walter Michaels, and J. G. A. Pocock have read parts of my work at various stages and have been influential in how I ultimately conceived my project. Tom Pegram, at Loyola, and Tom Herzing and Mark Kleinman, at the University of Wisconsin–Oshkosh, were also extremely generous in reading and commenting on parts of the work in progress. Finally, when I was an undergraduate at the University of Virginia, Charles McCurdy, William Lee Miller, and Peter Onuf inspired me, through their excellence in and dedication to undergraduate teaching, to become a historian in the first place.

My fellow graduate students at the Johns Hopkins University also deserve a huge thanks. Nancy Berlage, Lawrence Charap, Kelly Emerson, Mara Keire, and Lara Kriegel read chapters in progress and gave extremely valuable advice. In addition to this formal help, my work benefited greatly from many informal conversations over coffee throughout my graduate student years. I have had the opportunity to give parts of the dissertation-in-progress at forums outside of Johns Hopkins. I have benefited particularly from responses to presentations at the University of Delaware Department of History brown bag lunch, the New England American Studies Association "Fear Itself" conference, and the School of Criticism and Theory.

My archival research would not have been possible without generous travel grants from the University of Wisconsin–Oshkosh Faculty Development Program, the Littleton-Griswold fund of the American History Association, and the Iowa State Historical Society. A number of friends and relatives were good enough to take me into their homes while I was visiting archives and libraries and attending conferences. In particular, I would like to thank Winnie and Jay Ahn, Susan Cramer, Carl and Kathryn Frantz, Carolyn Frantz, Evelyn Holler, Susan and Josh Allen Nan, Charles and Marjorie Parsons, Judy and Ed Pilewski, and Peggy, Mark, Eric, Allyn, Tim, Emily, Anna, Kristin, and Rebeckah Weddle.

I have had the pleasure to work with a number of excellent reference professionals who have enriched my work greatly. I would particularly like to thank Tom Izbiki at Johns Hopkins, who, in addition to his friendship, has helped me in innumerable ways; Erin Czech in Interlibrary Loan at the University of Wisconsin–Oshkosh and Zack Jaffee at the Interlibrary Loans Department of Johns Hopkins; the Johns Hopkins Special Collections Department; Nancy Witman at the Michigan Law Library; M. Cody Wright, James Cohlmeyer, and Charles Cali at the Illinois State Archives; Jill Trueblood at the Illinois Supreme Court; Linda Robertson, Carol Emerson, and Timothy Gatti at the Iowa State Law Library; and Ed Frank in the University of Memphis Special Collections Department.

I would like to thank my colleagues at the University of Wisconsin–Oshkosh who have helped me to transition from graduate student to faculty member. The real commitment to supporting scholarship on the part of Lane Earns, the history department chair, and Michael Zimmerman, the Dean of Letters and Sciences, along with the support of my colleagues Franca Barricelli, Nikos Chrissidis, Don Haynes, Stephen Kercher, Michelle Mouton, Andrew Jackson O'Shaughnessey, Kim Rivers, and Tom Rowland made it possible for me to transform the dissertation into a book in a relatively short period.

I have very much enjoyed working with the Johns Hopkins University Press. Both Robert J. Brugger and Melody Herr have been helpful throughout the process, combining supportiveness with just the right amount of deadline pressure. Bob Brugger's advice to authors should be standard reading for anyone hoping to transform their dissertation into a book. It was also wonderful to have the opportunity to continue to work with Dorothy Ross, who has helped me to understand the broader implications of my own arguments.

I would also like to thank the *Annals of Iowa*, the *Journal of Social History*, and Purdue University Press for permission to include previously published material. Parts of Chapter 1 were published in a previous version in "Slaves to the Bottle: Smith's Civil Damage Liquor Law," *Annals of Iowa* 59, no. 4 (2000): 347–73. Parts of Chapter 2 were published in "Risky Business: The Uncertain Boundaries of Manhood in the Midwestern Saloon," *Journal of Social History* (winter 2001): 283–307. Parts of Chapter 4 appeared in an earlier version in "Fear of Seduction: The Allure of Alcohol in Late Nineteenth Century Temperance Thought," in Nancy Schultz, ed., *Fear Itself: Enemies Real and Imagined in American Culture* (Purdue University Press, 1999), 203–23.

I have had a great deal of support, both intellectual and emotional, from my family. My parents, Janet and Carl Frantz, and my sister, Carolyn Frantz, were always more than willing to listen to me talk through the difficulties I was having with the research, and always knew just what questions to ask and observations to make. They well know how many of my ideas emerge from conversations with them on the phone or around the dinner table. They also managed to find a way to encourage me to finish writing without putting on too much pressure.

My husband, Jotham Parsons, has assisted me with this book in every way. He was my main source of intellectual critique and inspiration. He was an ideal audience when I wanted to "talk things out," and he read through every word, often more than once. He cheerfully offered technical assistance with computer glitches, printing problems, and all sorts of other frustrating things that arise in the process of writing a book. He financially supported me through my last two years as a graduate student. Most important, though, he is always there for me emotionally, reminding me that there is more to life than the history of the temperance movement. I could not even begin to conceive of how I could have written this book without him.

Manhood Lost

Introduction

In 1899, by most accounts, Andrew Faivre was not a very impressive specimen of manhood (fig. 1). It had been different in 1878. Then, at the age of twenty-five, he had married a twenty-one-year-old woman named Louise, whom he had known most of his life, probably since his parents migrated with him from New York to Ohio in his childhood. Louise and Andrew pushed farther west after they married, making their way from Ohio to Iowa.[1] At the time of their marriage, according to Louise, she had no knowledge that Andrew was a drinker. Twenty years and four children later, however, Louise was all too aware of her husband's drinking habit.[2] The meager wages he earned as a low-skilled tailor in Sioux City were not sufficient to support their family. Louise took in washing, and their oldest daughter "worked out," presumably as a domestic servant.[3] As Andrew described it, he occasionally went on drinking bouts, during which he was incapacitated for up to a week: "I felt pretty mean and wasn't in any condition to work, and I lay around home." Not surprisingly, Louise and their working daughter were concerned about his drinking and financial irresponsibility. According to Andrew's account, the two tried to keep the family's financial information, and the little money they had, away from him. Whenever he asked his

Fig. 1. Andrew Faivre displays his frostbitten hands for his wife's civil damage suit. (Photo courtesy of Iowa State Law Library)

daughter how much she was earning, "she would give me a bluff."[4] At least once Louise visited Andrew's favorite saloons and warned the saloonkeepers, to no avail, not to sell her husband any more alcohol. On February 6, 1899, Andrew "patched together" with four of his fellow tailors to buy a bucket of beer to drink in the shop.[5] After drinking this beer, he headed to various local saloons with a friend to drink into the evening. It was a very cold night—ten below zero—and when a policeman noticed Faivre and his friend staggering about the streets, he warned them to go home.[6] Faivre's friend seems to have done so. Faivre, however, passed out and spent the night outdoors. When he was discovered the next morning, he had frostbite in his fingers and toes; a doctor amputated most of his hands and parts of his feet.

Even before the accident, Andrew Faivre, in the eyes of many of his contemporaries, had been lacking as a man. Tailors as a whole were little respected, and Faivre, with neither his own shop nor the skills to do more complicated and better-paying tailoring tasks, was on the bottom rungs of that trade. He clearly had little authority in his own home, even over his children. He had a well-deserved reputation for being a drunkard. The photograph of him included here was taken as part of a lawsuit brought by his wife against the saloonkeepers who had sold him alcohol the night he was injured. The saloonkeepers' lawyers condemned the photograph as a "parade of mutilation and suffering . . . taken in aggravated positions, making him look like a dumb supplicant for alms, posing at some street corner soliciting the charity and pity of the people."[7] The pitifulness of the figure Faivre cut makes him emblematic of a central issue in nineteenth-century culture.

Andrew Faivre perfectly represented the two aspects that temperance reformers believed to be the essence of the national drinking problem. Because of drink, he was unable to fulfill his gendered role as head of household, and he was rendered utterly helpless, seemingly unable to take responsibility for his actions. His failure forced the women of his household to assume culturally inappropriate roles, both as heads of household and as litigants in a suit against his saloonkeepers. When nineteenth-century Americans talked about the drink crisis, they were thinking of people like Andrew and Louise Faivre, and asking how the couple could have ended up where they did. Surely, the younger, hopeful Andrew would never have chosen to follow the drunkard's path. Somehow, many speculated, the alcohol Faivre drank must have fundamentally transformed him, his values, and his desires.

This book is about the power of a story. The story of hopeful young men like Andrew rendered helpless through drink led many nineteenth-century Americans to ask themselves how such falls occurred and how they could be prevented. Although stories similar to Andrew Faivre's had certainly been told in many other times and places, nineteenth-century Americans told, wrote, sung, drew, and performed them so often that they have to be considered one of the century's most frequently told narratives. This "drunkard narrative" came to prominence in the 1830s and remained extremely popular throughout the rest of the century. It became the central pillar of the temperance movement—arguably the largest social movement of the nineteenth-century United States. It was so ubiquitous that even those who did not actively participate in any of the intense public debates about alcohol policy were familiar with it. It was widespread enough that pamphleteers and the popular press felt comfortable alluding to it and parodying it in their pages without explanation.[8] Americans would not stop telling one another stories of the drunkard's decline. Recovered drunkards traveled from town to town giving their histories; drunkards' wives told juries, temperance reformers, neighbors, and officials of their plights; reformers repeated the stories of drinkers they knew or knew of; and temperance novelists, short-story writers, poets, songwriters, and playwrights presented fictional accounts of drunkards' lives. The drunkard narrative had very real consequences. Americans from all walks of life contributed to a series of slow but massive cultural changes that would culminate, above all, in a generally weakened belief in individual volition and in the fuller participation of women in public life.

The ways nineteenth-century Americans told the story of the drunkard's decline and the ways they attempted to counter it shed light on how they understood two of the most fraught intellectual problems of their time. On the one hand, Americans harbored serious concerns that individuals were so influenced and shaped by their environment that they had little control over their own character and actions. On the other hand, the nineteenth century saw conflict over women's (and, by extension, men's) proper roles within the family and within the public sphere. At first glance, these two problems seem to have little to do with one another. Drink debaters, largely through their tellings of the drunkard narrative, came to think of them as intimately intertwined. That is, they came to believe that the limited entry of women into the public sphere provided a way to reimagine how individual men and women could exercise their free will.

One pleasure and challenge in writing about the temperance movement and drinking culture in the United States is reckoning with the wealth of existing secondary literature on the subject. The 1970s saw an explosion of two largely separate bodies of scholarship: one on the temperance movement and the other on the working-class saloon. Since then, historians have considered alcohol's relationships to a vast array of topics including, but not limited to, ethnicity, class, race, religion, region, education, censorship, capitalism, legal culture, science, imperialism, and the family romance. Another considerable group of historians, rhetoricians, and literary critics has focused specifically on the discursive significance of the debate over alcohol. The study of representations of alcohol in literature alone has inspired monographs, a recent collection of essays, and even its own journal, *Dionysos*. Similarly, there is a substantial and growing literature on temperance forensics. Some of this scholarship has examined specific themes in the discourse. Harry Levine and Mariana Valverde, for instance, have written on the theme of volition in drink discourse.[9] Recently, some scholars have written about stories of the drunkard's decline. Although most of these studies have looked at the use of these narratives in twentieth-century Alcoholics Anonymous meetings, John Crowley has just published a collection of nineteenth-century drunkard narratives.[10]

There are good reasons that so many scholars have given so much attention to the debate over alcohol. Nineteenth-century Americans put an amazing amount of thought and energy into figuring out whether alcohol was a problem and if it was, what sort of problem it was and what to do about solving it. Scholars have been able to consider the relationship between alcohol and a seemingly endless number of other topics precisely because the alcohol debate was so strikingly pervasive in nineteenth-century culture. The social history of alcohol and temperance has already been so well and thoroughly analyzed that it is possible to jump off from the existing literature to explore how particular aspects of the debate functioned in the broader culture. Unlike most scholarship that deals with alcohol, this book is not chiefly concerned with explaining either drinking culture or the identities, tactics, successes, or failures of temperance reformers. Rather, it uses the drink debate as a means to the end of a richer understanding of how its largely rural and middle- and working-class participants thought about gender roles and the relationship of individuals to their environment. The final focus of the book is not on what reformers decided to do about the alcohol problem or how saloon supporters determined to thwart them, but rather on how drink debaters defined and attempted to solve these more abstract problems.

The pervasiveness and scope of the drunkard narrative are central to my argument. All Americans, not just those who particularly cared about temperance reform, knew the standard generic elements of the story of the drunkard's decline. As some of the vignettes that begin my chapters show, even those who disagreed vehemently with goals of the temperance movement were intimately familiar with the narrative that was its cornerstone and tried to refute it or even to adapt it to their own purposes. Yet even in the face of these oppositions and appropriations, the way nineteenth-century Americans told the drunkard narrative remained strikingly consistent across regions, decades, genres, and, to some extent, socioeconomic classes.

A good part of the drink discourse's success at crossing regional lines was doubtless due to the national circulation of temperance propaganda and the early growth of national temperance organizations. The temperance movement came to maturity in the 1840s and 1850s, as railroads and canals, telegraphs, new printing technology, and other changes in communication and transportation were integrating many aspects of the nation's cultural life. Of course, there was a serious breech in the intellectual cultures of the North and South in the years leading to the war. Recent scholarship, however, has argued persuasively that even though temperance was more popular in the North, the considerable southern movement that did exist largely shared values, ideas, and language with its northern counterpart.[11] The Washingtonians were, after all, organized in Baltimore, and groups like the Sons of Temperance and the Good Templars spread through much of the South in the 1840s and 1850s. As one Georgian temperance advocate indignantly insisted in 1887, the movement in the South was not "but lately transplanted to her borders—a kind of reconstruction fungus."[12] There had been serious statewide movements for prohibition in the early 1850s in some southern states, such as Tennessee. Even though antebellum southern movements had not had the same legislative successes as some of their northern counterparts, later southern temperance activists liked to insist that they had been making great progress until sectional conflict and war intervened.[13] There are some meaningful differences between the tendencies of northern and southern temperance sources, especially after the war. Southern reformers generally were more resistant than their northern neighbors to the idea that drinkers lacked responsibility for their own fates, and the question of whether the state should interfere in what many saw as a matter of private morality was more fraught in the South than in the North. In general, however, it is the similarities rather than the differences between the movement in the North and South that is noteworthy.

The drunkard narrative persisted over a chronological period straddling the Civil War. Although drunkard narratives evolved over time as they interacted with changing literary genres and with social and political realities such as the war, the process was slow and the changes often subtle. Many elements and characteristics of drunkard narratives endured throughout the century, or for much of it. The continuity of the drunkard narrative, and of the language of the drink debate more generally, was striking. The first half of this book describes a discursive system that was basically static, though it had numerous internal tensions. The last half homes in on two gradual, but significant, changes in the system that began before the Civil War but came into their own in the last three decades of the century: the shift from describing a drunkard's fall as a seduction to describing it as an invasion of the drinker's body and will; and the development of a counternarrative to the story of the drunkard's decline: the story of female invasion.

Just as the drunkard narrative persisted across regions and decades, so too it took root in diverse genres. I draw from drunkard narratives told in a wide assortment of texts: fictional forms, such as novels, short stories, poems, and song lyrics, and nonfiction forms, such as trial testimonies. To a lesser extent, I use memoirs, articles, and scientific treatises. Because I am chiefly interested in how nineteenth-century Americans told and responded to the story of the drunkard, it is not central to my analysis whether the stories they told were true, fictional, or (as was most often the case) somewhere in between. There were certainly differences between the ways jurors weighed wives' accounts of their husbands' dissipation, newspaper readers perused short stories of drunkards' falls, and members of reform groups sang "Father, Dear Father, Come Home With Me Now," but there were also important similarities. The great bulk of these accounts had elements in common: a familiar explanation of why the drinker fell, an account of how the family suffered in consequence, and similar language and metaphor used to describe the drinker. The wife who tried to explain what had happened to her husband faced many of the same challenges and resorted to many of the same methods as writers of short stories and song lyrics.

Of course, those who were writing fiction had more freedom to construct their narratives than did those who were attempting to recount true stories. Yet even persons testifying under oath about real people and real events had plenty of space to construct their own narratives through emphasis, inclusions and exclusions, and interpretation, not to mention imperfect memory and simple perjury. Some would argue that drunkard narratives in trial testimony and temperance fiction bore such close resemblance to one another because "that's how it really happened," and fiction writers represented these realities in their novels and short stories. Others, more discursively oriented, might suggest that the two resembled one another because plaintiffs understood their experiences in terms of available language and thus applied current literary tropes to their own lives. The truth is no doubt found somewhere between the two. Whether telling true or fictional drunkard narratives, people grappled to shape what they "knew" about how a particular drunkard fell, or how drunkards generally fell, into a cogent and familiarizing framework.[14]

One thing that is new about this book is that it relies heavily on the voices of immigrants and rural workers. It is difficult to address how current the drink discourse was among rural working-class immigrants and whether it assumed new forms or attributes when it left its native middle-class discursive home. Part of the problem is that such people left few written records of their thoughts and beliefs. Transcripts from alcohol-related trials provide a huge, and largely un-mined, treasure trove of working people's ideas about alcohol use. Of course, like any source, trial transcripts pose their own set of problems to the inter-preter. People surely spoke differently when testifying in a court of law than when casually talking at home or in a saloon. One of the ways in which the courtroom setting may have influenced rural working-class and immigrant wit-nesses is precisely by encouraging them to speak, as much as possible, in the language of the middle class. As a result, even though I draw heavily on the words of those who were decidedly neither native nor middle class, these sources cannot absolutely establish the extent to which immigrants or working people were fully integrated into the drink debate I discuss. The sources do, however, support two somewhat more moderate claims. First, rural working-class saloongoers and their families shared with middle-class temperance re-formers the concern that the figure of the drunkard destabilized both gender roles and ideas of individual self-control. Second, these saloongoers and their families were familiar enough with temperance reformers' language and tropes that they were able frequently to adopt them, often strategically, in the court-room setting.

That saloongoers and their families, when they appeared in the courtroom, had to work within certain formal constraints did not distinguish them from other tellers of drunkard narratives. It seems likely that the constraints imposed on them by the structure of questioning and courtroom rules were even stricter than, say, those imposed on novelists or poets by the expectations of readers and the demands of publishers. I rather suspect, however, that these class dy-namics within the courtroom were not dissimilar from those in the general culture. The drink debate was dominated and largely shaped by native middle-class voices. Immigrants, the rural poor, and urban workers participated in the debate, often extensively, but in doing so they usually adopted middle-class tropes and styles. Even when immigrants or workers explicitly understood themselves to be disagreeing with temperance movements dominated by the native middle class, they often found themselves adopting temperance language and answering questions the movement had posed. Their adoption of that language must often have been sincere, and at any rate it was a necessity if they were to be understood and taken seriously by those in power.

One genre I draw upon more sparingly is medical texts. In general, this book does not discuss the nineteenth-century debate over whether alcohol was a disease, and, if so, what sort of disease it was. I avoid this discussion for several reasons. First, it has been ably discussed by many historians of the temperance movement, and I have little to add to that discussion. Second, none of the sources upon which I most heavily rely—trial transcripts and fictional and literary writings—make heavy or meaningful use of medical or scientific discourse. Although temperance writers and civil damage litigants occasionally evoked scientific and medical language, the vast majority of them had little or no scientific training and thus made only a shallow use of scientific ideas. Third, I suspect that the medical discourse on inebriety in the nineteenth century derived from more than it contributed to the popular temperance discourse, largely dressing up drink discourse ideas in scientific language. I do occasionally refer to contemporary medical texts, largely to reveal parallels between the popular and medical discourse and to explain the broader intellectual context for the drunkard narratives I am exploring.

My focus on how nineteenth-century Americans told drunkard narratives to one another leads to some new conclusions about the significance of the drink debate. The most important has to do with the relationship of the temperance movement to the emergence of women's rights. One of the central tensions of the temperance movement's gender politics is that, while the movement ultimately contributed significantly to the broadening of women's roles and rights, reformers were largely motivated by the specter of families in which men became dependants and women were forced to take on traditionally male roles. The dominant interpretation of the relationship of the temperance and suffrage movements is that the temperance movement provided a relatively safe means for women to enter into public political life while claiming that they were merely fulfilling their traditional responsibilities as wives and mothers. Then, once women had entered the public sphere, they had taken a significant step toward the more radical world of suffrage. This basic description is well substantiated, but there has not yet been a convincing explanation of the discursive changes that accompanied these social behaviors. Rather, accounts of the move of temperance reformers toward suffrage often imply either that temperance leaders like Woman's Christian Temperance Union president Frances Willard deliberately used the temperance message to ease women into suffrage or that women who joined the temperance movement did so largely to justify their entry into the world of politics. I argue that because reformers condemned drunkards more for abdicating than for abusing their patriarchal roles, the gender politics implicit in sobering them up were decidedly ambiguous. Though my analysis accepts the conventional position that temperance women performed radical actions but explained them in traditional terms, I describe why the very idea of radical action in the name of conservative ends came to be considered necessary and how it came to be deeply embedded in temperance discourse. I argue that the relationship between the temperance movement and the suffrage movement was much more organic to temperance discourse than is generally understood.

A good way to get a sense of the basic structure of the drunkard narrative that loomed so large in the drink discourse and would have so many and varied consequences is to look at how temperance opponents parodied it. Kansan Charles Willsie, in an 1890 antitemperance pamphlet, hit most of the main characteristics of the genre in his cynical description of it,

> depicting in the most forcible and touching strains the evil of intemperance, citing in the most eloquent manner the cases of various talented young men once surrounded with pious mothers and beautiful sisters, who had been ruined by the intoxicating bowl and who finally filled drunkards' graves; and again carrying the listeners off to the scenes of the disgusting drunken husband with heartbroken wife, and ragged and starving children crying in vain for warmth and food, or to the saloon-keeper wearing diamonds and his wife and children arrayed in silks and fine linen, while the tippler, his wife, and children are in squalid rags and drinking the dregs of poverty, though born of respectable parents, and, perhaps, with the blood of the most noble ancestors coursing in their veins. It was asserted that thousands upon thousands of young men were filling untimely graves, or bringing down with sorrow the gray hairs of noble and pious parents, breaking the heart of that mother whose only hope was her darling son, the boy whose feet had slipped, who had gone wrong through the influence of the saloon . . . and, worse than all, that the rising generation of bright boys were [sic] being contaminated and ruined by the poisonous fumes of the dram-shop.[15]

Drunkard narratives, as Willsie suggested, generally began with a young man on the brink of adulthood.[16] Longing to exercise the privileges of adulthood and yearning for excitement, he allows himself to be lured into a saloon, usually by a "fast" young man. His entry into the saloon and his subsequent "fatal first drink" launch him into the downward spiral of the chronic inebriate. After describing the first drink, the story often jumps forward a few years, and we see the young man well along the road to ruin. His wife and children are suffering from hunger, cold, and his abuse. His parents have often gone to an early grave out of sorrow. He has drunk and gambled away any property that he has accumulated and everything that has been built up by ancestors and passed along to his family. Ultimately, after a dramatic bout of *delirium tremens,* the drunkard usually either dies or is reformed through some external power or the sudden shock of the death of a loved one.[17]

There are six key aspects of the classic nineteenth-century drunkard narrative. First, the drinker, before his first drink, is a particularly promising young man. Second, the drinker falls largely or entirely because of external influences. Third, if the story blames the drinker for contributing to his own fall, his weakness is a desire either for excitement or to please his ill-chosen friends. Fourth, after he begins to drink, the desire to drink overcomes all of his other motivations. Fifth, he loses his control over his family, his economic life, and/or his own body. Sixth, if the drinker is redeemed, it is through a powerful external influence. Although some texts that I consider drunkard narratives in these pages do not explicitly include all of these elements, most do, whether from the 1830s or the 1890s, from Iowa or Tennessee, from novels or courtroom testimony. Many contemporaries recognized the highly formulaic nature of this narrative. One temperance speaker in antebellum Mississippi, for instance, after giving the narrative at length, apologized to his audience for dwelling on such a "trite theme" but insisted that "all the substantial features of the portrait I have presented to you may . . . be recognized in every one who lives and dies a drunkard."[18]

The maleness of the subject of the drunkard narrative was central to the story's logic; therefore, I will, throughout the book, refer to the "drunkard" as "he." The fate of male drunkards was much more widely discussed in the nineteenth century than that of female drunkards. Everyone was well aware that there were female inebriates, but their stories simply did not work their way into public discourse to the extent that those of their male counterparts did. Even when nineteenth-century Americans did tell the story of female drunkards, they told it with different language and tropes.[19] One of the ways in which drink-debate innovators like Louisa May Alcott and Elizabeth Avery Meriwether began to dissect and ultimately transform the drunkard narrative was precisely by imagining what would happen if they told a drunkard narrative with a female subject.

Tellers of drunkard narratives often referred to the fall of the drunkard as a loss of "manhood." The word *man* had a double usage in the nineteenth century: the first, gendered; the second, encompassing both men and women. On the one hand, to be "manly" or to have "manhood" was to possess those physical and behavioral characteristics—strength, intelligence, ability, prudence, and the like—associated particularly with adult males. But the term *man* was also used more generally, as in "mankind" or in contrasting man and beast.[20] While it never lost its gendered valence, at times it meant "personhood" or the full humanity to which every individual, male or female, should strive. When drunkard narratives said that a drinker had lost his "manhood," they emphatically meant both his gender and his humanity. It was in the slippage between these two usages that temperance reformers ultimately began to imagine a solution to the problem of the drunkard. One meaning of the term *manhood* in both its gendered and gender-inclusive usages was a certain form of willpower. Independence and strength of will were highly gendered qualities, yet nineteenth-century Americans considered the possession of free will as a precondition of full personhood for both men and women. The drunkard narrative allowed Americans to reflect on this issue in two ways. On the one hand, they were rethinking the proper roles of men and women, and how those roles could be preserved or adapted in the face of drink. On the other, they were asking whether the power of alcohol over the drunkard made it necessary for them to rethink the nature and strength of individual volition.

Attempts to define manhood, womanhood, and the proper relation between the two caused no end of conflict in the nineteenth century. There was a growing sense that women should have at least somewhat broader rights, but there was no agreement on how this could be done without sacrificing the advantages that seemed to arise from a patriarchal system. Even before the Civil War, there were a number of signs that these roles were in transition. In the Northeast, the writings of Margaret Fuller, the increasing involvement of women in religious, benevolent, and reform groups, and the Seneca Falls convention signaled that change was in the air. In other regions of the country, the signal was more muted, but the observant could detect the subtle shifting of gender roles.

After the Civil War, throughout the country—though perhaps most obviously in the West—there was little doubt that the meanings of manhood and womanhood were rapidly changing.

At the same time, new scientific, religious, and social scientific ideas suggested that eighteenth-century ideas of the individual (regardless of gender) and his or her relationship to his environment would need to be altered radically. The attack came from all directions. Scientists and popular writers focused on the power of heredity to shape individual character and behavior. Social scientists and reformers increasingly emphasized the extent to which the environment in which people lived shaped their behavior and character. Social Gospel ministers unabashedly spoke of "social salvation" as though even eternal life was a collective prospect. Many feared that these new ideas implied that no person could possess individual volition.

The brilliance of the story of the drunkard was that it combined these two seemingly distinct problems, and in so doing suggested a new solution to both. In describing the drunkard's fall from "manhood," the story constructed the gender crisis as a problem of individual volition and the crisis of individual volition as fundamentally gendered. Of course, it was a consequence of deeply engrained cultural sexism that the term *manhood* referred to full personhood *and* maleness. Women had long been forbidden to participate in many of those political, intellectual, and social pursuits that their culture believed built and developed the human potential. Yet temperance women and their male allies would use this sexist exclusion to argue that women alone could restore the drunkard's manhood. Temperance reformers took advantage of women's exclusion from the public sphere by arguing that women's domesticity shielded them from a certain type of attack on volitional selfhood. From their sheltered position, they were particularly able to restore men and mankind to gendered "manhood" and to full humanity. This sounds to twenty-first-century ears like an argument about subalternity. Of course, temperance reformers did not understand it in those terms, but they did understand that not being closely involved in male institutions gave them a different, and privileged, way to look at the problems of which those institutions were a part.

It was from the intersection of these two problems that a new narrative emerged. The narrative of female invasion described how women could briefly and dramatically enter and transform dangerous male spaces like the saloon, then return to their domestic sphere unharmed. It proposed a gendered solution to a universal crisis of the individual. In so doing, it challenged and reconstructed "manhood" in both its gendered and its broader sense. In the 1840s and 1850s, there had been scattered instances of individual or groups of aggrieved women entering saloons, condemning their proprietors, and destroying their wares. These female invasions would escalate into a national movement in 1873–74 and continue until Carry Nation took them to a dramatic climax at the beginning of the new century.

If the discourse over drink served as a space in which a large and diverse collection of Americans addressed questions of volition and gender, it was neither a neutral nor an abstract terrain. Alcohol was not merely a symbol. Rather, the story of the drunkard was an allegory that operated on the literal level as well as the symbolic. Then, as now, alcohol dulled the senses and judgment of drinkers, and ultimately produced unconsciousness in them. Then, as now, some drinkers claimed with every appearance of sincerity to find it impossible to stop drinking once they had started, and regular heavy drinkers suffered physically when they attempted to abstain. Then, as now, the excessive drinking of a family's chief breadwinner could bring chaos and misery to a household. Because of these observable phenomena, alcohol caused people to think about the extent to which an individual could be said to be free, and to think about the benefits and limitations of patriarchy.[21]

There are two dangers in focusing on storytelling. First, the actual personal tragedies experienced by nineteenth-century Americans like Andrew and Louise Faivre, and the social crises to which men like Andrew contributed, can come to seem like they are *just* stories. Yet to say that drinkers and their families often understood their own lives in terms of the stories that circulated through nineteenth-century culture is not to say that their experiences were any less real or immediate. Second, I offer a largely discursive explanation of how temperance language changed or persevered over time. This explanation is sound only if read alongside, rather than instead of, social and political explanations of the nineteenth-century temperance movement and drinking culture. Stories are not independent of social and political events. It matters that drinking rates changed over the course of the century and that the economic and class structure of the nation went through a revolution in these years. It matters that the period saw a striking centralization and expansion of governmental authority. It matters that different groups of Americans vied for cultural status and political power throughout the century. This book supplements, rather than challenges, the literature on the social history of alcohol and temperance.

This broad understanding of the drink discourse's enormous cultural importance is supported by the understandings of nineteenth-century Americans themselves. Both sides of the debate over drink considered the question of temperance to be fundamental. They often portrayed it as an opening wedge for a much larger body of ideas and convictions with which it was interrelated. Advocates of temperance spoke of their "crusade" in religious and often millennial terms. Many opponents of temperance believed that, at the very least, the future of the nation hinged on the preservation of an individual's right to drink. Though the antitemperance predictions of the dire consequences to follow a temperance victory may seem as absurd as the temperance movement's glorious projections of a coming new age, it would be a serious mistake to dismiss either as merely rhetorical. Like temperance supporters, temperance opponents understood the saloon as a battleground in a much larger cultural and intellectual dispute. Both sides believed that drink encapsulated an entire set of issues relating to almost all aspects of social life.

This book draws upon drunkard narratives in many genres, including pamphlets, medical writings, poems, short stories, newspaper articles, and songs. Most of its analysis, however, draws from three types of texts: novels, plays, and trial transcripts. Novels are particularly fruitful for this sort of reading not only because of the detail with which they present the narrative but also because the novel as a genre was developed in part as an account of the nature of interiority and volition, and from its beginning focused on the problematic relationship between the sexes. The melodramatic play shared these characteristics, as the frequent and easy transformation of works from one genre to the other illustrates.

Transcripts from late-nineteenth-century "civil damage law" trials serve as both complement and antidote to the use of novels and plays. Civil damage laws, sometimes called dramshop laws, were passed in a number of states in the mid- to late nineteenth century, giving those injured by others' drinking the right to sue saloonkeepers for damages.[22] Under the common law, an injured party had the right to sue only the person who was most directly responsible for their injury. So if a drunken man assaulted someone, the drunken man himself would be the only person the assaulted party could sue for damages. Civil damage laws overrode this common law tradition: a person assaulted by a drunken man could still sue the man himself, but he or she now had the additional right to sue the person who had sold alcohol to the drinker. Today, civil damage suits are most frequently brought by those injured by intoxicated drivers, whereas in the nineteenth century they were usually brought by women whose drinking husbands had been injured or killed while intoxicated or had failed to support their families.

The civil damage laws largely had been advocated by temperance reformers and were popular among them throughout the late nineteenth century (though a few purists worried that the laws gave saloonkeepers the right to destroy men as long as they were willing to finance the consequences).[23] The Woman's Christian Temperance Union even commissioned a booklet instructing members how to assist drunkards' wives in bringing and winning the suits.[24] Yet the acts certainly were not universally popular. From the beginning, the farsighted appreciated how subversive they could be to gender roles. When confronted with an early proposal for a civil damage law in 1854, Horatio Seymour, then governor of New York, vigorously opposed it. In granting wives and children the right to bring suits to recover losses due to their husbands' or fathers' drinking, it unduly deprived "the lawful head of the family . . . of the respect and authority due to his position." Any suits that might be brought under the statute, Seymour continued, would merely indicate either that the man of the house was the "instigator of a dishonest prosecution on the part of his wife or children, or that he is to be made an object of contempt by them." The home of a family bringing such an act would be either "a scene of strife, or a place where fraud is plotted."[25]

Most witnesses in civil damage cases were family members, fellow drinkers, neighbors, or co-workers of the drinker in question. They gave their own, often extensive, accounts of when, why, and how much the man drank. In doing so, they frequently told a longer story of how the man had become a drunkard. The drunkard narratives presented by plaintiffs' witnesses closely resembled those presented in temperance novels and other genres. The transcripts illustrate that while drunkard narratives were heavily imbedded in, and indebted to, a discursive context, many of those who told them were combating what they believed to be a very real problem.

In this book, I portray the drink debate as a dispute between two parties, "temperance reformers" and "saloon supporters" or "temperance opponents." While this characterization is broadly accurate, social conflicts are never that tidy. To begin with, many people occupied positions between these two extremes. Some, for instance, countenanced alcohol use at home while opposing public drinking. Others disapproved of hard liquor but supported the use of wine, cider, and beer. Many others had shifting or incoherent positions. In fact, part of what I hope to convey is that people were drawn to the debate not only, perhaps not even chiefly, because of a love or hatred for drink or the saloon, but rather because the debate provided a forum to work through other, more abstract, issues. It is not surprising, then, to find a good deal of slippage between the positions. Not only were there a variety of positions between teetotalism and saloon advocacy, there were a number of deeply passionate participants in the drink debate who are impossible to categorize as either supporters or opponents of the saloon. Throughout my analysis, my too-convenient division of debate participants into two warring camps will be blurred and undermined by such line-crossers and fence-sitters.[26]

In writing about the wide-ranging and powerful story of the drunkard's decline, I found myself coming perilously close to presenting a discursive model that left little space for individual idiosyncrasy. Yet even as the drunkard narrative retained much of its basic shape as part of a collective discussion, each individual encountered it from his or her own perspective and integrated it into his or her own experiences and beliefs. To emphasize this point, I begin and end each chapter with a focus on individual participants in the drink debate, exploring how each encountered, adopted, and manipulated aspects of the drunkard narrative. Each of the six figures ending each chapter—Charles M. Sheldon, Jack London, Edgar Watson Howe, Louisa May Alcott, Elizabeth Avery Meriwether, and Carry Nation—were influential participants in the drink debate, all of whom held, and published, highly individual views of the topic. None of the figures who begin the chapters—Bissell Rice, Harry Summers, Clara Cramer, Eugenia and Thomas Peacock, Rose Ann and John Sankey, and Hattie and William Ferman—were public figures. Indeed, the only records that remain of their thoughts on the debate were others' accounts of their behavior or their own testimony in civil damage law trials. Yet their stories and their testimony reveal how they struggled with and manipulated aspects of the drunkard narrative in much the same ways as did their more influential peers.

CHAPTER ONE

Volition

Far away, up a great many pairs of winding-stairs in [the drunkard's] heart, is a door, and on that door is written: "MAN." And we must knock at that door once, twice, seven times—yea, seventy times seven, that it may open unto us.　　　JOHN B. GOUGH, quoted in *Templar's Magazine*, 1854

Could it be seen that there was any part of the man that could escape the ravages of the destroyer, that some little corner of the being somewhere would preserve its natural condition, and remain the same, we might say that there was some redeeming feature in the case, but it is apparent, beyond a doubt, that nothing is left untouched by the blighting, withering influence of intemperate indulgence.

　　　J. E. STEBBENS, *Fifty Years History of the Temperance Cause*, 1876

Bissell Rice of Illinois became the subject of a good deal of discussion about the relationship of alcohol to volition. Born in 1840 in New York, he had moved west to Illinois by the time the war started, and he married in 1862. At some point, he fought in the war on the Union side; perhaps he developed his drinking habit while in the service.[1] In the early 1870s, he fell and injured himself after drinking. His wife was one of the first to take advantage of the newly passed Illinois civil damage law to seek compensation from his saloonkeeper. Because this was a very early civil damage case, participants in the case discussed on an unusually theoretical level the idea of the drinker's volition embodied by the civil damage law. In particular, they discussed whether Bissell Rice himself had "will-power" and, if he did, whether it would be fair to require his saloonkeeper to pay for his injuries. In other words, the Rice case was a discussion of the logic and justice of the civil damage laws themselves.

Three major issues loomed large in the Rice case. First, the sides disagreed about whether Rice had been intoxicated when he injured himself; second, they disputed whether Rice was such a habitual inebriate that he had lost the power to stop drinking; and third, they debated whether, even if Rice had been inebriated and was a drunkard, it was fair to ask saloonkeeper Frederick Mapes to pay his damages. The first issue was difficult enough, not only because it was unclear how much Rice had drank at the time of his injury but also because the trial participants could not agree on how to define intoxication. When Mapes's attorney asked one of Rice's associates whether a person who had consumed only one drink would be under the "influence" of liquor, the plaintiff objected to the question on the basis that it was "irrelevant, incompetent, and seeking an opinion from the witness upon a matter in which he is not shown to be an expert." Even though the judge overruled this objection, the witness's answer, "Some is and some ain't," did not contribute much to the process of defining intoxication.[2] Bissell Rice himself was not much more help. He was not sure how much he had drunk, or how intoxicating the alcohol he consumed was. He did, however, concede that "it must have been intoxicating, else I shouldn't have fell down in the culvert."[3] Generally, however, this first issue was the saloonkeeper's weakest point, as the evidence tended to show that Rice had been under the influence at the time of the accident.

On the larger question of whether Rice was a habitual inebriate, the issue was cloudier. He was a regular drinker, and his neighbors did not seem to have a very high opinion of him. One said pointedly that Rice was "not a bright, active man." The defense, however, made much of the fact that Rice occasionally refused offers of alcohol.[4] It asked the court to instruct the jury that "a habitual drunkard is a person given to inebriety, or the excessive use of intoxicating drink, who has lost the power of the will by frequent indulgence" and that if Rice had ever turned down an offer of a drink, the jury should consider that evidence that he "exercised 'Will-Power' and was not a slave to his appetite."[5] The court, however, refused to issue this instruction. The plaintiff later defended the court's decision, arguing that just because Rice sometimes turned down offers of liquor and had "method even in his 'sprees'" did not mean that he "had will-power and hence was not a slave to appetite."[6]

The third point at issue in this case was whether it was fair for Mapes to be required to pay the cost of his customer's drunken behavior. Mapes, after all, was a man who had paid a fee to the state for the privilege of selling liquor. Toward the end of the trial, Mapes's attorney dramatically read Mapes's liquor license into the evidence.[7] The plaintiff had not gone to much length to establish that Mapes had ill intent when he sold the liquor to Rice, or even that he had reason to know that Rice was a habitual drunkard. Mapes, in the opinion of many, was a man lawfully and innocently pursuing his trade, and it was simply not fair to assign him the blame for his customers' actions. Furthermore,

Mapes's attorney reminded the courts, it was not just Mapes who was to be made the victim of the unjust new civil damage law. "This class of litigation is on the increase; our Circuit Courts *swarm* with the indicted."[8] The plaintiff's attorney addressed precisely this point in his own brief. The judgment, he insisted, was not only "necessary to attain the object of the new liquor law" but was also "just."[9] It was fair that Mapes be forced to pay these damages, because he, by selling liquor to a helpless Rice, had caused them.

As the case of Bissell Rice illustrates, the ways nineteenth-century Americans thought about the drunkard were closely interrelated with how they thought about free will. The drink debate was largely a conflict between one group of people that was more willing and another that was less willing to entertain the notion that individuals lacked moral responsibility for their actions. At the root of the nineteenth-century debate over individual responsibility was the question of whether it was possible to define the borders of the self, and, if so, whether that self generated its own actions or merely responded by necessity to external influences and inherited tendencies. Few people argued that individuals were purely autonomous: there was near-universal agreement that the environment influenced individual behavior both by limiting the range of possible actions and by alerting or reminding the individual of available opportunities. At issue in the drink debate and other similar discussions was not autonomy but the much more specific question of whether a given individual exercised *any* agency in navigating among those opportunities offered him or her or whether a person was best understood as part of a larger "social organism," with all of his or her actions emerging necessarily from the combination of inherited mental and physical capacities and exposure to external influences.[10]

The popular debate over volition in the nineteenth century, in other words, was fought over a rather narrow piece of ground. Because most participants conceded the immense power of the environment and often the immense power of hereditary forces as well, the debate frequently dissolved into whether there was, somewhere, squeezed between these forces, an embattled core of volition. To find and describe this elusive volition, debaters focused on marginal spaces and extreme situations. Drunkards—like slaves, women, children, and the insane—were useful illustrations in arguments about free will for much the same reason that the worm is useful in displaying the basic workings of nervous systems; their relationship to their heredity and environment seemed more apparent and significantly less complicated than that of others.

If they looked to these peripheral figures to understand how the will worked, nineteenth-century Americans often were actually much more interested in the application of their arguments to the center: adult, free, sane white men. The founding fathers had constructed the United States' democratic government around the belief that adult, propertied, usually white, men, unlike other people, were in a position to make independent political decisions. Of course, the electorate broadened in the first decades of the century, and apologists for this system insisted that many of those excluded from the voting process—wives, mothers, children, sisters—could wield indirect power by influencing the enfranchised. Still, it was the adult white male who ultimately sifted through this influence to make political choices in the nineteenth century. To imagine voting men as mere parts of a social organism, lacking individual responsibility for their decisions, was to pose a radical challenge to the democratic system, especially the privileged position of white men within it. Ultimately, the drink debate did just that.[11]

Temperance reformers were much more ready than their opponents to doubt the boundedness and volition of the individual. By the 1830s, and increasingly throughout the century, they tended to emphasize the power of heredity and environment and to believe that true reform would come not from individual decisions and acts but from social transformation and regulation. Temperance opponents, in contrast, placed more value on the freedom of the individual to make moral choices and stressed that true change had to come from private decisions and actions rather than from governmental regulations or social pressure. Because temperance reformers saw the individual as more vulnerable to heredity and environment than did their opponents, they also had much more sympathy with "drunkards" who, after all, were not to blame for inherited tendencies toward inebriety or for having been raised in "unwholesome" settings and forced to walk home from work through rows of brightly lit saloons. Yet, even as they were increasingly skeptical of the power of individual choice, reformers were not comfortable with the consequences of discarding the volitional self. Ultimately, by the end of the nineteenth century, they would work to construct a new basis for individual volition to replace the older ideal to which their saloon-supporting opponents clung. In the meantime, however, many of them followed their arguments to quite unorthodox and unwieldy conclusions about the nature of the self.

For the first few decades of the nineteenth century, before the drunkard narrative gained popularity in the 1830s and 1840s, most temperance reformers believed that, despite environmental temptations and inherited inclinations, the intemperate drinker ultimately bore moral responsibility for his or her act of drinking. Their practical agenda reflected this understanding. Because the blame for intemperance lay primarily in the drinker's viciousness, the fairest and most direct way to solve the problem would be to approach intemperate drinkers rather than, say, attempt to prohibit all use of alcohol. Many of these early reformers, then, both countenanced moderate drinking and themselves partook of "good creature." Although even these early groups, in the 1810s through 1830s, called on state and local governments to take steps to prevent public intemperate drinking, they put the most hope and energy into their attempts to persuade drinkers to drink moderately and privately or to abstain altogether. This "moral suasion" tactic, of course, assumed that a drinker would have the power to choose not to drink and the will to enforce that choice.

As early as the 1830s, just as the drunkard narrative was emerging, some temperance advocates publicly stated grave doubts about whether intemperate drinkers really possessed the strength of will necessary to benefit from moral suasion.[12] The more they began to doubt the drinker's volition, the more they began to assign responsibility to the drink purveyor rather than to the drinker. In 1837, for instance, a temperance novel entitled *Female Influence* asked, "Is it not just to compel men who take the profits of making drunkards, to support them and their families, when disqualified to obtain a livelihood?"[13] By the 1840s and 1850s, a growing number of temperance supporters were even more outspoken. "Moral suasion," had failed, they insisted, because the "rumseller" refused to give up his profits. If inebriates were to be saved, many came to suspect, it would be by cutting off their liquor at the source, not by redeeming them one by one.[14] That could only be done by the use of coercive power. As one writer of a Tennessee treatise (written in dialect) put it in 1859, "all legislatiff restrickshuns merely a-sisted by arts of moril swashun howsoever strong, are idle and grossly futil."[15]

Relocating the blame for intemperance from drinkers to drink purveyors implied a weakened belief in the drinker's capacity to make moral choices. Take, for instance, the comments of temperance physiologist Caleb Ticknor in his 1846 *Philosophy of Living*. "The greatest evil attendant on the habitual, though even moderate use of alcoholic drinks . . . results from the change it effects in a man's feelings, taste, and disposition. He seems, in fact, not to retain his identity."[16] Ticknor was not exactly saying here that even an habitual drinker completely lacked the power to make moral choices, and he made no claims whatsoever about the beginning drinker. In proposing that the inebriate loses his "identity," however, he developed an argument that would be a key component to temperance descriptions of the drunkard's lack of volition: the drunkard was unable to exercise volition largely because he lacked a sufficiently defined self. A few years later, just before the war, a southern temperance advocate insisted, in dialect but in earnest, that "those who fall under [alcohol's] onfluence looze all kommand of themselves, mentilly and fizzikilly."[17] The changing interpretation of the moral responsibility of the inebriate made the idea of stopping intemperance through methods of "moral suasion" (such as voluntary pledge signing) seem decidedly inadequate. Rather, reformers increasingly turned to prohibitory legislation. While voluntary measures like pledge signing would remain popular, temperance reformers put an increasing amount of their energy into what Joseph Gusfield has dubbed "coercive reform" tactics—most notably calling for state and local prohibition.[18]

This shift from moral suasion to coercive reform, and the changing ideas of the drinker's responsibility that the shift indicated were not without their opponents. Many temperance supporters, even those who agreed that coercive measures would be more effective than voluntary measures had been, were concerned about the implications of the change. They worried that the movement's new strategy and philosophy could have two dangerous consequences. Either the measures might actually limit opportunities for drinkers or potential drinkers to exercise the moral responsibility they did possess, or the philosophy that underlay the coercion might inspire them to stop feeling responsible for their own actions and to rely instead on the state to control their moral lives. In both cases, temperance reformers' own growing doubts that drinkers had sufficient strength of will to stop drinking would be a self-fulfilling prophecy. Walt Whitman expressed the second of these fears in his highly idiosyncratic early temperance novel, *Franklin Evans*. He confessed that he "had sometimes thought, that the laws ought not to punish those actions of evil which are committed when the senses are steeped in intoxication." Nevertheless, if failing to hold intoxicated individuals responsible for their actions was just, it was also practically dangerous: "if such a principle were allowed to influence judicial decisions, how terrible an opening there would be! How great a temptation, even, to the letting loose of the worst passions."[19] Reformers abandoned their faith in drinkers' moral responsibility gradually and reluctantly both because they feared the practical implications of the move and because they felt uncomfortable with the new intellectual terrain in which they found themselves.

Of course, drinkers themselves, reformed or otherwise, had reason to be particularly interested in changing views of the drunkard's responsibility. One foundational early drunkard narrative expresses some of the ambiguity with which inebriates themselves faced the question of responsibility for their falls and the extent to which they could claim credit for their redemptions. John B. Gough was probably the most famous reformed drunkard of the nineteenth century. He gained national fame as a lecturer traveling from one city to another telling audiences the story of how he had become a drunkard and how he had regained his sobriety. In 1845, Gough published an extended version of his story, in which he offered several explanations of how he became a drunkard.[20] First, he was thrown into temptation in his formative years when his English family sent him far from home to seek his fortune in New York. As "a stranger in a strange city, with no one to guide him, none to advise, and not a single soul to love, or be loved by," he was vulnerable to "circumstances" that "induced" him to stray from respectable paths. When Gough described his descent, he generally avoided either blaming himself or assigning fault to others by slipping into the passive voice. He "became exposed to temptation." He "got introduced into the society of thoughtless and dissipated young men." Yet, whoever was responsible for his being surrounded by such unwholesome influences, he blamed this corrupt environment for facilitating his decline. Indeed, as he began to realize that he was drinking too much and tried to stop, he found that he was "entangled" in the "fatal meshes" of a "dissipated social network." Finally, even as these fast friends slipped away, he described himself as "addicted" to alcohol and as a "slave of a habit."[21]

After Gough was reduced to pauperism, a temperance reformer persuaded him to sign the pledge. In signing, Gough recalled, he "exerted a moral power, which had long remained lying by, perfectly useless." This first signing of the pledge marked the end of his first fall. Afterward, Gough launched his career as a speaker on the Washingtonian lecture circuit. Yet even after he became a popular temperance lecturer, Gough went on two more drinking sprees in 1843 and 1845. He blamed his 1843 fall on the fact that he "had relied too implicitly on [his] own strength for support" rather than trusting in God. He confessed his error, signed the pledge again, and returned to the lecture circuit. His 1845 fall was more spectacular. According to Gough's account, drink purveyors and other enemies of temperance had conspired to discredit him by luring him into a drug store, drugging his soda water, setting him on a spree, and seeing to it that he was discovered in a compromising position.[22] Though many were skeptical of Gough's account of this final fall, it fit so well into some contemporary fears about plotting among liquor merchants that it undoubtedly seemed more plausible then than it does now.[23]

Gough offered three models of the drunkard's fall. His first he attributed largely to environmental influences, though he left open the possibility that he himself was partially responsible. Could he have prevented this fall by avoiding evil influences? The answer depends on how the reader interprets the space left empty by Gough's use of the passive voice. Could he have escaped earlier from his circle of corrupt friends or from his addiction to drink? On the one hand, his use of metaphors of entanglement and slavery imply that he could not. On the other hand, he ultimately did free himself by exercising his own "moral power," which strongly suggests that he could have done so earlier. He attributed his second fall to overconfidence and insufficient religious piety. He described this fall as almost entirely the consequence of his own weakness, though he vaguely insinuated that it may have been compounded by a blow to the head he suffered as a youth. For the third fall Gough would accept no responsibility whatsoever. However strongly determined Gough was to remain temperate, he could hardly have avoided his enemies' clever trap. Gough's diverse accounts of his three falls obscured and complicated the question of how much responsibility drinkers bore for their own plights.

If voluntary reform was highly appropriate for dealing with drunkards who fell due to their own moral and religious weaknesses, and occasionally worked to save drinkers like Gough who fell due to immersion in corrupt environments, it would never be effective against the deliberate and treacherous wiles of drink purveyors. Yet Gough was reluctant to advocate coercive tactics. Many within the Washingtonian movement with which he was so involved felt strongly that to use coercive tactics was to degrade the inebriate—to deny his manhood. As the introduction to the 1843 *Washingtonian Pocket Companion* put it, the drunkard "is a man; and all the other classes of society whom we wish to win over to, and enlist in this blessed cause are neither more nor less than men." Therefore, the introduction continued, "moral suasion, not force" was the proper way to approach the issue.[24] John Gough, to a large extent, agreed with the sentiment. An 1854 source quotes him as saying "Far away, up a great many pairs of winding-stairs in [the drunkard's] heart, is a door, and on that door is written: 'MAN.' And we must knock at that door once, twice, seven times—yea, seventy times seven, that it may open unto us."[25] Gough was clearly troubled over the dilemma; on the one hand it seemed that only coercive tactics would work, but on the other it seemed that in doing so they robbed the drinker of his manhood.

Ultimately, John Gough, the most famous living example of the success of moral suasion, alienated many of his temperance allies by calling for coercive reform in the form of prohibition. At the end of his autobiography, Gough offered a distinctly defensive account of his support for this legal coercion. He asserted that he had "advocated moral suasion *alone,* and in its fullest extent, too, in the case of the drunkard." However, he believed that the law ought to be brought into operation against "the rumseller . . . who sells that which causes his fellow man to become an inebriate" and "which unfits him for discharging the duties of a man and a citizen, towards his family and his country."[26] Moral suasion simply did not go far enough. Temperance advocates needed to "throw another wall of protection around the wretched and almost helpless child of intemperance." Gough never imagined the drinker as completely without responsibility—he hopefully slipped in a slender "almost" before his "helpless child of intemperance." Yet he believed moral suasion to be "as useless in the effort to remove drunkenness, as it would be ridiculous to attempt to empty the ocean drop by drop."[27] Drinkers, at least in most situations, might just barely possess the ability to save themselves, but to rely on that ability as part of a strategy for meaningful large-scale social improvement was "ridiculous."

As temperance reformers like Gough lost faith in the drinker's power to resist alcohol, they struggled to find a way to describe the relationship between drinker and drink. One metaphor they frequently turned to, probably more than they did to any other, was that of slavery. Just as John Gough had described himself during his first fall as the "slave of a habit," so many antebellum reformers began to describe the relationship of the inebriate to his drink as one of slavery. In Ronald Walters's description of antebellum temperance rhetoric, "temperance writers pictured alcohol as a form of tyranny, resembling slavery in depriving people of their ability to act as morally responsible creatures. Giving in to it meant destruction of one's autonomy."[28] Just as slavery imposed external restraints on individual freedom, so the excessive use of alcohol worked internally to paralyze or subvert the will. To drink was to enslave oneself to alcohol and to yield one's volition.[29]

The use of slavery as a metaphor for the relationship of the drinker to his drink raised its own set of problems. To begin with, if there was one figure in antebellum America whose volitional status was more ambiguous than the drinker's, it was the slave. Many white people doubted slaves' volitional capacity for two reasons. First, their status as slaves put them in a position in which they frequently could not execute their wills. As or more importantly, however, many whites questioned the volitional strength of African Americans just as they did their intelligence and morality. To compare a white drunkard to a slave, then, was a complicated proposition.

One way to approach the power of the slavery metaphor is to look at how Southern courts dealt with "slaves to the bottle" who actually *were* slaves. Ambiguities about slaves' status often left Southern judges scratching their heads about how to treat slaves under the law.[30] Two cases that involved intoxication left them even more confused. In *Harrison v. Berkeley* (1847) and *Skinner v. Hughes* (1850), slaves had purchased alcohol from white men, became intoxicated, and died in alcohol-related accidents. In both cases, the courts required the men who had sold the alcohol to compensate the owners of the slaves for having caused the intoxication leading to the deaths.[31] The judges argued that slaves would naturally drink alcohol if it were offered them; they lacked the willpower to abstain. In *Skinner*, for instance, the court held that the death of a slave who had become intoxicated "was a *natural consequence* of the act of the defendant in providing him with the means of intoxication." A slave's drinking to excess was not a volitional act that interrupted the chain of causation. Rather, it was simply part of the "usual course of nature," the inevitable consequence of giving him access to liquor.[32] The judges claimed that offering a slave a drink was tantamount to restraining him and pouring it down his throat. Strikingly, *Harrison* is still occasionally cited as a precedent in alcohol-related suits today.[33]

A second problem with the slavery metaphor was that it fed the temperance movement's connections with a political issue even more controversial than prohibitionism. Many temperance and antislavery activists, black and white, recognized the similarities between the goals of the two movements. In 1849, for instance, the African-American paper *The North Star* approvingly reprinted an article from the *Pennsylvania Freeman* describing a set of resolutions made by a meeting of African-American reformers in Ohio. The group first resolved that "it is their duty to organize themselves for the promotion of the cause of temperance, and the liberation of their brethren in bondage." Their next resolution was "that all intoxicating liquors as a beverage, are hurtful to man, and tend to injure health, destroy the mind and demoralize and corrupt his nature." Third, they declared "that whoever will not assist to save the intemperate and relieve the slave is no philanthropist."[34] This promiscuous intermingling of the two subjects was far from an isolated case.

Some antebellum temperance reformers went so far as to argue that intemperance was worse than chattel slavery. As one temperance reformer and slavery opponent explained, as immoral and debasing as the slave trade was, intemperance "fetters the immortal mind as well as the body."[35] Important temperance leaders in the late antebellum North tended to support antislavery measures, and leading antislavery activists generally supported temperance reform. The same was true in the general population; as Robert Dykstra has shown in his work on antebellum Iowa, those who supported prohibition were likely also to oppose slavery and vice versa.[36]

Even though the language of slavery often fed the connection between the temperance and antislavery movements in the North, to call an inebriate a slave did not necessarily have antislavery implications. Claiming that various institutions and practices made white men into "slaves" was, after all, a staple of antebellum Southern political rhetoric. Even temperance reformers who advocated slavery frequently referred to white inebriates as "slaves," meaning that through drink they had lost their appropriate status as free men and descended to the degraded and unfree status of slaves. In using the language they were not calling for the end of the institution of slavery but for the restoration of white men to the full, free manhood considered appropriate to them.

It is true that temperance organizations suffered in the South, even more so than in the North, as sectional tensions increased in the 1850s. Some Southerners had looked at temperance with skepticism due to its unsavory northern connections, and at any rate their attentions were increasingly absorbed by the impending conflict. Still, even during the war temperance discourse persevered to some level in the South. Though they provided liquor rations to their troops, the Confederacy, like the U.S. Army, had an interest in promoting as much temperance as possible in its ranks. Probably because they hoped it would have military utility, Southerners dedicated a share of their limited printing supplies and facilities to the production of temperance literature during the war, including at least one standard drunkard narrative.[37] Even in the heat of wartime, in a passionately pro-Southern press, the slavery metaphor endured. As one wartime Southern temperance pamphlet put it, "better had we bowed the neck to Lincoln's yoke, than made ourselves the willing slaves of groveling passions, and depraved appetites."[38]

One of the more striking things about drink debaters' use of the slavery metaphor is that it continued well after emancipation, even to the end of the century.[39] In 1880, the *New Englander and Yale Review* published a lengthy article on just that topic. "The Analogy of Slavery and Intemperance Before the Law" discusses the popularity of the metaphor and of temperance reformers' frequent claims that intemperance could be killed just as "dead" as slavery had been. There were differences between slavery and intemperance, the author insisted, that made the latter less amenable to legal solution. "The radical difference between slavery and intemperance is that the victim of the former is involuntary, forced, while the most conspicuous victim of the latter keeps up at least the semblance and goes through the motions of being voluntary in his subjection and loss."[40] Without the cooperation of the "prisoner" of drink, who continued to "hug his chains" rather than assisting in his own liberation, society would find it a much more difficult matter to end intemperance than it had to end slavery.[41]

The slavery metaphor persevered with particular force in two genres: popular fiction and the courtroom. Grace Strong, in an 1886 novel, suggested that one drunkard was alcohol's "slave, vainly trying to free himself from . . . bondage."[42] Neither Strong nor most of the thousands of other temperance reformers who used the language of slavery were merely thoughtlessly continuing to use figures of speech that had been popular before the war. Rather, they frequently reflected on and extended the meaning of the slavery metaphor. In the last years of the century, for instance, temperance novelist Jane Collins wrote a volume, *Free At Last,* focusing on the story of an emancipated slave who celebrated his freedom only to discover that many blacks and whites alike were "slaves to drink." "Were colored people really free? Were they not bound down by a *more cruel* bondage, learned from white folks' customs and habits?" Collins further hoped that "surely these poor ones will not again be permitted to be bound down by a worse bondage to their appetites and passions. God forbid that another Abraham Lincoln should have to be raised up to emancipate the millions enslaved to rum."[43]

Litigants, attorneys, and judges in postbellum alcohol-related cases also frequently metaphorically described drinkers as "slaves." The judge in Bissell Rice's case, remember, instructed jurors to take evidence that a man exercised "Will Power" as proof that he was "not a slave to his appetite for intoxicating liquor."[44] A lawyer in an Iowa case in 1880 described drunkards as "slaves to their appetites." Louise Faivre's lawyer argued, about twenty years later, that "habitual drunkards" such as Andrew Faivre were "slaves of the saloon keeper."[45] Another case suggested that a man's drinking had "fettered his will."[46] The language of slavery, then, with all that it implied about volition, endured within the drink discourse long after the institution of slavery had ended.

Temperance reformers' approaches to the question of drinkers' volitional strength continued to evolve after the war. In particular, temperance reformers were influenced by the emergence of both a new religious movement and a closely related new intellectual discipline: the Social Gospel movement and social science. The Social Gospel movement came to prominence in the post-war years and reached its height at the century's end. What distinguished this movement theologically was the extent to which its members were willing to understand religious events such as salvation as collective or social rather than individual. This theological shift went hand in hand with Social Gospellers' increasing focus on social reform. Social Gospellers were skeptical of the power of individual conversion. Without wider social change, they feared, converts would soon slide back into their old ways.[47] The only effective salvation was that which embraced an entire community. Important Social Gospel minister Walter Rauschenbusch, for instance, referred to sin and salvation as "social force[s]."[48] Washington Gladden similarly insisted that "the individual cannot be separated from the society in which he lives and retain his individuality."[49] Phillips Brooks's sermon collection, *Perfect Freedom,* developed his assertion that the individual could only find "freedom" to the extent that he participated in the social body.[50] Temperance reformers imbibed these ideas directly and passed them along in their own writings. For instance, the Woman's Christian Temperance Union organ, the *Union Signal,* published an article in 1892 which put the position succinctly: "Dogmatic theology has iterated and reiterated the injunction 'save your own soul' but the most ideal salvation is the forgetfulness of the 'own soul' in the general soul."[51]

The social sciences, which gathered data and developed scientific strategies to bring about social reform, emerged in partnership with the Social Gospel movement. Thomas Haskell, following Robert Wiebe, suggests that this new body of expertise was called forth by social change. As they argue, at the beginning of the nineteenth century, America was composed of a collection of island communities in which each member had some personal knowledge of most of the people and institutions whose actions seriously affected his life. By the century's end, through speedier transportation and communication and through the rise of big business and government, American communities were increasingly "interdependent." More and more, decisions made and actions taken a long way off, perhaps in Washington, D.C., or New York City or on the Chicago Board of Trade, could have a direct and vital impact on an individual. Haskell refers to this phenomenon as the "recession of causation." As it became increasingly difficult to decide how and where consequential decisions were made, and, more importantly, to predict what consequential events would occur in the future, social scientists emerged and offered to explain and predict political, social, and economic change.[52]

The social sciences posed a serious challenge to individual volition.[53] Herbert Spencer asserted in his 1897 *Principles of Psychology* that it was certainly true that "everyone is at liberty to do what he desires to do." That, he insisted, was not at issue. Rather, the problem of free will was in the nature and origins of desire. He emphatically denied "that every one is at liberty to desire or not to desire, which is the real proposition involved in the dogma of free will."[54] Franklin Giddings's important *Democracy and Empire* (1900) similarly maintained that "it seems to be agreed on all hands that in any case the ego is nine-tenths or more somebody else."[55] Others were less willing to jettison ideas of individual free will. While Richard Ely talked a great deal about social solidarity and insisted in 1893 that the "salvation of [a] soul is not purely an individual process" he insisted that, in his schema, "individual responsibility can scarcely be said to be lessened. If it is lessened at all, it is lessened for those who are so low down that they scarcely feel their responsibility for their position."[56] Still, Ely's statement is best read as a heartfelt protest against an intellectual trend that he suspected had come to stay.

Sometimes social scientists drew on the drunkard narrative to make their arguments about the nature of the individual. Thus, Lester Frank Ward wrote in his 1883 *Dynamic Sociology* that, while people want to believe that the consciousness is sovereign, "there are many substances which, taken into the system in various ways, instantly rob us of all control of the mind." The fact of mind-altering substances like alcohol led him to the unpleasant conclusion that "Finally, the will, that highest power of mind of which we boast so much is, if not a chimera, at least a far different thing from what it appears to be."[57] Ward was no stranger to the drink discourse. A few pages before this passage, he cites state civil damage laws as exemplary legislation because, unlike prohibitory legislation, this type of law draws on the pecuniary interests of plaintiffs and thus "executes itself."[58]

Perhaps the most striking aspect of this new challenge to individual volition was the practice, particularly among Social Gospellers and social scientists, of referring to groups of people as an "organism." Social Gospeller Walter Rauschenbusch often did so. Another important Social Gospel minister, Phillips Brooks, invited his listeners to equate themselves to pieces of metal, useless by themselves but capable of being integrated into a larger machine.[59] Similarly, social scientists made claims about the "social organism" central to their projects. Josiah Royce maintained that "the ties which bind various finite individuals together are but hints of the unity of all individuals in the Absolute Individual."[60] Ward, in *Dynamic Sociology,* took the idea furthest when he suggested that the entire world, both animate and inanimate, be seen as one living organism. He posited a "universal soul in inanimate nature" which humans were unable to perceive.[61] Once one accepted society as the organic unit, imagining it as the seat of will was an easy and obvious step.[62]

The imaginative rethinking of the organism also worked in another direction. While some thinkers imagined an "organism" consisting of many individuals living interdependently with one another, others suggested that ancestors and descendents be understood as comprising a single "organism." Popular hereditarian writer Robert Dugdale wrote in 1877 that "any given series of social phenomena—as honest childhood, criminal maturity and pauper old age, which sometimes occur in the life of a single individual—may be stretched over several generations."[63] An 1891 *Harper's* article popularized the theory of "the continuity of the germ plasm," suggesting that though individuals might be mortal, their "germ plasm" passes from one generation to the next. This "germ plasm," the author argued (presumably following Lamarck via Aggasiz), was permanently marked and altered by the behavior of each individual. Drawing on studies of "lower animals," the author suggests that "animal immortality, as regards its substance at least, is to be regarded as fully proven."[64] In an 1882 temperance pamphlet, "The Effects of Alcohol on Offspring," Nathan Allen showed how explicitly this idea could be tied to the question of individual volition. "Connected with this law of heredity, a very important question arises: What is man's *free agency* and *accountability* in the matter?" Allen asked. "Modern science is teaching us every day that there is a most intimate, direct, and legitimate connection between the parent and the child."[65] Arguments like these, which implied that an individual life ought to be seen as extending over multiple generations, only increased drink debater's fears about the weakness of individual volition.

Some temperance reformers who adopted this Lamarckian idea of the transmission of acquired traits soon found themselves in an uncomfortable position. On the one hand, as Nathan Allen's remarks suggest, Lamarckian ideas could be preferable to Darwinian ones precisely because they allowed individuals to imagine that they were not merely helpless recipients of some preordained set of traits and characteristics. Temperance reformers often used such arguments to counter those who fatalistically denied responsibility for their actions and entirely undermined the possibility of reform. On the other hand, reformers tended to tell drinkers that they must choose not to drink so as not to condemn their children to inebriety. This entreaty led to a rather awkward and inconsistent notion of will and heredity. So "The Effects of Alcohol on Offspring" exhorts the reader to "take into account fully his own responsibility in the matter." "By his own nature he is created a free moral agent," but "he has, in a great measure, the character and destiny of his offspring," either for "*weal or woe,*" under his control.[66] The author struggles against the logic of his own argument to maintain a slender, if inconsistent, space for the possibility of individual volition.

It would be easy to read too much into these applications of the idea of the organism and the individual life. They are best seen as poetic representations of the far-reaching consequences of popular scientific and theological ideas. However, they do reveal that social science and Social Gospel theology challenged traditional notions of the individual and that social thinkers found these challenges evocative and powerful. In the late nineteenth century, the idea of the volitional individual was increasingly attacked by hereditarian and environmental thinkers. Since the idea formed a basis of many aspects of American culture—most notably political theory—challenges to it were fraught with consequence and never taken lightly.

Postwar temperance reformers adopted many new ideas from the Social Gospel and the social sciences and used them to reimagine and reinvigorate ideas inherited from the antebellum drink debate and the slavery conflict. These influences nudged the movement towards a more explicit recognition of the drunkard's volitional failure. Because many reformers believed that an individual could inherit an alcoholic tendency so strong that drinking one drop would bring to life an uncrushable inner demon, and because they believed that environmental influence could be irresistible, reformers frequently asserted, in the strongest possible terms, that the drinker had no will at all.

Writers of postbellum temperance fiction were even more apt than their antebellum predecessors to depict the drinker as lacking willpower and, hence, moral responsibility for his actions.[67] Prolific temperance novelist Mary Dwinell Chellis had a character in an 1874 novel claim that "when one's brain is heated with wine, the power of self-control is lost."[68] Novelists like Chellis were quite deliberate in their attempts to describe the state of the drinker's will and the technical processes by which it was compromised. Many writers of temperance fiction also wrote or lectured on the science and hygiene of alcohol.[69] Elizabeth Meriwether (author of the play *The Devil's Dance*) armed herself with "numerous large color charts" and gave many public lectures in St. Louis in the mid-1880s on "Alcohol and Health." In one, she claimed that "the most prominent physicians agreed that drunkenness caused automatic cerebration, that is, the action of an individual automatically—without using his brain."[70] In her 1880 temperance hygiene textbook for children, Julia Colman (author of the play *No King in America*) insisted that "the drunkard has no *will* left. He has given it up to the drink so often that the will-power is gone."[71] Physician William Hargreaves (author of the novel *Lost and Found: or, Who Is the Heir?*) agreed in an 1884 popular scientific book, *Alcohol and Science; or Alcohol: What It Is, and What It Does*, that when an individual became intoxicated, "the controlling influence of *will* and *judgment* are lost."[72] Meriwether, Colman, and Hargreaves used their fiction to illustrate their "scientific" ideas about the relationship of the inebriate to his drink, particularly their ideas about the drinker's will. These and countless other writers were quite straightforward in their claims that drunkards lacked both will and the moral responsibility for their actions.

Writers of temperance fiction made these claims about the drinker's volition by asserting that the drinker was radically alienated from environment and memory, and that after a certain point the drinker lacked a "self." In doing so, such writers anticipated the ideas of Frank Lester Ward, who argued in *Dynamic Sociology* that "truth is the natural nourishment of the mind, and, when not fed by it, the mind becomes superficial and impotent."[73] Of course this was not really a new idea; a long tradition of theorists had claimed that an individual could possess free will only insofar as he or she had an accurate understanding of the environment with which he or she was interacting. Older republican notions of prudence here intersected with ideals of individualism and moral freedom. To drink, many temperance advocates claimed, was precisely to cut oneself off from "truth," both from sense data and from memory. The prototypical *delirium tremens* scene, in which the drunkard is unable to recognize his own home and family, was the most common fictional depiction of this. As one temperance playwright put it, "there is no feeling in him; his brain's turned —his senses fled—he is unconscious of everything around."[74] At the heart of the drunkard's lack of will is his failure to perceive truly, and thus to have his own reactions appropriately influenced by, his environment. A man can become a drunkard through insufficient resistance to a corrupt environment or through an inordinate desire to please his friends and acquaintances, but at the end his will fails because he is insufficiently aware of and in harmony with his environment. The drunkard withdraws into himself, creating his own world of fantasy and imagination.[75]

It is a common trope in temperance writings that the drunkard "forgot" his familial and social relationships. As a prominent theorist of medical jurisprudence put it in 1871, the heavy drinker "is entirely beside himself, memory and judgment having abandoned him. . . . The past has gone from his mind, and he cannot be influenced by considerations which he no longer remembers."[76] Another temperance theorist stated the same idea even more pointedly thirty years later. Exploring the consequences of drinkers' memory losses, he concluded, "the self shrinks with the memory."[77] Temperance literature frequently echoed the idea that drink caused forgetfulness. Martha E. Whitten's 1887 poem, "The Drunkard's Wife," lists the many things and people—his wife, his children, his promises, his sense of shame and ideas of virtue—the drunkard forgets in taking a drink. Similarly, in *The Itinerant's Daughter* (1908), Albert forgets "his manhood, his late promises to sweet little Helen Judson . . . his pledge . . . his mother . . . everything."[78] Of course, many temperance writers realized that "forgetfulness," and, for that matter, alienation from their real environment was exactly what drinkers were seeking when turning to the bottle. Terribly worried about the overwhelming influence of the environment, temperance reformers suggested that in the moment of *delirium tremens,* the drinker utterly cut himself off from it. Yet it was in exactly that moment, when the drunkard was finally, radically alone, that temperance reformers imagined that he most entirely lacked free will.[79]

To writers of temperance fiction, the drunkard's experience of alienation during spells of *delirium tremens* did not count as autonomy because, reformers believed, he had lost a "self" in which autonomy could reside. This trope came through frequently in drunkard narratives. As Mary Dwinell Chellis described one habitual inebriate in an 1876 novel, "there was not much left of him." Characters in an 1872 temperance play said of an inebriate that "all his thoughts, feelings, and actions begin and end in the bottle."[80] A novelist in 1902 similarly described a drunkard's "rum-soaked person."[81]

Writers of temperance fiction, though, were often troubled by the implications of their belief that inebriates lacked free will and moral responsibility. In works prior to the 1880s, many temperance writers asserted, often against the apparent logic of their own stories, that the drunkard was not entirely devoid of free will. Mary Dwinell Chellis's 1879 novel *From Father to Son* is one of the more strained of these attempts. In this story, a moderate drinker's older three sons become drunkards, while the younger three are saved only by the impressive moral exertions of their father's teetotaling new bride. Chellis's narrative seems to blame inebriety both on the habits of drunkards' ancestors and on their parents' moral instruction. At the same time, however, Chellis attempts to leave space for individual moral responsibility. When inebriate son Caspar (who, according to Chellis, has "the power to will, without the strength to perform") bitterly asserts that "parents sow for their children," his temperate brother argues that each individual is able to determine his own destiny.[82] A mere seven pages later, however, the book ends with a tearful scene in which the father takes responsibility for his boys' declines.[83] Like Chellis, many temperance fiction writers were uncomfortable arguing that drinkers entirely lacked volition. Just as John Gough left in his account a narrow space for the possibility that they could save themselves, writers often declared that inebriates possessed some modicum of moral responsibility. Yet even if they inserted such careful statements, the logic of their stories seemed to insist that the opposite was true.

As temperance reformers became a more powerful social force, the doubts they had voiced about drunkards' volition in their novels, plays, and tracts began to shape how drinkers were treated under the law. Widespread cultural belief that drinkers were unable to take responsibility for their actions made the lives of excessive, and even moderate, drinkers more difficult. The most immediate social impact of this philosophical shift was that reformers called increasingly for coercive reform in the postbellum era. Even before the war, of course, many states had passed some form of liquor legislation—whether hard-core total prohibition Maine Laws or weaker laws that allowed local governments to decide to license liquor sellers in their areas, or that increased liquor license fees so much that only the most prosperous liquor purveyors could stay in business, or that forbade the sale of liquor "by the glass."[84] Whatever form prohibitory legislation took, it was the product of the public's increasing willingness to hold drink purveyors responsible for the making of drunkards and for the consequences of inebriety.

The spread of civil damage laws was a subtler but perhaps equally significant policy consequence of the growing belief that inebriates were neither responsible for nor able to stop their own destructive drinking. Versions of these laws were passed in Pennsylvania, Ohio, New Hampshire, Nebraska, and Kansas in the 1840s and 1850s, and in Iowa and Massachusetts during the Civil War. In the 1870s and 1880s the laws were not only strengthened in these states but also spread throughout the country, especially in the North. By 1890, twenty-one states had enacted civil damage laws. All six New England states adopted the laws, along with the mid-Atlantic states of Delaware, New York, and Pennsylvania, and eight Midwestern states: Illinois, Indiana, Iowa, Kansas, Michigan, Nebraska, Ohio, and Wisconsin. Four states from other regions—Colorado, North Carolina, West Virginia, New Mexico—also adopted civil damage laws.[85]

These laws varied from one state to another. Some allowed exemplary damages, and others did not. Some specifically held saloonkeepers' landlords liable for damages along with their tenants, while others did not. The most important difference among them was in what sorts of sales they made actionable. Most states' laws held that any sale made a saloonkeeper potentially liable for damages caused by his customer. Ohio, Colorado, New Mexico, and Wisconsin, however, held drink purveyors liable only if they had received written notice not to sell to an individual. Michigan, Delaware, North Carolina, and Pennsylvania held saloonkeepers liable for damages arising from intoxication only if their sales were to known drunkards or minors or were in other ways illegal. Rhode Island held saloonkeepers liable only if they sold illegally or in violation of a written request.[86]

Whatever the differences, in states with civil damage laws, citizens damaged by others' drinking could require that saloonkeepers pick up the tab. By the 1870s and 1880s, enough people thought that this was a fair arrangement that legislatures were willing to pass it in twenty-one states. When legislatures considered these acts, they explicitly evoked the language of the drunkard narrative. Take the temporarily successful but hotly contested struggle in the Wisconsin legislature in 1872. Members who endorsed the act submitted an impassioned and lengthy supporting statement. Intemperance, they explained, was a "monster vice" carrying "misery" into the "very heart of otherwise happy families." They made some effort, probably as a concession to the strength of opposition to the temperance movement in the state, to distance themselves from some of the more extreme elements of the standard drunkard narrative: they admitted that some people drank voluntarily. Many heavy drinkers were inebriates, however, and in their cases, alcohol caused the "complete disarrangement of the whole physical, mental, and moral being," to the extent that they could no longer be held accountable for their actions. The "seller . . . is the only *voluntary* agent" in the inebriate's purchase of alcohol, the legislators insisted. The inebriate's "power of *will* is gone," and he is unable to resist when "the tempting bowl is placed within his grasp by one whose only aim is gain." The victim of intemperance, they continued, is "an abject slave to his appetite, who seeks in vain to liberate himself from its galling chains. . . . He has foes within to embattle and foes without seeking to decoy and seduce him from the path of sobriety." They proceeded, with a nervous but defiant eye to Milwaukee, to label liquor purveyors and manufacturers as "artists in human slaughter."[87] In spite of opposition by the ethnic Germans who formed a minority of the committee and who later issued a report insisting that such puritanical legislation would only drive drinking underground and make it more pernicious, the House passed the bill and sent it on to the Senate.[88]

A majority of the Senate committee to which the bill was referred heartily agreed with the position taken by the assembly and wrote their own statement in concurrence, emphasizing that the bill was "a *just* measure." They acknowledged that "It is claimed to be unjust, in that it makes the seller responsible for the results of the sale," but countered that the liquor traffic is like a "vampire," leaving his victims and their families "bleeding and helpless." When families of drunkards were reduced to poverty, it was the "legitimate, natural result of the vending of spirituous drinks." "Is it just," they continued, "that the *innocent* should suffer, and the *guilty* go free?"[89] Opponents of the bill in the Senate protested more vehemently than had their peers in the assembly, calling the bill "an insult on the character and good reputation of the people of this state." They insisted that it was "unjust" because it punished law-abiding saloonkeepers for wrongs committed by others. Civil damage act opponents also argued, practically, that legislative attacks on the industry would cripple the thriving brewing business in the state.[90] Illustrating their sense of the injustice of the act, they proposed an alternate bill. The first section of this substitute read, "Drunkenness is hereby prohibited in this state," and the rest continued along the same lines, making the drinker rather than the saloonkeeper legally responsible for the consequences of his drinking.[91] The minority's attempts to derail the civil damage act, however, were to no avail; it was passed and signed into law later in the session.[92]

Another way to appreciate how civil damage acts were tied to a particular understanding of the drinker's volition is to look at a much-cited 1888 decision by the supreme court of Alabama—which, like most other southern states, did not adopt a civil damage law. The case was brought by Susan B. King, the widow of James King, against Benjamin Henkie, a saloonkeeper who had sold James the alcohol with which he apparently drank himself to death. Because Alabama did not have a civil damage law allowing wives to sue saloonkeepers, Susan King brought the suit in her capacity as the administrator of James's estate. It is not surprising that Susan King ultimately lost. Even in states with civil damage laws, drinkers themselves, and hence those acting as the administrators of their estates, were excluded from the provisions of the acts and rarely won when they tried to bring cases under the common law or other statutes. What is interesting about the case is the wording of the court's decision and the strength of its insistence on drinkers' control over their own fates. Even if James King was "helplessly drunk when he purchased and drank the liquor, so much so as to render the exercise of ordinary care by him impracticable, if not impossible," and even if he was so intoxicated when he took his fatal last drinks that he was "morally unaccountable," the court insisted that his death "was not 'caused' so much by the wrongful act of the defendants in selling him whiskey, as by his own act in drinking it after being sold to him." The court concluded with an even more general statement of the drinker's moral responsibility for his fate: "A drunkard, or one in a state of voluntary intoxication . . . has by his own agency, either wantonly or negligently, brought about his own misfortune."[93] This was exactly the sort of attitude and the sort of justice that civil damage law advocates wanted to expunge from the courts.

The civil damage laws were innovative in their assignment of responsibility for the actions of drinking men. In the common law tradition, generally one was held civilly responsible for an injury to another only if one's own act was the "proximate" cause of the injury. As one civil damage act court explained to the jury, "an act is the proximate cause of an event only when in the natural course of things. . . . such an act would or might naturally produce the result, or event. . . . If a new force or power intervene of itself sufficient to stand as the cause of the mischief or injury the act complained of is not the proximate cause."[94] Under common law, as one can see from Susan King's case, the drinker's consumption of an alcoholic beverage was considered to supercede the saloonkeeper's sale of the beverage as the proximate cause of intoxication.[95] Civil damage laws required that courts not consider drinkers to be the "proximate cause" of their own intoxication. The Connecticut Supreme Court explained that their state's 1872 civil damage act "displaced the common-law rule that the proximate cause of intoxication was not the furnishing of the liquor but its consumption."[96] The Illinois act was based on the idea that "a person . . . selling or giving intoxicating liquors" could "cause the intoxication" of the drinker.

Civil damage laws were, and still are, a cause of great confusion and annoyance to many legal scholars who argue that they are jarringly out of accord with the rest of the U.S. legal tradition.[97] A 1910 authoritative work on liquor law, Woolen and Thornton's *Intoxicating Liquors,* complained that "much confusion has resulted from the loose way in which the term 'proximate cause' has been used by courts and writers" in civil damage cases.[98] Somehow, in the middle of the nineteenth century, a number of state legislatures passed a type of law that appeared to be based on a different notion of legal responsibility than the rest of American law.

Civil damage laws seemed fair to lawmakers and to many of their constituents for the same reasons that prohibitory legislation seemed necessary: they had come to believe that drink purveyors bore a large degree of responsibility for their customers' drinking. Court officials in civil damage cases often claimed that habitual drinkers, at least, lacked free will and moral responsibility. In a decision on an 1876 civil damage case, the Iowa Supreme Court insisted that some drinkers' actions could not be seen as voluntary. Responding to the saloonkeeper's attorney's argument that *"involuntary* whiskey drinking is something foreign to human experience,"[99] the court insisted that "it is one of the saddest facts in human nature that many persons do both buy and drink intoxicating liquor who, spontaneously, of their own will, without being influenced or impelled by others, would not have done so."[100] A doctor testifying for a plaintiff in 1874 claimed that "although the will [of a drinker] may be in existence still it is perverted."[101] Similarly, a plaintiff's attorney more than twenty years later cited a legal treatise that suggested that when saloonkeepers sold alcohol to a man until he was drunk, they made "the will theirs and not his."[102] The judge in *Lafler v. Fisher* (1899) instructed the jury that an intoxicated man's "usual will power is temporarily suspended."[103]

Plaintiffs and court officials frequently stated their conviction that inebriates lacked willpower. Some used an array of degrading metaphors to describe drinkers' failure of will. One saloon lawyer complained that "the underlying idea [of the civil damage act] is, that a drunken man is a sort of ferocious animal, and whoever puts him in that condition, must answer for his violence; the same as the owner of a vicious beast, who lets him loose to gore or injure others."[104] A plaintiff's lawyer compared a drinker to "an infant of tender years, or an idiot, or a person NON COMPOS MENTIS from any cause."[105] Others said that drinkers were not "themselves." In an 1875 trial, for instance, plaintiff Elizabeth En- gleken bemoaned that her husband was "not near the man he used to be a couple of years ago."[106] James Rush's brother-in-law claimed, more colloquially, that when drunk, James was not "at himself."[107] Witness John Funk claimed that a drinker "didn't have any use of himself."[108]

Civil damage law plaintiffs, court officials, and juries increasingly worked under the premise that at least some drinkers lacked the strength of will neces- sary to resist alcohol. They did not excuse drinkers; courts generally still held drinkers criminally and civilly responsible for their acts while intoxicated. Plaintiffs could sue drinkers as well as saloonkeepers. Still, the law imposed a double responsibility on the drinker and on the drink purveyor. While courts had not entirely excused drinkers from the consequences of their actions, they had moved to complicate the relationship between the drinker and his deeds. Courts increasingly adopted an understanding of the drunkard as lacking will and took unprecedented steps to deal with him accordingly.

In other words, those who supported civil damage laws had accepted the underlying logic of drunkard narratives like Gough's and Chellis's. Indeed, laws themselves inspired many plaintiffs and their lawyers to tell drunkard narra- tives that closely resembled those from temperance fiction and propaganda.[109] Civil damage act lawyers understood the power of the drunkard narrative, and their attempts to evoke temperance melodrama were both frequent and bla- tant. One plaintiff's lawyer, in an 1890 case, begged the court's pardon for beginning his argument with a "brief summary of the humble lives of the plaintiff and her husband, the two principal characters in this tragical case." He went on to describe how "whiskey, the demon of man," deliberately proffered by a saloonkeeper, destroyed the "happy little home" of a "strong, able bodied, healthy, hard working, laboring man . . . honest and industrious" and his "dar- ling wife . . . spotless in the crowning glory of woman."[110] In 1873 another plaintiff's lawyer asked, "How long shall these breathing-holes of hell be per- mitted to curse the land with their woe and desolation?" He continued by summarizing the key points of the drunkard narrative: "Men, debased by na- ture, with passions ever prone to evil, have those passions flamed by the fires of alcoholic spirits. . . . Wives are driven homeless upon our streets. . . . Children . . . are thrown with feeble minds and frail bodies upon the charities of the state." After wreaking this havoc, the saloonkeeper "continues his traffic. His coffers are filled with gold, and the land with sorrow."[111] A third brief quoted the Michigan Supreme Court's telling of the narrative, "In an evil hour [a man] is led astray and commences the use of intoxicating liquors. Unable to control himself in their use, he becomes a drunkard . . . his wife is neglected and his children become outcasts."[112]

The language and the larger structure of these arguments, even to the extent of discussing the plaintiffs as "characters" in a story, moved the jury into the melodramatic realm of the fictional drunkard narrative. Civil damage act lawyers presented their clients' husbands as acting according to the conventions of a drunkard's decline. These men had indeed sunk low—as plaintiff Elizabeth Engleken's attorney put it, "Could he be very far from the lowest depth who would rob his children of their treasured pennies to barter with defendant for his vile potions?"[113] Yet these same men had been exemplary husbands before they turned to drink. Plaintiff Amanda Parker, for instance, said of her deceased husband, "I don't think there was a kinder man."[114] Plaintiffs' lawyers portrayed saloonkeepers as melodramatic villains, "chuckl[ing] . . . with glee" while pocketing the money from desperate drinkers' wives' "toil at the washtub."[115] Attorneys described drinkers' wives and children as long-suffering victims of saloonkeepers' deliberate attempts to oppress them. An attorney in an 1874 case claimed the plaintiff was "turned penniless upon the world, to satisfy the grasping avarice of the rumseller."[116] Drinkers' wives approaching saloonkeepers in plaintiffs' narratives were entering an unequal power relation, in which they were forced to throw themselves on the mercy of the merciless. Plaintiff Amanda Woolheather in 1874 testified that she had "begged of [defendant Frank Risley] not to sell liquor to my husband or anyone that belonged to the house. He made no reply, but turned upon his heel and laughed me in the face."[117] Louise Faivre's attorney asserted that saloonkeepers "fill the windows with bright lights and gaudy signs, for the purpose of enticing" drinkers from the path of rectitude.[118]

Saloonkeepers' lawyers frequently complained about plaintiffs' use of the language of the drunkard narrative. They argued that evoking such melodramatic stories prevented juries from rationally deliberating on the facts of the case. As a saloon supporter wrote in 1884 of the temperance movement, "prohibitionists never had facts on their side, but they have had, and have, an abundance of theories and a world of sentiment at their command."[119] In an early Iowa civil damage case, the counsel for the defense predicted that the plaintiffs' attorneys would "rely mainly, from necessity, on arguments addressed to the prejudices and passions of men as against the evil of intemperance, and the heinousness of selling liquor."[120] Another Iowa attorney asserted in 1878 that juries in liquor cases "however rational they may be upon other subjects, upon the subject of liquor they become at once monomaniacs. . . . Their reason is dethroned, their better judgment is gone, and their petty preferences, passions, and prejudices gain sway."[121] Decades later, a third attorney complained about his opponent's blatant appeal to the jury's emotions. The plaintiffs' lawyer had, apparently, "carve[d] the air, reeking with sweat, charging up and down as if the whole object and purpose of the trial were to still further inflame and make mad the jury he was addressing."[122] A fourth, similarly, though less dramatically, accused his opponent of the "tendency to drift away from the facts and draw upon the imagination."[123] In each of these cases, plaintiffs' lawyers harnessed the immense cultural power of the drunkard narrative; often, the best the saloonkeepers' lawyers could do was complain that they weren't playing fair.

An 1873 cartoon in *Harper's Weekly* took a wry view toward the civil damage laws that were then spreading across the country. It depicted "an intoxicated gentleman" expressing his approval of the legislation (fig. 2).[124] In expressing the sense that civil damage laws improperly forced others to pay the consequences of irresponsible drinkers' actions, the cartoonist voiced a common objection to the laws and to the ideas of moral responsibility that undergirded them.

Temperance reformers' denial of drinkers' willpower and hence of their responsibility for their own actions, served as the chief rallying point for their opponents. Antitemperance thinkers attacked temperance reformers' understanding of drinkers' volition. They insisted that reformers were incorrect in asserting that drinkers lacked will, and they pragmatically argued that adopting such an understanding would dangerously undermine the American tradition of freedom.[125] They admitted, as it would have been difficult for them to deny, that some individuals drank to excess and that their families and communities suffered for it. However, they argued, excessive drinking was only one among many vices in which imperfect men and women chose to indulge. People drank to excess because they were sinful. It was true, they often acknowledged, that it became progressively more difficult for frequent drinkers to stop drinking but that was because indulging any sin increased the sinner's desire. They believed that the habitual drinker did not lose his ability to stop drinking; he did not become "addicted" or "enslaved" to drink. There was no rift between will and

Fig. 2. Harper's Weekly cartoon, vol. 17 (1873), 560 (Photo courtesy of the Newberry Library, Chicago)

desire. Rather he repeatedly opted to sin because sinning became increasingly attractive to him.

Prohibition opponents' view of excessive drinking as the product of a sinful rather than an impotent will often led them, unlike temperance reformers, to impeach the general character of excessive drinkers. In 1888, Edgar Watson Howe, a prominent critic of the temperance movement, argued pointedly that temperance reformers glorified drinkers. As he put it, "When a man disgraces himself in any other way, we insist that he must be humiliated . . . but when he becomes a disgusting, beastly drunkard, we tell him in confidence that he is not to blame, and that his enemies the saloon-keepers, are responsible."[126] Saloon defenders, like temperance reformers, emphasized that those who drank excessively often chose to partake in other vices as well. Yet whereas reformers saw the other vices as proceeding from the paralysis of the will caused by drink, saloon proponents believed that sinful men chose to drink to excess, just as they chose to indulge themselves in other ways.[127]

Saloonkeepers' lawyers took a clearly pragmatic but strikingly critical stance toward excessive drinkers in civil damage suits. "He's a shiftless, lazy, drinking sort of a creature?" asked one lawyer of a drinker in 1877.[128] Another described a drinker as "accustomed also to gambling and practicing other evil vices, [who] was also a spendthrift and devoted his time to drinking, gambling, and idleness."[129] A third referred to one excessive drinker as an "old bum" and another as "vicious."[130] A fourth, in the 1890s, described a subject of a suit as "one of this class of boys that are brought up in town that do not work."[131] Indeed, it was the norm in civil damage suits throughout the late nineteenth century for saloonkeepers' lawyers to take a much more negative view of the drinker than did the lawyers for drinkers' wives. Of course, much of this was strategic; some judges instructed juries that if a drinker's actions were caused not by his drunkenness but by his "natural inclination or general depravity," plaintiffs could not recover losses.[132] However, it also fit into the larger cultural tendency of temperance opponents to hold excessive drinkers more accountable for their own vices than reformers did.

The pro-drink insistence on the drinker's personal responsibility for his actions was both religious and political. Like present-day opponents of gun control who insist that "Guns don't kill people: people kill people," prohibition opponents took issue with the idea that the availability of alcohol caused individuals to act immorally. One antiprohibitionist, writing to a temperance newspaper in 1869, complained that "Much is said of Alcohol destroying such vast numbers of lives, as if it was the active agent in the matter."[133] Many temperance opponents also voiced their passionate rejection of the perfectionism they understood to be pervading the temperance movement. As one antiprohibition pamphleteer wrote in 1884, "Prohibition was first tested in the Garden of Eden —and failed. The fall of man and his free agency were the results. All the imperfections of our moral nature are, according to the Scripture, consequences of this first failure of prohibition; for had not Eve plucked and eaten the forbidden fruit, man would be perfect. As it is, we are foredoomed to sin and suffer for sinning, but we are free agents."[134] Because they were based on a flawed perception of the nature of sin, opponents believed temperance reforms would fail.

Neither a judgment against a saloonkeeper nor any larger prohibition agenda would be an appropriate way to help the drunkard and his family.

Prohibition opponents further argued that temperance reformers' position on volition was more than wrong; it was dangerous. Acting as though drinkers lacked responsibility for their actions would only encourage them to pursue viciousness, secure in the belief that they would be neither punished nor blamed. Much of Edgar Watson Howe's opposition to temperance rhetoric operated along these lines. In lifting blame from drinkers' shoulders, reformers took away incentive to improve. The biggest danger to the path temperance reformers were pursuing, however, was that in falsely imagining that a class of people lacked free will, they threatened actually to rob them of the freedom to exercise that will. In an 1886 report to the St. Louis, Missouri, school board, a Dr. Starkloff argued against prohibitionist teachings, claiming that they would "rob" students "of will-power and self-control."[135] The freedom to choose sin, prohibition opponents argued, was an essential aspect of moral liberty.

They also believed that, in partially letting the drunkard off the hook for his behavior, reformers threatened to erode the basis of American political liberty. Much to the discomfort of temperance advocates, organizations of saloonkeepers and their supporters frequently evoked the language of freedom and liberty. Critics of coercive legislation like prohibitory laws and civil damage acts tended to call their organizations such names as "Personal Liberty Leagues" and give speeches with titles like "Prohibition versus Personal Liberty," evoking constitutional rights.[136] The temperance movement, throughout the nineteenth century, had been gradually using the term "liberty" to mean not "freedom from governmental interference" but rather "freedom from enslavement to alcohol."[137] Their opponents, by reappropriating the terms, challenged this discursive move. Saloon supporter George Maskoff, for instance, had a character exclaim in his 1890 play, "The only analogy I see between slavery and prohibition is that both are an outrage against human liberty."[138] Similarly, a sympathetic character in an 1893 antitemperance novel cited Blackstone's dictum, "every man's house is his castle," to underline the novelist's argument that the temperance movement was violating the boundaries of men's sovereignty.[139]

Prohibition opponents saw the implications of the widespread erosion of belief in the drinker's volition. The ability, freedom, and obligation to take responsibility for one's own actions was a prerequisite not only to morality but to political liberty. If people came to accept that individual drinkers were not responsible for their own actions and the consequences that might arise from them, it was hard to imagine what limits might remain on the power of the government to interfere with them. As Dr. Starkloff continued in his recommendation that the St. Louis school board not include total abstinence advocacy in the curriculum, "To make this republic strong and lasting we, above all, need men and women who can exercise self-control."[140] Indoctrinating schoolchildren with temperance principles, like pushing prohibition in the political realm, was a first step toward political tyranny because it robbed individuals of the power to make their own moral choices.

It probably came as no surprise to antiprohibitionists when some temperance advocates began quite explicitly to claim that inebriates had no political rights. In 1892, prominent temperance-reformer physician T. D. Crothers blatantly insisted that "the moment a man becomes a drunkard he forfeits all rights to liberty."[141] This extreme position was exactly what prohibition opponents had understood to be the consequence of denying drinkers' volition. But many critics of temperance tactics felt that depriving inebriates of all freedom and depriving all men of the freedom to drink were only first steps in a larger project to deprive all men of political and personal freedom. The challenge to drinkers' volitional manhood, they claimed, threatened all men, largely because determining who was an inebriate, or even who was intoxicated, was so imprecise.

In that pre-Breathalyzer and blood-test age, determining whether a man who had been drinking was drunk was absolutely subjective; if the most credible people around a man were willing to testify that he was drunk, then he was. Determining whether someone was "a drunkard" was even more ambiguous. Far from constituting a distinct and recognizable category, drunken men were impossible to identify accurately. The question of whether a man was intoxicated at any given moment, and whether he had thus forfeited his autonomy, was a very difficult one. Simply asking him would not necessarily help, given intoxicated men's well-known tendency to claim sobriety. Any attempt to encroach on his freedom would likely be met with a defense of his rights. Would-be assistants simply had to rely on his appearance and behavior.

Despite some judges' hopeful assertions to jurors that the meaning of "intoxication" was so obvious that it need not be defined, saloongoers and other witnesses repeatedly complained that they did not know what it meant to be "intoxicated" or that their definition of "intoxication" differed from what they thought the court or other witnesses meant by it.[142] Some felt that they could tell accurately when some men were intoxicated: one man apparently peppered his conversation with the word "galvanize" when he was drunk; some "wiggle-waggle[d] around"; some forgot to wear their hats; some had a peculiar red or glassy-eyed look; one was unable to use eating utensils when drunk; others became either unusually belligerent or sociable.[143] Yet these were exceptions. Most saloongoers insisted categorically that they could not tell if someone else was drunk or even if they themselves were drunk. They pointed out that a man could pretend to be drunk or could seem "duly sober" even while intoxicated, and that each person behaved differently when drunk.[144] Even if they were sure what it meant to be drunk, they could not with certainty testify whether another person fit into that category.

In this period of the rise of the "expert," some lawyers tried to get around this problem by setting up certain witnesses as particularly experienced in defining and identifying intoxication.[145] Law-enforcement workers sometimes filled this role, but in most rural communities, policing was a part-time job and lacked professional status. Some lawyers brought in physicians to testify, but physicians who themselves were not drinkers found their authority called into question, while those who were risked having their sobriety challenged.[146]

The other obvious experts were saloonkeepers or heavy drinkers. One attorney asserted in a brief that the testimony of abstainers "upon the question of intoxication is not to be relied upon when opposed by that of others who have been in the habit." Similarly, one drinker in an 1874 case said to a nondrinking lawyer, "If you drank liquor yourself you could help me tell what effect it has on a man, but when a man don't drink any it is hard to tell a man or satisfy him what feeling it has on one." Although they were most experienced with the effects of alcohol, drinkers and saloonkeepers were suspect for that very reason.[147] Not surprisingly, they were also notoriously uncooperative with plaintiffs' lawyers' attempts to define intoxication. Their testimony was frequently vague and highly idiomatic. Take, for instance, the testimony of bartender William P. "Kid" O'Connell.

Q. What is your idea of intoxication?
A. What is my idea of intoxication?
Q. When is a man intoxicated?
A. When is a man intoxicated?
Q. Yes.
A. When he is full. When he has enough. Got enough to drink.
Q. What do you mean by when he has got enough to drink?

A. Not give him any more. I never sold a drunken man a drink in my life.

Q. When is a man drunk?

A. When you see him come in and staggering around.

Q. A man is not drunk until then?

A. You can always notice when a man is full and he has got enough.

Q. Describe a man's appearance when he has got enough or is full.

A. Why, he just walks up to the bar and slaps on it, and wants a drink, a little whisky. I would say, "You got all you want."[148]

Though "Kid" O'Connell claimed that he could tell when a man was drunk, and suggested that "staggering around" was one mark of intoxication, his maddeningly circular definitions contributed little to the attorney's efforts to define the signs of intoxication. His employer, saloonkeeper Peter McCarthy, complicated matters even further, insisting that though some men "can drink thirty [beers] and then they are not intoxicated," other men "are intoxicated when they do not drink anything."[149] One lawyer in another case grew frustrated that his saloongoing witnesses refused to testify like experts. Commenting on their ceaseless use of local slang to describe states of drunkenness, he sarcastically asked a witness, "Is the term 'beastly sober' recognized in the saloon as a technical term?"[150]

The civil damage act and the philosophy behind it threatened the legal status of most men, as it was hard to see whom, besides teetotalers, the category of "drunkard" might not ultimately encompass. As civil damage act litigants and temperance writers pointed out from time to time, even the smallest amount of liquor altered the "natural state" of a drinker and began the process of transformation. When asked in an 1899 case "What quantity of alcohol can a man take into his system and have it produce no effect upon him?" one testifying physician replied simply and chillingly, "No quantity."[151] Even social prominence or wealth did not protect a man from being labeled a drunkard. A few of the "drunkards" in civil damage cases were, or had been, quite affluent. One was described as "a man of full habit and portly, and a man of urbane manners."[152] Another had recently bought a yacht ("like Jay Gould had, only not quite so elaborate").[153] In a Massachusetts case, a wife accused her husband of pawning several expensive and irreplaceable items including "a certain bisque statuette," "coral ornaments of great value," "a ring containing a topaz set in diamonds," "two diamond bracelets," and "a certain cross set with pearls."[154] Some civil damage act drunkards had held positions of responsibility within their communities. The drunkard in one Iowa case, in fact, was a lawyer who had defended a saloonkeeper in an earlier civil damage suit.[155]

Ultimately, if a reasonable observer judged that a man was drunk, that observer had a right and often a responsibility to attempt, often by force, to save the man from himself. Because of the extreme subjectivity of drunkenness, any man entering a saloon and taking a drink put himself in a position in which others—not only fellow saloongoers, but also family members, neighbors, and even, in a broader way, the government and temperance activists—could label him "drunk" and interfere in his affairs. Saloon supporters knew that the subjectivity of "drunkenness" made even moderate drinking potentially perilous.

Indeed, many temperance advocates contemplated the possibility of free will much more generally in their writings. A medical journal specializing in alcoholism, the *Quarterly Journal of Inebriety,* evoked Spinoza in an 1890 article, asserting that his "saying, that 'Our Illusions of Free Will are but our ignorance of the motives and influences which enter into our acts' is true among inebriates."[156] Another temperance polemicist leapt from an argument that weak liquor license laws had contributed to making men drunkards to a more general assertion that "mortal man is the creation of influences which have followed him through life."[157] J. T. Crane began a chapter of his 1870 temperance book, *The Arts of Intoxication,* with some philosophical speculation. "The union of the soul with the body in which it dwells is an unfathomable mystery. What tie binds them? . . . how shall spirit be welded to matter?"[158] Before discussing the drunkard's loss of willpower, George D. Lind's temperance-heavy physiology textbook (1892) muses that "[v]olition . . . seems to come from within and be independent of external stimuli, yet we do not know but that it is a result of impressions *previously* received through the sensory nerves and stored up in the cells of the brain, to be given out later in the form of voluntary motion."[159] George Cutten, in his 1907 *The Psychology of Alcoholism,* insisted that while he did not "believe in the 'freedom of the will,' " because this phrase has become meaningless, he believes "both from the standpoint of psychology and of ethics in the 'freedom of the self.' "[160] With that helpful clarification, he declared "the subject, as far as we are concerned, is dropped." These temperance thinkers, just as their opponents feared, saw the problem of the drunkard as potentially opening into a more general understanding of the nature of the human will and hence a changing view of the possibilities of human freedom.[161]

The intersection of alcohol and free will was a central theme of one of the best-selling novels in the late-nineteenth-century United States, Charles Sheldon's

In His Steps: What Would Jesus Do? (1896). Sheldon, a Congregational minister, was a leader of the temperance and other social reform movements in Kansas.[162] His novel tells the story of a group of Midwestern churchgoers who attempt to live as Jesus would if he found himself in their situation in life. They ultimately determine that Jesus would fight against a rather eclectic collection of social ills, including poor labor conditions, violations of interstate commerce laws, newspaper coverage of prizefights, and unscientific housekeeping among poor immigrants. Many of them, however, determine that Jesus would chiefly work for an alcohol-free United States. Therefore they work to rescue from drink those who live in areas they consider "stronghold[s] of the devil" like a neighborhood called the "Rectangle" in their own town, and vice districts in Chicago.[163] The key to the book's popularity may be that, like the temperance movement generally, it participated in, articulated, and worked to resolve the question of how to account for the self as a responsible moral actor in the face of environmental influences that were perceived as increasingly powerful.

"Who could tell what depended on their environment[?]" one of Sheldon's characters exclaims despairingly, "the environment does have a good deal to do with the character."[164] Sheldon illustrated this power in stark terms, though he never explicitly articulated how environmental influence worked. As a Social Gospel minister, he particularly emphasized the power of the environment when discussing residents of vice districts, which he described as possessing a kind of collective agency. "The Rectangle" lived a "brutal, coarse, impure life." It "start[ed] in with vigor on its usual night debauch." It "seemed to stare as with one great, bleary, beer-soaked countenance." It "never took itself seriously when it was drunk." "The Rectangle was drunk and enraged." Not only was the Rectangle drunk corporately, it was saved corporately. It "lay like some wild beast at [an evangelical singer's] feet." Later, even more strikingly, "the Rectangle for the time being was swept into the harbor of redemptive grace."[165]

This phrasing was not just quirky use of language. In Sheldon's narrative, it is impossible for residents of neighborhoods like the Rectangle to save themselves individually. People from these neighborhoods can only "be saved" by reformers who physically and forcibly remove them to middle-class neighborhoods or enclaves like settlement homes. Prayer, conversion, and faith can take residents only so far, and ultimately they fail to make lasting changes as long as they remain in their corrupt environments. "What can [an evangelist] do with his gospel meetings when half his converts are drinking people, daily tempted and enticed by the saloon on every corner?"[166] Loreen and Burns, the only named vice-district residents who are rehabilitated in the novel, are literally dragged or carried by evangelists to islands of middle-class domesticity. In Sheldon's world, environment has everything to do with character.

Although Sheldon portrays the power of environment most strongly when describing vice districts, he suggests that the influence of a middle-class or affluent environment can also determine the character of those who live in it. Occasionally, though less frequently than with residents of the Rectangle, Sheldon describes the behavior and thought of middle-class and wealthy churchgoers corporately. On one occasion, for instance, "the First church of Raymond came to the morning service in a condition that made it quickly sensitive to any large truth."[167] Throughout, Sheldon emphasizes how the competition and influence of comfortable society blinds its members to the world beyond their sphere and to the true Christian message. If vice-district natives like Loreen and Burns have to move to middle-class neighborhoods to be saved, most middle-class Christians in Sheldon's book have to move in the opposite direction. A few of the church members who decide to live as Jesus would (like young heir Roland Page, who witnesses to members of his elite social club) find that they can be Christians while remaining within "society." For most, though, the answer to the question "What Would Jesus Do?" involves moving out of prosperous neighborhoods and into revival tents, storefronts, and settlements in poor neighborhoods. One character refers to his move to a Chicago settlement as having "left the world."[168] For poor and prosperous, abject sinners and churchgoers alike, one key to salvation is to leave the home environment behind.

Sheldon's willingness to minimize individual responsibility for sin and to question the possibility that preaching could bring about individual salvation may seem to have been an unwise choice for a minister. Not only did he potentially detract from his own authority, he also challenged a belief deeply held by many of his congregants. The idea of the responsible individual was one of the central pillars of Protestant Christianity. In imagining neighborhoods rather than individuals as willing units, Sheldon suggested that all people were not merely influenced but largely or completely controlled by powers greater than themselves. Yet as disruptive as Sheldon's message potentially was, it clearly attracted and inspired a large segment of progressive-age American readers. Because the American public had become familiar with the rhetoric of the drunkard narrative, the radical view of manhood implicit in *In His Steps* raised few, if any, eyebrows.

CHAPTER TWO

Manhood

Harry Summers, a successful young builder and bricklayer in the village of Weldon, Illinois, spent the last Christmas day of the nineteenth century in a bar and an adjoining upstairs "club room." He had chosen not to work on Christmas, and by 8:00 A.M. he was drinking whiskey and playing cards with his friends in the town's only saloon. By most accounts, Summers drank a lot throughout the day; thirty-one-year-old day laborer Henry "Chicken" Johnson claimed to have seen him drink "15 to 20" drinks before 11:30 A.M.[1] At some point in the afternoon, one of Summers's card-playing companions, C. C. Murdock, accused Summers of cheating. Summers denied it. Doc Marcum, a day laborer from out of town who knew Murdock, had wandered in to watch the game, and he apparently encouraged Murdock to stand his ground. So far, this sounds like the script for a classic saloon gunfight. Summers and Murdock, however, resolved their dispute peacefully. The fight that did break out was between Summers and Marcum. Summers was more willing to overlook Murdock's insult to his honor than Marcum's interference in his business. He "spoke up and asked [Marcum] what was his business, and [Marcum] says 'It is some of my business' or something." Summers threatened Marcum, stood up, and headed toward him. Marcum pulled out a gun, but Summers, unfazed by the weapon, said "You've got a gun, but it don't make any difference" and continued approaching.[2] Marcum then fatally shot Summers, but before he died, Summers managed to give Marcum a "light lick at a high point," knocking him to the floor.[3] Observers testified to their sense that Marcum, by interfering in the dispute over cheating, had seriously violated saloon norms and invited Summers's attack.[4]

The criminal case that followed the attack was open and shut. Marcum—who was smaller than Summers, whose exit was blocked, and who shot Summers while holding his left arm in front of him to ward off his blow—had clearly killed in self-defense.[5] The civil damage suit brought by Summers's widow, Emma, was more complex. She asked for a judgment against the saloonkeeper on the grounds that the death of her husband was caused by the intoxication of her husband and Marcum, who had been drinking his liquor. She won her case on both counts, and the appellate court upheld the district court decision, but the Illinois Supreme Court, when they heard it in 1903, reversed and remanded the case on the grounds that the trial judge had issued faulty instructions to the jury. It is unknown what happened to Emma after her husband's death. She may have moved, since neither she nor her son appear on the June 1900 census of Weldon.[6]

Harry Summers's fatal encounter with Doc Marcum seems to have been caused largely by his failure to recognize the limits of his autonomy. Surely he had not stopped to reflect that his judgment was too impaired by alcohol to enable him properly to take care of himself. More immediately, his fatal failure to acknowledge that Marcum's gun "made a difference" suggests a blind confidence in his own power to bring his will to fruition. Many nineteenth-century men like Summers felt similar tensions between their desire to imagine themselves as possessing autonomous manhood and the stubborn fact that they were often distinctly not in control of their affairs, or even of their own bodies. While most men did not experience this tension as dramatically and momentously as did Harry Summers, many found themselves unable to come to terms with the forces that impinged on their autonomy. For many, the use of alcohol brought this tension to a crisis.

Harry Summers's sudden death illustrates the extent to which the idea of "volition" in the 1800s was interrelated with culturally prescribed gender roles. It was widely believed that men had both a privileged relationship to volition and a weighty responsibility to preserve their volitional independence. Because women and children depended on husbands and fathers for sustenance and protection, and because they were shielded from engagement in business, politics, and much other social interchange, both their thoughts and actions were to some extent controlled by adult men.

Americans of the period often wrote and spoke of volition in gendered terms. They frequently, for instance, expressed the division between the public person and the interior self in the gendered language of domesticity.[7] They commonly compared an individual's interior to the interior of the bourgeois home, using the analogy to the point that "middle class woman emblematized interiority itself."[8] The idea that the skin covering the human body or the walls surrounding the middle-class home protected spaces of "interiority" from the potentially corrupting forces of society was a mainstay of nineteenth-century thought. This widespread association of femininity and interiority caused debates over gender roles and the status of the volitional individual to flow seamlessly into one another. As Americans wondered aloud whether individuals possessed some core capable of resisting environmental influence, they began to see women, who traditionally were protected from exposure to the public environment, as possessing a privileged relationship to interiority. This is one of the reasons that the drunkard narrative was so strongly gendered. Increasingly, drink debate participants asked one another not only whether drinking men could be said to possess any volition but also whether any man, exposed as men were to constant environmental influence, was truly safe from the allure of alcohol.

The problem of the drunkard, to many temperance advocates, was a matter of both manhood and volition. To be more specific, it was a failure of volition that *caused* a failure of manhood. The drunkard, in the eyes of reformers, was not a true man because he was unable to exert his will over his own body and interests. This theme of lost manhood was key to the logic of the drunkard narrative. Nevertheless, the cultural association between manhood and volition, and the suggestion that drunkards had lost both, were by no means limited to temperance circles. These fears eventually came to be shared even by many saloongoers and would ultimately play an important part in undermining the saloon culture from within.

The problem of influence was central to the connection between the gender and volitional crises expressed in the drink debate. The basic presupposition behind the idea of "influence," given that people were largely shaped by their environments, was that it was possible for others who were part of their environment to plan deliberately to shape them in particular ways. This could often be a force of good. The virtuous could, by setting an example of moral conduct, spread moral behavior to the less moral. Moral suasion relied on this idea.[9] Through the conscious exercise of influence, women, though lacking more overt forms of political and social power, could guide their husbands and children, and therefore shape their own environments. The model of female power as influence posited that women should exercise their power indirectly, by inculcating moral principles into their husbands, sons, and fathers, who would in turn bring those principles to bear in the world of public affairs. Influence, because it was indirect, solved the problem of allowing women to affect the world without being corrupted by it.[10]

Yet this model of "influence" had some troubling implications. First, to the extent that moral suasion was effective in causing men to behave differently than they would have behaved without it, it called men's volitional independence into question.[11] A reformer's attempts to persuade a working man to take the pledge or a wife's concerted efforts to influence her husband to abstain might have been more morally commendable than a party boss's attempts to win a drinker's vote or a saloonkeeper's efforts to influence him to drink, but were the actions of the reformer and wife really that dissimilar in kind from those of the demagogue and saloonkeeper? Ironically, just as many reformers were determining that the power of alcohol was so strong as to impede the drinker's volition and render "moral suasion" useless, some temperance opponents were arguing that reformers' "moral suasion" efforts themselves so overpowered pledge signers as to prevent them from exercising their own volition.

Opponents of the temperance movement began to make this point as early as the 1830s. Consider, for instance, the objections of a Virginia antitemperance pamphleteer in 1836 to the pledge. "As a moral agent, [man] is endowed with both reason and appetite . . . through fear of his ruin, shall we impose on him restraints in advance? Then suppress all his appetites . . . reduce him at once to a mere stock and stone; he then will be safe."[12] In the same year, Harper and Brothers in New York published an anonymous antitemperance society tract in which the author, "A Protestant," similarly argued, "Who that has put his name to [a temperance pledge] can say that his conscience is in his own keeping; or that he is at liberty to use his own judgment?"[13]

These antitemperance writers, like many others, were beginning to imagine that influence could be so powerful as to amount to coercion. This belief, of course, closely resembled temperance advocates' growing conviction that alcohol did not so much tempt the drinker as enslave him. The close parallel between the two opposing groups' ideas of the power of influence soon led to a rather complicated discursive situation, as another passage from "A Protestant's" tract shows: "The demand [to sign the pledge]—for demand it virtually is—is made in such circumstances and under such influences, that not one in ten, probably not one in a hundred, could avoid yielding to it, however they might desire to escape." As she put it, "They are literally dragged to the sacrifice. . . . having once submitted, there is no more to be said; the triumph is complete; the victory is proclaimed. . . . The victims are bound—there is no escape. Conscience, and reason, and judgment are all taken away."[14] This passage, no doubt inspired by anti-Catholic seduction literature, is almost indistinguishable from the inevitable "fatal first drink" scene in the drunkard narrative. At the time the pamphlet was written, the drunkard narrative was just emerging; if it had been written even ten years later, the passage would almost certainly have been read as a deliberate parody of temperance literature.[15]

In the antebellum years, both temperance opponents, in their antipledge writings, and reformers themselves, in their drunkard narratives, expressed deep concern about the nature of influence and worried that it could potentially interrupt its object's volition and become coercion. After the Civil War, the equation of influence and compulsion became much more a part of the temperance argument than of the antitemperance discursive arsenal. Reformers backed away from the "pledge," instead calling for coercive tactics like prohibition. In contrast, prohibition opponents extolled old influence tactics as preferable to the antidrink legislation. They devoted considerable energy to maintaining precisely the distinction between influence and compulsion that their antebellum precursors like "A Clergyman" and "A Protestant" had blurred.

The antebellum drinker's self-mastery, then, was threatened both by the liquor that threatened to make a "slave" of him and by those, whether family members or reformers in the community, who hoped to "influence" him to remain sober. Neither of these threats were alleviated in the years following the war. Rather, temperance reformers stepped up their rhetoric on the coercive power of saloons and used this rhetoric to call for even more ways to "save" drinkers that took account of their volitional failure. As women emerged as leaders of the temperance movement after the war, the battle over drink and the volitional issues it involved came to be seen as strongly gendered.

The cultural debate over the relationship between alcohol and gender roles was not limited to the pages of temperance pamphlets. Rather, drinkers expressed their concerns over these relationships every day through their saloon behavior. Rather than changing suddenly, the mixed-gender "tavern" dominant at the beginning of the century gradually evolved over many years into the homosocial "saloon" characteristic of the postwar period. Even so, the typically male saloon took on its classic character and became an important American institution at about the time the Civil War ended.[16] In the wake of the homosocial camaraderie of the war, returning soldiers (who were, notoriously, saloons' best customers) seem to have sought out and created such (almost) all-male spaces. An image of a late-nineteenth-century Midwestern saloon looks at first like the epitome of a male space, but there is a certain symbolic significance to the fact that out of a curtained window above the saloon, presumably the saloonkeeper's home, there looms a white-clad female figure (fig. 3). Like the war itself, the saloon would prove to be a space in which gender roles were challenged, threatened, and reimagined.

Two images of nineteenth-century saloongoers coexist uneasily within our historical imagination. One is of a strong, swaggering, whiskey-tossing gunslinger; the other, of a red-nosed, unshaven, flabby fellow wearing a misshapen hat and slumped against a lamppost. Those images competed as much with one another a century ago as they do today. Their coexistence points to an apparent paradox: many Americans saw the saloon as both confirming and threatening manhood. The very qualities that marked the saloon as a quintessentially manly space—the rawness of the exchanges among its patrons and its homosociality—simultaneously threatened manhood. As Catherine Murdock has aptly put it, "alcohol use was a male attribute that destroyed masculinity." The tension between these two images resonated with the saloon's critics and even more significantly with male saloongoers themselves. As he swaggered about the barroom's sawdust floors, the saloongoer cast an anxious glance over his shoulder, always fearing that his manly pretense would be exposed.[17]

It is impossible to pin down standards of male behavior in the late 1800s. Such ideals are always contested and variable, and this period was a particularly volatile one for gender prescriptions. The social chaos brought about by the Civil War and Reconstruction destabilized gender relations, often making it impossible for men and women to fulfill prewar gender expectations. There was also a dramatic change in the nature of men's work; by the end of the century, a much smaller percentage of men could claim either the independence of self-

Fig. 3. Oshkosh, Wisconsin, Phoenix House Saloon and Patrons, 1890 (Photo courtesy of the Oshkosh Public Museum)

employment or the prospect of upward mobility. As men moved from self-employment as farmers or tradesmen to subordinate positions within larger business organizations, older notions of self-sufficiency lost their cultural viability. In the face of these changes, many turned from grounding their manhood in their economic lives to grounding it in their leisure, bodies, and desires. Though middle-class, urban, Eastern men formed the backbone of support for this "passionate manhood" or "masculinity," the masculine exemplars they celebrated were often quite different from themselves. In particular, those sympathetic to the cult of masculinity often found themselves uncomfortably admiring, even emulating, uncivilized "savages," unrefined workingmen, and coarse Westerners. The Midwestern saloon, with its culture of rough male competition and camaraderie, played an important role in this construction of masculinity.[18]

Though many men in this period certainly did move from countryside to city, and from self-employment to salaried work, many others continued in agricultural and small-town self-employment. Though some of the Midwestern saloongoers in this study were railway workers, governmental employees, and the like, most were farmers or self-employed tradesmen like barbers, tailors, builders, day-laborers, blacksmiths, or plasterers.[19] They did not face with the same intensity the challenges that undermined traditional notions of manhood for so many others. For that reason, many of their countrymen idealized the Midwestern saloon as a haven for untroubled, traditional manhood. Saloongoers, however, were far from realizing the stable ideal of male behavior their contemporaries sought.[20]

In hindsight, we know that the saloon itself was a doomed institution that would collapse within the lifetimes of many of its patrons. Though the forces that brought down the saloon were largely external—launched by temperance men and women—they were so devastating largely because of what Madelon Powers, following Perry Duis, has called the saloon's "decay from within." In using this phrase to explain the surprising lack of effort saloongoers exerted to resist prohibition, Powers has argued that the saloon had so effectively organized its customers that they had taken over many of its social functions themselves. However, Midwestern saloongoers' own descriptions of saloon life suggest that this "decay" was as much discursive as it was functional. Many patrons found it impossible to reconcile saloon culture with their own standards of proper manhood. The attacks on the saloon that began in earnest in the years immediately following the Civil War exposed and exploited existing contradictions within saloongoers' own customs and gender identities.[21]

To appreciate what many nineteenth-century Midwestern men thought of as manly behavior, it is essential to investigate not only how they acted when they gathered together in the saloon but also the language they used to explain and justify their actions. Saloongoing witnesses' trial testimony reveals how Midwestern men talked about the line between acceptable and unacceptable male saloon behavior.[22]

In many respects, the saloon was a place where men could be men. Towns-men stopped by for a quick drink, sometimes looking for work or workers, or doing some other business, and met up with their neighbors and with farmers in for the day. Together they enjoyed a glass of beer and perhaps some bologna and boiled eggs, as well as plain talk and other amusements. It was unques-tionably a male space; Powers' recent revelation that the bars of some saloons were lined with "urination troughs" for customer convenience is certainly jar-ring but not really surprising. In rural areas, the homosociality of the saloon was, if possible, even more pronounced than in more anonymous urban areas. Male camaraderie in spaces like saloons helped working men to maintain their sense of manhood. As they drank, swore, smoked, gambled, told bawdy and exaggerated stories, and sang maudlin tunes together, they confirmed one an-other's identities as men. Trial testimony gives us a window into the substance of these identities.[23]

When Midwestern saloongoers talked about male norms and behavior, they did not use the language historians have used to describe them. They rarely talked about "honor," for instance, or "autonomy," "self-discipline," "indepen-dence," or "courage." Rather, the phrase they used most often to distinguish proper from improper male behavior was "minding your own business." They described their behavioral norms in terms of male control over a fairly well-de-fined social and physical space. This space at the very least included the man's own body, and usually encompassed his family, household, property, and eco-nomic interests. To fail to "mind one's own business" was to be like a slave, a woman, or a child—to lose one's claim to manhood. The saloon was a place for men to establish and defend, through both words and actions, the boundaries of their business. By spending his leisure time doing this, the saloongoer marked himself as a member of a dynamic manly community. Nineteenth-century sa-loongoers used "business" both in the sense of commercial interests and in an older, broader sense encompassing all of the activities and affairs in which an indi-vidual had an interest or responsibility. When they evoked "minding one's busi-ness" normatively, their meaning was closer to the older, second meaning. As such, they sometimes applied it (negatively) to women who were looking into the conduct of others instead of working to maintain their own households, as well as to men who were interfering in others' affairs instead of supporting their families. In the usage of saloongoers, however, "business" continually slipped into com-merce, and (as we shall see) into a wide variety of other highly male-gendered activities such as gambling, violence, and, of course, drinking. Thus, "minding one's own business" could become the governing norm of the all-male saloon.

If being a man meant "minding your own business," however, the saloon was also a space of threatened manhood. Popular explanations of the effects of alcohol suggested that alcohol brought saloongoers' primal bellicosity to the surface only by incapacitating certain aspects of their minds, wills, and persons. Writers often described alcohol as "an intruder." It was an "enemy . . . seductive in its advances . . . insidious in its influence, and . . . terrible in its triumph." Any man might unknowingly harbor an inherent weakness for alcohol, "lurking in [his] blood, ready to master [him] when opportunity invites." Once consumed, alcohol disabled or subverted the drinker's "controlling power," releasing the "brutish part of human nature." One 1862 temperance short story, John B. Gough's "Risky Business," personified alcohol, suggesting that it threatened to take over a drinker's business.[24]

According to one contemporary popular theory, then, alcohol itself could "mind the business" of a drinker and cast his manhood into doubt. More concretely, the physiological and psychological effects of drinking opened up men's business to interference by others, both inside and outside the world of the saloon. With his "controlling power" disabled, the drinker risked falling out of the norms of independent social control altogether. To drink was to risk becoming drunk and thus incompetent to mind one's business. Such incompetence invited, even required one's fellow saloongoers, wives, and other interested parties to intervene in one's affairs. This might take the form of individual and personal interference with a single drinker, or it might take the form of a massive social movement aimed at restricting the freedom of all drinkers and at destroying the saloon as an institution. While jostling with one another over position and authority, then, saloongoers risked losing mastery over their "business."

When saloongoers talked about "minding your business," which they did incessantly, they meant it in both a positive and a negative sense. Each individual had an obligation to attend to his own responsibilities and defend their boundaries, and he was to avoid becoming involved in those things that were rightly the responsibilities of others. Saloongoers were quite sensitive to perceived intrusions on their autonomy or that of their neighbors. The man who interfered with another's business faced the possibility not only that his target would defend himself by force but also that fellow saloongoers would take the part of the would-be victim, restraining, criticizing or ostracizing the aggressor, or even mobilizing forces outside the saloon to punish him.

The saloon was a location of the enactment of manhood. Men in Midwestern saloons saw one another as comrades as well as competitors for power, status, and money. They joked, sang, and relieved themselves together, but they measured themselves against one another, attempting to define and defend their own areas of control and to challenge those of others. Some of this competition and violence served to exclude outsiders—those of different ethnic or political identities—or those who were considered habitual drunkards. Most of it, however, worked to shape and foster relationships rather than end them. Saloongoers challenged, clarified, and ultimately strengthened the boundaries of each individual's business. Except in the rare cases where things went too far, the "friendly scuffle[s]," or competitive jockeying for position among saloongoers encouraged camaraderie by assuring that each man knew the relationship in which he stood to the others.[25]

Recent saloon scholarship, perhaps in reaction to the "Wild West" image of the barroom as a site of violence, has so emphasized fellowship and camaraderie that it has downplayed this vital element of competition. Firsthand accounts of Midwestern saloon life, however, include stories of manly competition so blatant that they make cinematic depictions of machismo-run-amok seem almost subtle. G. H. Crawford, a butcher, described one such episode in Illinois in the 1890s. "There was a good many in the [saloon], the house was nearly a third full. They were talking and [Thomas] Webber [a thresher] was going about measuring arms and saying he could reach further than anyone else, telling what a man he was and asking the boys up to drink." Later, according to another man present, "they went to [measuring] pool sticks." Another man showed off his muscles and lifted heavy furniture to prove his strength, and still others bragged about how much alcohol they could drink without effect.[26]

In this atmosphere of competition, men who perceived that others were encroaching on the boundaries of their "business" often moved beyond playful competition to initiate violence to defend their interests. Threatening and insulting one another, they got into fistfights, broke each other's bones with their bare hands, hit one another with metal bars and pieces of lumber, threw stones, and occasionally drew knives or shot somebody. (Sometimes they regretted the violence, blaming it on their use of alcohol. After breaking his friend's leg, A. A. Free apparently sobbed that it was the third time he had broken someone's leg while drunk.)[27]

Many barroom quarrels emerged out of a perception that one saloongoer was interfering with another's business or boundaries. A drinker named Dewey became angry with a man named Ropp, because he "thought Ropp was interfering with his business."[28] Douglas Reneer, who shot and killed two men at a keg party outside an Atchison, Kansas, brewery at the turn of the century, complained that the men had been threatening him about his failure to join a union.[29] The fight that may have led to the deaths of two young Norwegian immigrants, Ole Hobbet and Andrew Larson, in the late 1880s, appears to have begun with a barroom shoving match over the affections of Hobbet's wife, Tarjon.[30] A group of saloongoers in Michigan in the 1880s precipitated one dispute by failing to yield the sidewalk to another group.[31] There are countless such examples in civil damage transcripts from the 1870s to the century's end.

Observers often described not only the causes of saloon violence but the violence itself in terms of violations of space. In a turn-of-the-century case in Washington State, a witness recounted Jacob Woodring's (a farmer and notorious bully) threats to Pete Grosjean, a younger man with whom he was quarreling in the street outside of the saloon. Woodring moved closer and closer to Grosjean as he backed up again and again. On a previous occasion, Grosjean had run away in the face of Woodring's threats, and he had even fruitlessly asked the justice of the peace to intervene. This time, in front of the many townspeople who had assembled to watch the confrontation, he decided to defend his ground, picked up a two-by-four, and sliced it across Woodring's face, killing him.[32]

Both the camaraderie and competition of saloon life could serve to affirm saloongoers' status as men, but the alternate image of the saloongoer as unmanned was never far away. Of course, temperance reformers were happy to embrace the view that saloongoing endangered manhood. They regularly referred to saloongoers as having lost their manhood. An 1869 temperance newspaper proclaimed, typically, that "No man can drink intoxicating liquors . . . without doing violence to his manhood." A sketch in an 1871 pamphlet-in-verse put out by the Sons of Temperance dramatically illustrated the lost manhood of the drinker; note the suggestive placement of the bottle in the drawing may be significant, though it was probably not intentional (fig. 4).[33] One female author of an 1875 temperance novel, quoted a despairing drunkard: "My manhood . . . it is a thing of the past." Another novelist, ten years later, wrote of a drinker, "his strong desire to be a man was overcome by an unquenchable thirst." A third, in her portion of a novel collectively written by a Kansas chapter of the Woman's Christian Temperance Union in 1908, had a promising young man take a drink and in so doing forget "his manhood." As he proceeds down the drunkard's path, he cries "As long as Christian men vote to protect the places whose only and sole object is to despoil manhood, what hope is there for me?"[34] In postwar temperance fiction such allusions to drinkers as "unmanned" were a staple.

In fact, the idea of the "unmanned" drinker was also something of a commonplace outside of temperance circles. Even that decidedly drink-friendly venue, the vaudeville stage, seemed to insinuate a conflict between alcohol and virility. The vaudeville drinking songs performed by cross-dressed women like Miss Betty Bonehill, Elsie Holt, and Emma Grattan suggested that the drinker in question preferred alcohol and male companionship to his wife.[35] Throughout the country, advice-manual writers, political leaders, reformers, and pundits of all kinds asserted that true men did not spend their evenings together (particularly in saloons) but rather spent time within their family circles. Many nineteenth-century Americans saw a connection among drink, saloongoing, and the loss of manhood. Midwestern saloongoers themselves appreciated and feared this connection.

Just as the image of the saloon as manly related to its usefulness as a space where men could make visible, define, and seek to enlarge the boundaries of their "business," the image of the saloon as unmanning was tied to "minding one's business." To many Midwestern saloongoers, the very definition of intoxication or drunkenness was the inability to "mind one's business." When William Ferman, an Illinois barber, was asked by an attorney whether he had ever been drunk, he replied, "No sir but what I knew what I was doing and could attend to business."[36] W. H. Parker, a tinsmith from Illinois, said of another man in an 1885 case, "I don't know as you could call him drunk, he knew enough to tend to his business."[37] Charles McRoberts, who seems to have been a rather feckless drifter, testified in an 1886 case, "I was under the influence of liquor, but wasn't drunk. Could attend to my own business; knew what I was doing. . . . I might not have seen Mr. Bell as others might have seen him. Others might have seen him and called him drunk; but I called him a man that was able to attend to his business."[38] Sometimes lawyers made the same equation between drunkenness and the inability to mind one's business. One Michigan lawyer in an 1891 case asked a witness "[have you seen him] what we call drunk—staggering, or so that he couldn't do business?"[39]

If an individual did drink so much as to prevent him from "minding his business" properly, not only saloon norms but also wider cultural norms called

Fig. 4. "John Swig," from a Sons of Temperance Pamphlet by Edward Carswell called *John Swig: The Effect of Jones' Argument* (National Temperance Society, 1871) (Photo courtesy of the Oshkosh Public Museum)

upon his acquaintances to assist him, particularly when it came to his getting home after a night out. Managing a horse, team, buggy, or cart while intoxicated could have fatal consequences to the driver and to others. Midwestern roads were sometimes difficult to navigate even for the sober, with mud, ditches, narrow bridges, and unexpected obstacles complicating any trip. Horses proverbially disdained to be controlled by drunken men. Men who opted to walk home often had to go miles through sparsely populated countryside, over railroad tracks and bridges, sometimes in bitterly cold and icy conditions. Either way, for a drunken man to leave a saloon for home was potentially disastrous. If he did assist a belligerent drunken man home, a saloongoer sometimes felt called upon to remain to protect his family from him.[40]

Saloongoers were expected to intervene on the behalf of a drunken man in other ways as well. Many felt compelled to protect drunken friends from making bad business deals. "He wasn't so drunk but what you were willing to do business with him?" one defense attorney asked in an 1899 case. "I done business with him," the witness agreed.[41] Villains in temperance fiction frequently got men drunk in order to trick them into ruinous business deals.[42] When a man was drunk, unable to "mind his own business," it was not only socially acceptable but socially expected for others to intervene benevolently in his business.

But men who seemed to be incapable of minding their business often resisted assistance, manfully maintaining their boundaries and insisting that they could take care of their own affairs. Remember that on the night that Andrew Faivre, the tailor discussed in the introduction, developed frostbite in his hands and feet, a policeman had seen him and his friend "hanging onto one another" and "told them to get off the street and go home." They had responded that "they were capable of taking care of themselves." Similarly, when William Blakesley offered assistance to a seemingly intoxicated Frank Huff, Huff replied "I ain't drunk. I can take care of myself. I don't need any help." To Warren Harris who suggested that Huff had drunk enough and ought to go home, Huff responded, "Go to hell! I will go home when I get ready." When W. W. Buell saw twenty-eight-year-old laborer Michael Judge collapsed on the street on a cold night and sought to bring him indoors, Judge grabbed him and tried to wrestle with him. Like the policeman who confronted Faivre, Blakesley, Harris, and Buell backed off when the drinkers rejected their advice or assistance. Like Faivre, Michael Judge stayed out on the street all night and developed frostbite; he lost a leg. Huff was even less fortunate; he soon after fell off a bridge to his death.[43]

One might blame the would-be assistants for allowing themselves to be so easily rebuffed by their drunken friends. In their testimony, one can sense regret. However, they were in a very awkward position. They knew that when a man was drunk and incompetent to conduct his business, failure to assist him could lead to tragedy, but they also knew the consequences of attempting to interfere in a man's business as long as he considered himself competent to conduct it. The problem became even more complicated in light of the second meaning of "minding one's own business." The drunkard, in the eyes of Midwestern saloongoers, failed to "mind his own business" both in that he was incapable of tending to his person, property, and affairs, and in that he so often seemed inclined to intervene inappropriately in the affairs of his neighbors. Saloongoers asked to explain why they considered one of their companions to have been drunk often said that they could tell he was drunk because he interfered in others' business.[44] If a saloongoer, who might well have been drinking heavily himself, involved himself in the business of a man he perceived to be drunk, he ran the risk of being labeled unable to "mind his own business." Even nonsaloongoing or nondrinking witnesses who perhaps came upon drinkers on the street often found that juries looked skeptically at those who claimed sobriety but had involved themselves in the affairs of intoxicated men.[45]

Drinkers and nondrinkers alike found it impossible to agree on a definition of "intoxication." Civil damage lawyers and judges faced still other obstacles to determining whether the subject of a given suit had been intoxicated. Saloongoers, respecting barroom norms, were frequently careful to insist that they had not been paying too much attention to others' affairs. Often they claimed that they had not noticed a certain man's behavior and that they did not consider it their "business" to observe him.[46] The discomfort many of them felt in having been caught watching, or worse, interceding in, another man's behavior is manifest in the confused testimony of Joseph Williams, a barkeeper who had cut off a patron, in an 1896 case.

> Q. Why did you tell him he had enough?
> A. It's my business to look after such men.
> Q. Was his apparent condition that of intoxication?
> A. Well, no, he was not intoxicated.
> Q. You did not tell him not to drink any more?
> A. I did it with all men.
> Q. That would cut your business down?
> A. That's my business . . .
> Q. The reason why you told him was because he was in an intoxicated condition?
> A. No sir. He was a long ways from home and it was very cold and it is a man's business to look after such things when they are in his business.[47]

Of course, as the barkeeper claimed, it literally was his business to monitor the intoxication of his customers. Still, he was defensive about the position in which he found himself, and not merely because his employer was arguing that the man had not been intoxicated.

Because intoxication was so subjective, because witnesses appreciated that labeling a man drunk allowed all manner of incursions into his business, and because they were committed to maintaining the boundaries of each man's business, saloongoers tended to be extremely reluctant to label their fellows as drunk. In one 1890 case, the plaintiff's exasperated lawyer, after fruitlessly attempting to get a witness to say that his client's husband had been drunk, finally erupted, "I will ask you this: Do you consider a man drunk as long as he can lay with his face down, and hang to the grass and holler?" The witness, unmoved, replied, "I don't know; he might be sober and holler."[48] Though an extreme example, this was consistent with most saloongoers' unwillingness to label anyone who had not actually collapsed, and some who had, as drunk.[49] Iowan David Livingstone, for instance, maintained, "I call a man under the influence of liquor when he gets like a beast and can't stand erect or walk erect; when a man stands on all fours."[50] Illinois gas fitter and plumber John Gross similarly insisted, "I never call a man drunk unless I see him falling over; that is the only time I say I am drunk when I stumble or happen to fall on my nose or something like that."[51] Bernard Worth of Michigan agreed, insisting that "when a man is drunk he will lie down; as long as he stands up and does his own business, walking around and doing his own business and talking, [I] don't consider him drunk."[52]

Drinkers like Livingstone, Gross, and Worth chose to evade the tension between drunkenness and the volition necessary to manhood by defining drunkenness as narrowly as possible. What is most interesting about this approach is the path that they did not take. It might have been possible for saloongoers to negotiate, or at least contain, the conflicts between intoxication and manhood. The meaning of manhood in the late nineteenth century was highly contested and constantly in flux. Though "minding one's own business" had tremendous cultural resonance, saloongoers could have worked to reshape or reformulate such notions of manhood when they became unsustainable. Becoming roaring drunk, for instance, has often been seen as an indication of, rather than a bar to, manliness. As Elliot Gorn pointed out in his work on antebellum Southern rough-and-tumble fighters (and Gunther Peck in his on Western miners), some men considered risky and self-destructive behavior an assertion of their freedom to use their own bodies as they saw fit—reaffirming their status as independent rather than enslaved.[53]

Occasionally, civil damage transcripts do reveal something of this sort. Certainly some witnesses made inflated claims about how much alcohol they had consumed *without* becoming intoxicated. When called to account for their sa-loongoing, moreover, some men boasted about their incapacity. Joseph Hermes, a "section boss," volleyed with the plaintiff's lawyer in a case early in the 1890s: "Q. You take your drink? A. You bet I do. Q. Taken it today, haven't you? A. Yes sir."[54] In another 1890s case, George Webber claimed, "I did not draw a sober breath for six weeks."[55] Fifty-year-old farmer and West Virginia coal miner G. B. Duckworth and some of the witnesses in his 1908 case similarly seemed to take pride in their extreme intoxication. Duckworth claimed to have gotten "about as drunk as a man could get." When discussing his failure as a provider in later testimony, however, even he volunteered that "he had no business to get drunk."[56] Examples like this can occasionally be found in transcripts through-out the late nineteenth century. Most Midwestern saloongoers, however, per-sisted in a definition of manhood precariously grounded in the language of "business." They were unwilling to forsake the ideals of rationality, independence, and freedom implied by that definition even under the pressure of legal action.

The very structure and intent of the civil damage acts challenged drinkers' control of their business still further. In many civil damage cases, the male drinkers were clearly objects of contempt in the eyes of their families and of their communities. Some plaintiffs were widows of drinkers killed in alcohol-related accidents, and some had been abandoned by their drinking husbands, but in many cases, these failed patriarchs watched, and even testified in, their own wives' trials. To make their cases, plaintiffs often presented their husbands' failures in stark terms. Martha Duckworth's declaration in her 1908 trial typ-ically described her husband G. B. as "feeble and helpless . . . disordered and disabled."[57]

Some inebriates cooperated with their family members' cases, testifying to their own degradation. Even those men who cooperated, however, often re-vealed discomfort with the situation in which they found themselves, par-ticularly with the fact that so many others suddenly had the right to intrude into their business. When asked about his drinking habits, for instance, Duck-worth, who had admitted that he had been "arms length acting the fool" said snidely, "Probably there is witnesses that would know more about it than I do—because they have kept an account of it and I have not." Other drinkers rejected their families' characterization of them as drunkards and sided with their sa-loonkeepers,[58] an alliance which often did the saloonkeepers' cases more harm than good by illustrating to juries the extent to which the drinkers lacked concern for their own families' financial well-being.

The very fact that drinkers found themselves testifying about their lives to hostile juries suggests that their attempt to hold to their definition of proper manly behavior had failed in the larger culture. The laws and even the court proceedings seemed designed to attack the manhood of drinkers. Once in the courtroom, testifying saloongoers (who usually addressed court officials as "sir," a courtesy rarely reciprocated) were often subjected to humiliating skepticism, mockery, and insult by lawyers from both sides and even, occasionally, by judges. Twenty-seven-year-old James Powell, for instance, could not have been pleased with an exchange during his testimony in an 1891 case:

> The Court: Are you right now? Are you drunk or sober?
>
> A. I am all right now.
>
> Q. There is a little defect in your speech, isn't there?
>
> A. No sir.
>
> Mr. Withey: I thought you were a little tongue-tied.
>
> Court: It would be a good thing if he was, *and* his mouth tied too, for a while.[59]

Court officials often suggested that saloongoing witnesses were unreliable, dishonest, lazy, and incompetent. One official, in an 1874 case, referred to a (living) drinker's body as a "rotten . . . putrid . . . and repulsive carcass." Another, a year earlier, referred to a saloon patron as a "miserable, unwashed, uncleansed, unannealed and graceless scamp." In 1885, a third claimed that a witness was a "horse-jockeying, gad-about sort of man, a frequenter of houses of ill-fame, a runner of a threshing machine."[60] Considering that often all of the witnesses, lawyers, jurors, and observers in these courtrooms knew one another, being a witness could hardly have helped a saloongoer maintain the already tenuous boundaries of his manhood.[61]

Given all that they had to lose from being identified as drinkers, it is perhaps not surprising that some witnesses went to great lengths to assert that they were abstinent. Rarely did drinkers or saloonkeepers defend their habits or seem offended that their presence in a saloon rendered them suspect and subject to contempt and ridicule. Rather, they attempted to dissociate themselves from the saloon. One barkeeper insisted in an 1899 case that, "no sir, I never drink nothing. I never have for years. I want this Court to know it."[62] The attorney for another saloonkeeper, twelve years earlier, asked his client's twenty-six-year-old assistant, "Did you drink or have you for 11 years drunk intoxicating liquor of any shape?" Though the plaintiff successfully objected to the line of questioning before the barkeeper responded, we can assume that the barkeeper had planned to claim that he had been a teetotaler since he was fifteen.[63] Others testified that, though they went to the saloon daily, they never drank intoxicating liquors there; they drank only soda pop, had since gone teetotal, had stopped into the saloon for just a moment looking for a man, or were only looking through the doorway.[64]

Saloonkeepers sometimes attempted to extend the patina of sobriety over their entire establishment, by claiming that they only served "BB" (birch beer?), which was non-alcoholic. Other excuses were that the beer they served was so weak that "a man could drink a barrel of it and not get drunk," and that men mainly came to their places to read newspapers, socialize, have lunch, and "warm their shins" but rarely drank.[65] Of course, some of these disclaimers probably had elements of truth, given the many social functions of the saloon.[66] They were certainly tactical, since many of the witnesses had interests or sympathies in the cases. They were also, however, attempts by saloonkeepers and saloongoing men to distance themselves from a damaging association with alcohol.

Late-nineteenth-century Midwestern saloongoers were in an awkward position. Though many of them, whether farmers or self-employed tradesmen, continued to lead lives closer to traditional ideals of independent manhood than their contemporaries, their ideas of proper manly behavior were confused and contradictory. Try as they might to "mind their own business," they were chronically unsure who was capable of doing so and when outside intervention was required. When called upon to make such distinctions and to justify saloon codes in public, they failed or evaded the question. The central role of competition and the enactment of manhood within the saloon seems to have made it almost impossible for these Midwesterners to reach a consensus on limits to autonomy which the law insisted—and which they were forced to agree—must exist.

The drinking men of the rural Midwest, as of much of the rest of the late-nineteenth-century United States, were handicapped as well by the fact that they shared much of their rhetoric and ideology with elites and women who were becoming increasingly vociferous in their opposition to drink. Temperance reformers worked tirelessly to uphold an ideal of manhood centered exactly on the concepts of economic and political autonomy and control over a household that constituted the "business" of the saloongoer. That witnesses in civil damage cases were so often at pains to distance themselves from the consumption of alcohol suggests that even within the saloon, the contention that alcohol was inimical to responsible, independent maleness had considerable resonance. In the end, the temperance movement's success in destroying the premier male space of the late nineteenth century depended not so much on attacking as on exploiting contemporary ideologies of manhood.

One writer who considered the relationship of ideas of manhood to drink and intoxication was Jack London. For him, alcohol had everything to do with gender. London was famously obsessed with determining what it meant to be a man.[67] His works celebrated the idea of "physical manhood" so prominent in the late nineteenth and early twentieth centuries, and his popular writings did much to promote that view of manhood in the wider culture. The men in his accounts rippled with muscles, fought at the drop of a hat, and tested themselves against the most extreme conditions nature had to offer. London made himself into a living symbol of the masculine life. Yet when he wrote his fictionalized autobiography, *John Barleycorn*, he wrote it as what can only be called a drunkard narrative, replete with all the genre's gender ambiguities. He sarcastically contemplated calling it "Memoirs of an Alcoholic."[68]

Like so many late-nineteenth-century saloongoers, London associated the barroom with masculinity.[69] "Drink," he claimed, "was the badge of manhood."[70] "Men gathered to [the saloon] as primitive men gathered about the fire of the squatting-place or the fire at the mouth of the cave."[71] The saloon was, above all, where he "escaped from the narrowness of woman's influence into the wide free world of men."[72] London participated in all aspects of saloon life: treating rituals, violence, bonds of trust among drinkers and between drinkers and the saloonkeeper. The saloon helped London to become a man, but he was also convinced that it was destroying him. He accepted much of the logic and language of the temperance movement. Alcohol, he mused, "can throw the net of his lure over all men. He exchanges new lamps for old, the spangles of illusion for the drabs of reality, and in the end cheats all who traffic with him." Once alcohol entered a man's system, it planted its "seeds of desire" for itself within him. Here, London suggests alcohol's seduction of and compulsion over the drinker ("the net of his lure"). He points to alcohol as a deceiver ("spangles of illusion"). He implies that his own desire for alcohol was of foreign origin, in some sense *not* his own: "the seeds of desire." (Though it is not clear from this passage, London imagines that the "seeds of desire" were of external origin, and had been planted when first he began to drink.) In this one brief passage, as in many others, he accepted and used temperance reformers' metaphors of seduction and of invasion. He certainly did not accept the popular idea that a man who consumed even the smallest amount of alcohol risked losing his volitional independence. "Twenty years of unwilling apprenticeship had been required to make my system rebelliously tolerant of alcohol, to make me, in the heart and the deeps of me, desirous of alcohol."[73] Yet if he insisted that alcohol enslaved men slowly, he came perilously close to agreeing that its control over its victims could become total.

London, however, was unwilling to follow temperance logic to its conventional conclusion, and he was too deeply committed to the idea of moral autonomy to imagine himself as a slave to drink. He explicitly differentiated his book from a drunkard narrative, beginning his final chapter by informing readers that the book will not end as they expect. "Of course, no personal tale is complete without bringing the narrative of the person down to the last moment. But mine is no tale of a reformed drunkard. I was never a drunkard, and I have not reformed."[74] When he says that he is not a drunkard, he means that he has determined that he drinks not because he is addicted to alcohol but rather because he continues to prefer life with it to life without it. While he admits that alcohol influences or even controls his desires, he insists that in drinking he is exercising his own free will.

In a sense, that answer should have resolved the problem. Drink and the saloon freed man of woman's influence, but they did not themselves compromise his volition. However, London was clearly not satisfied with this potential resolution. Though he refused to concede that alcohol had mastered his will, he believed that its mastery of his desires was powerful enough that he could not save himself. If he were to be saved, he believed, it would have to be through some external agency. The only such force that could save him from the "net" of alcohol's "lure," he believed, was reforming women. "It is the wives, and sisters, and mothers, and they only, who will drive the nails into the coffin of John Barleycorn."[75] London framed this novel with the idea that only women could save him from alcohol's grasp; the book begins with London explaining to his surprised wife why he has gone to the polls to vote for woman suffrage. He explains that he has done so because if women get the vote they will usher in prohibition and save him from his own desires. The saloon had made London a man by saving him from women's influence, but only women had the power to save him from the saloon. The quest for manhood had alienated London from his own desires; only by surrendering to the influence of women could he be made to desire what he wished he desired.

CHAPTER THREE

Contentment

There is no more blessed boon given to man for his earthly condition than
home. There is no one provision which so completely meets the varied
wants of his nature as this; and he who allows the tendrils of his heart to
spread the farthest, and take the deepest, strongest hold of this, is the man
who is most secure against all the temptations and evils of a siren world.

> J. E. STEBBINS, *Fifty Years History of the Temperance Cause*, 1876

[In the temperance utopia, our descendants] shall dwell in the splendors
and happiness of the palace of purity. . . . They will go up to it over the
broad white flag-stones of perfect desires.

> SAMUEL W. SMALL, "Deliverance From Bondage:
> A Temperance Sermon," 1890

On January 5, 1891, Charles W. Danielson allegedly sold two bottles of whiskey
to a minor named Albert Rhino in Genessee County, Michigan. When Albert's
friend Frank found him out at the saloon in a condition which he "called . . .
drunk," he brought him home. It was not an easy task. "He didn't want to go
any too well, I pretty nearly had my hands full to handle him, to keep him up
on his taps."[1] When Albert approached his home, he was "singing and danc-
ing." According to his mother, he was "intoxicated, dreadfully intoxicated."
After he entered his home, his mood became violent. He "pitched at" his
mother and told his step-father that he would "knock him over." After menacing his thirteen-year-old brother, he threatened to slap his sister and called her a
"dirty bitch." It was a scene of a household gone completely awry.[2]

In response, Alfred's mother, Clara Cramer, brought a civil damage suit
against Charles Danielson. Unlike most civil damage litigants, Clara Cramer did
not base her suit on the financial loss her family member's drinking had caused
her, presumably because she had no evidence that it had cost her anything.
Indeed, Albert awoke the next morning and went to work as usual, though he
didn't eat much breakfast. Rather, Clara charged that Danielson had broken

Michigan liquor laws by selling to a minor and that in so doing he had upset the tranquility and order of her home, causing her personal embarrassment, mortification, and distress. More than many other civil damage cases, Clara's rested on the notion that when their products upset domestic contentment saloonkeepers owed drinkers' female relations compensation.

However, Clara Cramer's domestic situation was by no means standard. The attorney for the defense attempted to prove throughout the trial that Clara Cramer's home was "a house of prostitution" in which she herself "was the prime inmate."[3] Clara's husband, whom Albert had drunkenly threatened, was much closer to Albert's age than to Clara's: he was twenty-one to her thirty-nine.[4] The saloonkeepers' attorney, Clarence Tinkler, mocked what he saw as Clara's brazen attempts to set up her home as a domestic space and to pose as the injured mother of a son who had been corrupted by the wiles of the saloonkeeper. Repeatedly, he insisted to the jury that Clara was no natural mother, alleging that she herself had "fed liquor to him as mothers usually feed their child milk from childhood up."[5]

Whether or not Clara was actually running a house of prostitution (and it seems likely that she was), she was locally reputed to be a prostitute. The fact that the judge and jury did not dismiss her case out of hand points to the power of the ideal of domesticity in nineteenth-century culture. Clara Cramer met with a surprising degree of success in her efforts to save her home, however disreputable, from the demon drink. The judge repeatedly refused to allow defense attorney Clarence Tinkler to ask questions that would establish Clara's prostitution. He insisted that it was not relevant to introduce facts about the moral quality of Clara's home, unless Tinkler could show, which he could not, that Clara had contributed to her son's intoxication on the day in question. Ultimately, the judge strongly rebuked Tinkler for his attempts to discredit Clara, insisting that "the statute does not except a prostitute's son from the operation of the law. . . . The law protects the rich man's son and the poor man's son and the prostitute's son and all of them."[6] As this statement reveals, the judge saw the civil damage acts as a way to protect drinkers by dissuading merchants from violating liquor laws as well as a way to compensate injured family members. However far from the ideal drinkers' homes might be, their families had the right to protect them from evil external influences.

It is difficult to say exactly what motivated Clara Cramer to bring her civil damage suit. Her motives could have been simply financial; under Michigan's civil damage act, the jury had to award the plaintiff a minimum of fifty dollars if they found that a liquor seller had broken the law. It is also likely that Clara was truly concerned about her son's drinking habits and hoped to protect him from evil external influences a little while longer. A more interesting possibility is that Clara brought the suit playfully and with a proper sense of its absurdities. Her case revealed with striking clarity the fallacies in reformers' often blind idealization of the domestic space as a haven from the evils of the public sphere.

The jury's award to Clara was considerably lower than most, but Clara had claimed no pecuniary damages, her son had sustained no injuries that evening, and she had made no argument that he had become a habitual drunkard. The only claim she made was for the fifty dollars required by law in a case of illegal sale and for an additional sum to compensate her for the events of that one drunken evening. Significantly, however, the jury doubled the minimum that the law required, awarding Clara one hundred dollars. In large part, the jury was no doubt interested in punishing Danielson for selling to minors, but fifty dollars was not an inconsiderable sum, and might have served that purpose adequately. Furthermore, the jury was willing to see that money go to a woman of ill repute who had asked them to compensate her for her trauma and for drink's disruption of her extremely unconventional domestic arrangement.

Ultimately, the supreme court reversed the lower court's decision. It did so partly on the grounds that the judge should have allowed Tinkler to introduce his testimony regarding Clara's character and profession, so that the jury could factor that in its assessment of how much damage Clara suffered through her son's intoxication. In an unusually constructed decision, the court gave Clara the option of accepting the fifty dollars that had been automatically awarded for Danielson's lawbreaking and giving up on the fifty dollars awarded to compensate her for the disruption of her household and for her personal mortification. Whether Clara Cramer proceeded with her suit or not, her case reveals both the surprising ubiquitousness and strength of the drunkard narrative—not only could a reputed prostitute think to use it to defend her son against the wiles of the saloonkeeper, but a judge and jury could take her claims seriously.[7]

The idealization of contentment and of the domestic space in which many Americans believed contentment to reside was central to the drink debate. Temperance reformers used the drink debate to express their dissatisfaction with both gender roles and contemporary theories of the nature of individual volition. They hoped that by addressing these issues they could usher in significant social improvement. Yet their own dissatisfaction troubled them because they believed it to be a form of desire similar to that at the root of the drink problem. Many reformers believed that men became drinkers and drinkers drunkards largely because their desires, their wills, and the realities in which they lived were in discord. Reformers gave different accounts of the cause of this misalignment. Some depicted the drinker as tricked into acquiring unrealistic desires. Some imagined that alcohol paralyzed the drinker's will, making him incapable of behaving as he desired. Others argued that alcohol rendered the drinker incapable of experiencing and understanding his real environment. Most, however, agreed that the drunkard's inability to keep his wants and will in accord with the reality in which he existed was both the primary cause and the most damaging symptom of his drinking.[8]

Nineteenth-century Americans referred to the harmony of desire, volition, and reality as contentment. As one temperance play put it, "Happiness proceeds from a contented mind. Contentment with our lot in life is to be rich in happiness."[9] Pleasure that was not properly moored to "our lot in life," such as the pleasure of imagination, could be at odds with contentment. A truly contented individual's volition and desire were "contained" by his or her situation in life. To be contented was to will and desire what one already had and did, or what one could reasonably expect to do or to acquire through steady, traditional forms of labor appropriate to one's position in life.[10] The problem of contentment—its nature, how to achieve it, and how drink threatened it—was crucial to the drink debate. Americans expressed their concern that young people were losing their ties to traditional ways. Increasingly, many complained, instead of "plodding along," working patiently, remaining close to home, following familiar paths, young people were setting off to the city, engaging in risky business practices, and living "fast" lives. Temperance reformers and saloon defenders alike used the drink debate as a forum to discuss their concerns about this seeming attrition of "contentment." They wrote about it in fictional and nonfiction literature, sang about it in drinking songs, discussed it in the text of alcohol advertisements, and even evoked it in court.

Because of their obvious concern with this issue and the thick air of nostalgia it gave to some of their writings, temperance reformers have often been mistaken for social conservatives vainly trying to hold back the tide of modern culture. This is misleading in two ways, however. First, temperance reformers' opponents often shared their concerns with the problem of contentment. Second, temperance reformers were not so much concerned with preserving a specific set of cultural customs and values or with blocking all forms of "progress"—they were, after all, reformers—as with preserving some level of social stability and rootedness.[11] The attempt to reconcile this tension between reformers' idealization of contentment and their commitment to change would drive many of the movement's intellectual innovations over the course of the century. Temperance reformers and their opponents expressed highly ambiguous, at times even painfully contradictory views of the nature of contentment and the possibility of achieving it. Both sides, however, agreed that alcohol and temperance were central to the problem of contentment. Drink discourse participants bemoaned that society seemed to lack it, and questioned whether the home could be restored as its focus.

Although it was particularly prominent within the drink discourse, concern about contentment manifested itself in many areas of American life. This is not terribly surprising; historians and contemporaries alike have understood the nineteenth-century United States as a culture of extreme mobility and insecurity. In her monograph on Midwestern Gilded Age success manuals, Judith Hilkey shows that they, far from advocating unlimited ambition, suggested that young men should proceed "in the old-fashioned way—not only by employing honesty, frugality, and hard work but by an ethic of decency, fair-mindedness, conservative investment, and patient contentment with modest returns." She recounts a story popular at the time about a man who sets off to find his fortune and in so doing fails to discover that his own field was filled with diamonds, which he would have found if he had contented himself with farm work.[12] The theme of contentment in the texts Hilkey studies is so interesting precisely because one would expect that success manuals would be the last place such a theme would appear. Throughout the period, however, writers and thinkers of all kinds were in search of some sense of calm and solidity to counterbalance a society many perceived as fast-paced and unstable.[13]

If the contented person was the reformer's ideal, his or her opposite was the risk-taker. Drink discourse participants imagined that there were two ways to react to the chaotic forces that threatened both individual and political stability. "Discontented" people chose to embrace "fortune" because they were so profoundly dissatisfied with their situation in life that they welcomed instability. Drink debaters contrasted this sort of person with the truly virtuous person, who had come to terms with his or her situation in life and was contented.[14] In opposing "contentment" and "risk," drink debaters evoked the long-lived republican opposition of "virtue" to "fortune." That is, they believed that the world was full of chaotic forces that could either elevate or destroy people with a seeming randomness. Republican thought, on an individual level, suggested that a man should strive to achieve virtue—in the form of such things as knowledge and ability—so as to remove himself as much as possible from the realm of fortune or chance.[15] This understanding of the individual was closely tied to a body of political ideas, such as an interest in the rise and fall of historic republics and an attempt to imagine how a republic could achieve such virtue as to avoid sinking into the luxury and corruption that heralded its fall.[16] Temperance reformers, and to a lesser extent drink supporters, embraced many of the major aspects of republican political thought—most obviously the concern about the rise and fall of republics, luxury, and the fear of corruption. Sometimes this intellectual context was quite explicit, as when an 1887 newspaper noted that temperance activist and women's rights advocate Anna Howard Shaw had delivered a lecture on "The Fate of Republics."[17] The interest in contentment was part and parcel of their embrace of this republican discourse.

Besides this political dimension, the problem of contentment also had a gendered aspect. Some thinkers believed that the failure of "contentment" was fundamentally a male problem. According to this theory, women, by their nature inwardly oriented and rooted in the domestic sphere, did not suffer as men did from the desire to explore and acquire. This concept was potentially useful to female temperance reformers, and they made some use of it as they worked to develop a gendered solution to the drink crisis. They never were comfortable, however, with the idea that desire was a strictly male characteristic. Rather, in their own writings, they showed that women's discontent could be just as strong and just as dangerous as men's, though it tended to take a different form.[18]

In temperance accounts, "discontented" young men tended to become gamblers and speculators, or to go off to the city to "seek their fortune." In "trying their luck," they courted social chaos by throwing themselves into the thick of it. Their female counterparts closely resembled the protagonists of early American novels of sexual seduction.[19] While they did not have the freedom to leave their homes in search of novelty on their own, they attempted to create their own adventure at home or to latch on to a man who would take them to new and exciting places. They were "silly" or "giddy," and much interested in social intrigue and romance. They preferred the strange to the familiar, read too much sentimental fiction, and chose to marry their "flashy" risk-taking counterparts over less exciting, steady, hardworking suitors.[20] Such women hoped to climb dramatically out of their class position.[21] These risk-takers' discontent with their present state and desire for excitement and for immediate and great prosperity was so strong that they were willing to lose the things, such as their inheritances, that they already had.

The virtuous man acted in such a way as to tame, or at least remove himself from, the forces that threatened his comfort and stability. As much as possible, he stood on solid ground, remained prudently aware of his surroundings, and planned for any contingencies he might face in the future. He was likely to be a farmer or a solid businessman, to be geographically stable, and to be well integrated into family and community life. He carried through all of his work, as Hilkey has described, "not only by employing honesty, frugality, and hard work but by an ethic of decency, fair-mindedness, conservative investment, and patient contentment with modest returns."[22] When gamblers and speculators met him, they criticized him as a "slow coach" and found his "plodding" lifestyle unbearably dull.[23] His female counterpart was practical, dressed for comfort and respectability rather than fashion, and was similarly diligent in fulfilling her duties. She avoided reading novels, was not "giddy," and did not have social pretensions beyond her station. These contented men and women would probably ultimately succeed in their pursuits, gradually accumulating capital and mellowing into a comfortable and respectable old age. If they did meet with some unpredictable crisis, they would face it calmly and carefully. Because they had avoided taking risks, however, they would never become fabulously rich, and they would know that they had worked hard for every dollar.

The basic difference between the contented and the discontented person was that the former's hopes were "contained" by the reality of his or her situation in life while the latter's hopes were shaped by artificial, imaginary, or foreign ideas and images. Temperance reformers, in particular, associated alcohol with discontent precisely because alcohol encouraged dreaming and imagination. As Jack London put it in 1913, alcohol "exchanges . . . the spangles of illusion for the drabs of reality."[24] While intoxication might temporarily bring about a feeling of joy or even of contentment, a reformer wrote in 1870, this feeling was merely a "counterfeit" of "the golden coin with which God pays the worthy laborer."[25] To temperance reformers, the equation of alcohol with imagination became most apparent in the moment of *delirium tremens*, which, as one writer on the legal aspects of drink claimed in 1881, "bears a strong resemblance to dreaming."[26] True contentment could arise neither from men's artifice nor from the consumption of a substance but only from the true knowledge of having acted properly within one's rightful sphere. Temperance reformers saw alcohol as foreign and artificial. Although they knew that some drinkers claimed to find pleasure in the bottle, they understood this pleasure as the drinker's doomed attempt to escape his situation in life, at least imaginatively. To them, it was a form of risk-taking and therefore a threat to true contentment.

The idea that alcohol increased desire and destroyed contentment remained prominent within the drink discourse from the antebellum period through the progressive era. In one of the earliest temperance fictions, Lucius Manlius Sargent's 1833 short story "My Mother's Gold Ring," a young husband takes his fatal first glass, returns home and immediately announces to his wife that he "meant to have [her] and the children better dressed" and to buy a "horse and chaise."[27] Decades later, an 1895 pamphlet advertising the effectiveness of a popular cure for inebriety, the Keeley Cure, contained numerous testimonials from former Keeley patients, each under its own catchy subheading: "Contented and Happy," "Desire Gone and Health Good," "No Desire of Any Kind," and "Contented and Doing Well."[28] Of course, "desire" here primarily refers to the desire for drink, but there seems to be much more going on here as recovered drunkard after recovered drunkard testifies that he can now, as a sober man, thoroughly enjoy the situation in life in which he happens to find himself. The Keeley Cure did not simply cure drunkards of their uncontrollable thirst for drink, it reconciled them to their lot.

In response, opponents of the temperance movement both defended alcohol as a legitimate part of, or even as an aid to, domestic contentment and argued that it was the reformers themselves who were attempting to impose artificial and visionary schemes. Because drink supporters saw alcohol as traditional, natural, and domestic, they understood the pleasure brought about by drink as contentment. As one prohibition opponent wrote in 1859, "a moderate use of pure and unadulterated spirits may be fairly set down as one of the comforts of the present life."[29] An advertising booklet published by the Pabst Brewery in 1894, entitled "Ominous Secrets," took on temperance reformers on their own turf. In a section entitled "Nervous as a Witch," the writer agrees with temperance reformers that "fastness" is a serious problem in modern life but shifts the blame from alcohol use to other causes, including reformist busybodies: "The fact of it is that we live too fast. . . . Besides this, we Americans worry too much. Why, people even take up the affairs of their neighbors and fret their souls about them! Worry, too much care, business, sudden shocks, crossed purposes and aims, unrequited hopes, the gambling spirit that enters into all speculation . . . induce nervousness, even to prostration—sometimes death." He went on to propose Pabst Malt Extract, "The 'Best' Tonic," as a cure for this dangerous condition.[30]

Temperance opponents like the writer of this advertisement suggested that it was reformers who represented the true threat to contentment. Beer-industry writer Gallus Thomann, in an 1884 booklet, gathered statistics to oppose what he characterized as the "highly fertile imaginations" of temperance reformers.[31] Temperance reformers, as opponents described them, were basically a motley collection of failed housewives, spinsters, hen-pecked husbands, and ne'er-do-wells unhappy with their place in society. Prohibition foes alleged that participation in temperance reform was often a strategy for social climbing. One wrote in 1893 that "Several leaders in temperance work, who, ten years ago, were poor and obscure, now wear satins and jewels, take long and expensive journeys to Europe, and get their friends and children into soft places under the government."[32] To saloon supporters, social reformers, not alcohol itself, were the real propagators of discontent and instability. The Pabst "Best" Tonic advertising pamphlet also included a section on the dangers of the imagination, which, like "fastness," it attributes to temperance reformers rather than to drink. "Imagination is a siren, whose playful song leads the mind far from truth," the section begins, and then goes on to tell a rather complicated fable about a cow who died from fear of an imaginary danger. The analogy to temperance reformers' irrational fear of the dangers of alcohol was obvious, particularly when he summed up, "Now, don't make a mistake by imagining that The 'Best' Tonic is anything but a Malt Extract made exclusively for medicinal purposes. It is a food."[33] Both of these alcohol supporters were insisting not only that temperance claims were false but also that they were potentially dangerous. If enough people believed them, policy decisions would be made on the basis of imaginary dangers rather than realities.

Temperance supporters and saloon defenders alike associated the use of alcohol with the choice between coming to terms with one's situation in life and struggling to escape it. Because economic status was an important aspect of each individual's situation in life and because it was often more visible, representable, and quantifiable than other aspects, drink debate participants frequently focused on economic mobility over other types of attempted self-transformations. The young, white, promising, middle-class man was the ideal figure for exploring the problems and possibilities of transformation because he was understood to be at once marginal and empowered. Whether they were talking about the downward mobility of the drunkard, the vulnerability of the ambitious young man headed to the city, the special allure of alcohol for the creative, or the dangers and pleasures of dreams, imagination, or alcoholic hallucination, temperance reformers associated drink with the possibility of escape from the familiar. Conversely, drink defenders associated alcohol with groundedness in the familiar—relating alcohol to nostalgia for a homeland, depicting drinking as located in the home, or presenting the saloon as a place where hardworking laborers could find some comfort with their lot.

Thus, when drink debaters discussed the relationship of alcohol to contentment, they frequently discussed it in terms of class mobility and insecurity. Temperance reformers and saloon defenders alike often talked about their own positions in terms of class and class mobility. Temperance reformers touted their cause as a road to economic security and success and disparaged intemperance as the road to economic ruin.[34] A young man who wanted to establish a reputation as a reliable business associate could advance his cause by "signing the pledge." Opponents argued that certain legislation backed by temperance reformers, such as high license fees, and antisaloon movements were attacks not on alcohol itself but on alcohol consumption by the poor and working classes. Some reformers argued that individuals undergoing transitions in social status were at high risk of becoming drunkards. Temperance opponents argued that the saloon was one of the few comforts reserved for the working man. When drink debate participants wrote about economic and class mobility, however, they often conceived of it as part of a larger complex of ideas—as one aspect of the more general problem of contentment.

The most immediately obvious sign of the "drunkard's decline" in the standard narrative was that he and his family descended from a condition of "comfort," a state of contentment, though seldom of opulence, to a condition of "want," a state of perpetual desire. In the first act of temperance plays, stage directions almost invariably called for those who would suffer from others' drinking to wear "comfortable" or "old-fashioned" clothing and for the future drunkard himself to wear either "comfortable" or, ominously, "flashy," "fashionable," or "modern" costume. The astute observer of a temperance play could usually predict the level of culpability of each character by where his or her first-act costume fit onto the continuum of comfortable to flashy. Later acts, of course, would see the drunkard and his family in rags. If the drunkard reformed in the course of the play, the last act often restored the whole family to comfortable clothing.[35] The same held true for temperance stories and novels, in which drinkers and their families almost invariably suffered a plummet in economic standing, from comfort to want, losing not only inherited property and homes but also clothing, food, and all of the basic necessities of life.

Redressing the move of drinkers and their families from comfort to want was a primary concern of state civil damage laws, whose direct goal was to restore drinkers' families to the situation in which they had been before drink intervened. Plaintiffs in these cases often began their declarations by emphasizing the relative comfort of their lives before their breadwinners' alcohol-related decline or death. Samantha Rosecrants's declaration in an 1886 case claimed that "Clinton Rosecrants was an industrious man and hard working, and abundantly able by his labor to support this plaintiff and their said children in comfort, except for his habitual intoxication."[36] In a case three years later, Olive Bell similarly maintained that before his death, her husband John, a poor sharecropper, "made a comfortable living for himself and his family" and "did all he could to render his family comfortable."[37] About a year later, Nettie Brockway claimed that her husband, a twenty-nine-year-old laborer and ditcher, had supported his family "in comfortable circumstances."[38] Other plaintiffs had been in better financial shape to begin with. According to a neighbor's testimony in an early-twentieth-century case, one drinker's home had been "warm and comfortable always, and there always seemed to be plenty provided ahead."[39]

Whatever plaintiffs' condition in life had been before their husbands' falls, courts trying civil damage cases aimed to restore the complainants to stability and comfort. An Iowa judge ratified this idea in 1902. He maintained that the jury should grant a financial judgment to the plaintiff such as would fulfill the responsibility her drinking husband had neglected—to "provide the wife with a reasonable support according to her rank and station in society, and to provide her with the comforts and surroundings reasonable for the position in which she lives."[40] The wealthier a plaintiff could demonstrate herself to have been before her husband's decline or death, the larger the judgment to which she was entitled. Alcohol had disrupted economic stability and the ability to satisfy reasonable material desires; the court's business was to restore these things.[41]

The drunkard narrative prepared jurors to blame saloonkeepers for men's declines into dissipation and their families' declines into poverty; however, it contained some elements that saloonkeepers could, and did, mobilize in their own defense. There was a significant slippage, even in drunkard narratives produced by the most solid temperance supporters, between understanding drink as the *cause* of discontent and instability and as its *effect*. Writers and tellers of drunkard narratives often quite literally meant to convey that alcohol was at the bottom of all social evils and that the individual's willingness to take a drink was the Achilles' heel of his otherwise unassailable moral self. In this reading, the bottle contained all forms of moral and social evil, including "discontent." Yet many, perhaps most, tellers of drunkard narratives at times used alcohol and the "fatal first drink" as a sort of synecdoche or shorthand for a much more general process of embracing "discontent." Drinking, in this understanding, was a moment of discontent, a sign that the drinker had chosen to abandon comfort, home, and steady security in favor of risk and mobility.

To the extent that tellers of drunkard narratives meant the "fatal first drink" more as shorthand for a process of discontent than as the literal cause of all of the drinker's woes, they often marked the drinker, even before he consumed his first drink, as "discontented," "ambitious," "fast," or "fanciful." When a temperance novel introduced a character as "a restless, ambitious boy" or a character in a temperance play was described as "hankering for a chance to try his fortune among the money-catchers," readers and audiences knew that these were future drunkards.[42] In Walt Whitman's early novel, *Franklin Evans,* for instance, the eponymous hero is made vulnerable to the seduction of drink through his ambition to leave his hard and thankless farming life for a chance of success in New York.[43] In William Comstock's 1875 *Rum: or, The First Glass,* one character agrees to take his fatal first drink out of a desire to remain on good terms with a man who offers to help him out of a failing speculation.[44] Narrators frequently depicted the drinker, shortly after his consumption of his first drink, as engaged in multiple forms of risky behavior such as gambling and speculation. There was rarely a "fatal first dice throw" or "fatal first risky business deal" in these narratives. When there was, it utterly lacked the weight of the "fatal first drink." The reader simply assumed that, having taken a first drink, the protagonist had completely given himself over to risk and chance. Read literally, the drunkard narrative suggested that alcohol was fully responsible for the drinker's decline. Read as a synecdoche, however, the same narrative suggested that both his drinking and his decline were a natural result of certain related and preexisting character traits such as discontent, ambition, and fastness.

The association between drinking and discontent also had some adherents in the medical community. A tendency toward chronic inebriety was sometimes understood to be a consequence of neurasthenia. Physicians believed that neurasthenia was caused by the excessive speed and uncertainty of modern life, and therefore an individual could be made vulnerable to drink through participation and mobility in economic and social life. An 1871 medical treatise

told the story of two young men who became raving inebriates as a consequence of having too rapidly advanced to positions of responsibility and
power.[45] A 1905 medical textbook explained further why something like this
could happen. "The elevation of an individual out of the sphere into which he
was born may impose a tax upon the functions of his nervous system which
may eventually expose him to serious temptations." Men "attempting . . . to
better their condition, are thrown out of sympathy with their surroundings and
they become subjected to excessive nervous strain."[46] These writers were very
much in accord with the way George Beard (the coiner of the term *neurasthenia*)
and his many followers understood the relationship between social mobility
and alcohol throughout the late nineteenth century.[47]

On this point the arguments of some temperance advocates and supporters
of moderate drinking became indistinguishable from one another. Temperance
novelist Mary Dwinell Chellis had a wise character argue that promising and
ambitious men "are the ones that make the worst drunkards. . . . The slow and
plodding are more moderate in drinking, as well as in all other things."[48] Temperance foe Gallus Thomann, in an 1884 report sponsored by the U.S. Brewers'
Association, cited a physician's claim that one major cause of inebriety was the
"incredible activity and frantic struggle for gain" characteristic of U.S. culture.[49]
The idea that drink was only a symptom of a larger social problem or common
character trait cast doubt on prohibition as a silver bullet, but temperance
reformers were sometimes unwilling to shape their writings to fit the needs of
the movement. Many, like Chellis, found the explanation compelling and considered it in their writings even when it contradicted their other arguments.

Saloonkeepers' lawyers often played off this second reading of the drunkard
narrative. If they could demonstrate that alcohol was not the sole cause of the
drinker's decline, their clients would be free of liability. They argued that the
drinkers themselves had been involved in reckless economic behavior, either
engaging in risky financial speculation in hopes of getting rich quick or living a
lifestyle above what they could afford. These attorneys often suggested that the
plaintiffs' breadwinners had actually lost their money through business and
property speculation or, more commonly, gambling. In an 1879 case, the defense argued that the plaintiff's husband "was a spendthrift, squandering
nearly all of his earnings in other ways than inebriations." Similarly, a witness
in an 1896 trial consented that the drinker in question "was rather extravagant
for a farm boy." When the defense lawyer asked the drinker's wife if he had been
"reckless in other directions than in liquor," however, she cannily worded her

answer to shift the emphasis from drink as part of a pattern of risk-taking to drink as cause of risk-taking: "He might have when he was intoxicated he might have gambled."[50] In these cases, saloonkeepers' attorneys evoked the common idea that drinking was only one part of a complex of excessive and damaging behavior in order to argue that the drinkers' financial losses had more to do with other parts of the complex than with drink itself.[51]

If the drunkard-narrative drinker could be read either as a sympathetic victim of the bottle or as a risk-taker who had brought his trouble upon himself, so could his wife. On the one hand, the drunkard's wife was an innocent victim of a failed husband, to be pitied and assisted. On the other hand, however, drunkard narratives sometimes suggested that she found herself in such an intolerable situation because she had chosen a "flashy" and "fast" young man for a husband rather than a farmer or steady business or working man. Like Louisa May Alcott's doomed "Fair Rosamond" who, having declared "good people are dismally dull. . . . A short life and a gay one for me," headed off on the handsome yacht with a wealthy and mysterious man, some wives paid the price for choosing excitement over comfort and stability.[52] A young woman in an 1854 novel, *Fashionable Dissipation,* foreshadows her relationship with a drunkard when she complains, "I feel dull—miserably dull—stupid—listless! I long for something to thrill, to excite me; to startle my pulses, my fancies and feelings into new life. I wish I had a glass of wine to-night." Because she is female, her troubles ultimately arise from her romantic connection to a drunkard rather than from her own drinking, but the parallel is obvious.[53] Similarly, in Mary Dwinell Chellis's *Wealth and Wine* (1874), a young woman chooses future drunkard Hastings Warland over the sober Dr. Saunders. "In the flush of his manhood's pride, Hastings Warland had wooed her to a home of wealth and elegance; charmed her by his devotion; and dazzled her by fancy sketches of their future happiness."[54]

Civil damage lawyers capitalized on the idea that the drinker's wife was, like her husband, a fortune-seeking risk-taker by claiming that plaintiffs were deliberately misstating their previous class position in hopes of making a profit. Rather than asking to be restored to the comfort of their rightful place in society, these lawyers claimed, plaintiffs were using the civil damage laws—sometimes in collaboration with their husbands—in an attempt to exceed and escape their rightful place in society. In making this argument, defense lawyers often imagined marriage as a sort of business contract. Occasionally, they even used the highly charged language of speculation to describe plaintiffs' actions. According to one saloon attorney in an 1873 Illinois case, plaintiff Phoebe Arnold and her husband had brought the suit "for the purpose of speculation off of the saloon keepers of Mattoon." He admitted that Phoebe Arnold's husband's habits had injured her materially: "Her means of support have been diminished . . . by reason of having to winter him over each successive year. He diminishes her means of support by eating out her substance, and his absence would manifestly inure to her benefit." Still, he maintained, it was unfair to ask his client to compensate Arnold for her husband's general worthlessness, predicting that "this practice of making merchandise of a worthless husband, is likely to assume fearful proportions."[55] Arnold's husband had never been of any worth to begin with, so any money she gained from his client would not restore her to a former state but rather give her value for nothing.[56]

A lawyer in an 1875 Iowa case used a similar argument to defend his saloon-keeper client. He claimed that if the court upheld the jury's award to plaintiff Carrie Kearney, "she could sell her husband, *an old pickled drunkard,* to ten different men, and get full value and full exemplary damages each time." On the one hand, he was objecting to an interpretation of the law making multiple parties each fully liable for civil damage law damages. His larger objection, however, was that Carrie Kearney was not trying to return to some previous enjoyment of domestic comfort but making savvy business decisions about how best to profit from her seemingly worthless husband. "It *was money* she wanted, and not the reformation of her man Kearney. She wished to use him as her stock in trade, to speculate on his thirst for strong drink."[57] An attorney in a slightly later Iowa case argued in the same vein, insisting that the drunkard's wife "chose a drunkard for her means of support, and ought not to ask [the saloonkeeper] to help her out of her bad bargain."[58] Attorneys in many other cases either explicitly or implicitly made the same argument, producing testimony that the drunkard in question had never been profitable and that the wife had known this before their marriage.[59] In all of these cases, defense attorneys asked the courts to think of the plaintiffs' marriages as failed *economic* contracts that they were attempting, through abuse of the civil damage acts, to transmute into profit. Like stockholders who purchased shares in the Erie railroad, these wives had greedily procured what turned out to be worthless contracts, which they were now illegitimately attempting to "sell" to saloonkeepers.

Both in fiction and in the courtroom, temperance advocates and saloon defenders frequently understood the drink debate to be intertwined with the problem of economic mobility. Literal readings of drunkard narratives and the logic of the civil damage acts suggested that the bottle contained and caused economic dislocation. Readings of the drunkard narrative as synecdoche for discontent and risk, and saloonkeepers' civil damage defenses suggested that heavy drinkers and their families were speculative, thereby rejecting the stability and comfort proper to their station in life. Both readings assumed that society's ultimate goal was to prevent undue social mobility, either upwards or downwards. The civil damage acts were intended and used largely to keep people in their economic places. Rather than challenging that goal, saloon lawyers argued that collecting damages from their clients would not serve it. The pro- and antisaloon movements as a whole shared a commitment to economic stability grounded in the ideal of peaceful, stable, and highly risk-averse communities and domestic spaces.

Drink debaters' fears of economic mobility were matched by their concerns about geographic mobility. They worried that people were insufficiently grounded in their homes and communities; that is, people were too apt to break free and head off alone, leading to general social instability.[60] Those on both sides of the debate understood themselves to be working to preserve stable homes and communities, and to staunch the flow of rootless individuals moving from countryside to city, from one region to another, or peripatetically from one town to the next. Alcohol advocates suggested that drink, whether served at home or in a saloon, could breed conviviality and thus help preserve loyalty to home and community. Their opponents insisted that it did just the opposite, unsettling and destroying homes, and sending families wandering.

If someone had asked a nineteenth-century American to associate "contentment" with a place, he or she probably would have responded "the home," though "the countryside" would have been a close second. The idea of contentment was fundamentally domestic, tied to the image of the middle-class couple and their two to four children cozily gathered around a fireplace engaged in improving or productive, but not arduous, activities. The comfortable home became an extremely important symbol within the drink debate. While advocates of alcohol frequently represented drinking as a family-centered activity, adding to the coziness and conviviality of the domestic scene, temperance reformers' drunkard narratives frequently argued that men's drinking made this epicenter of comfort far from comfortable.

Drink defenders insisted that home consumption of alcohol could be an important part of family life. Advertisements for beer and malt liquor often depicted drink in domestic spaces. In different ads, two alcohol manufacturers depicted a child or cherub delivering a crate of alcohol to a bourgeois woman in a substantial home surrounded by lush foliage.[61] Many brewers advertised their beers "For family use."[62] Some producers and distributors of alcohol were even more direct in challenging temperance reformers' assertions that alcohol could disrupt and disperse the home. An advertising booklet for Moerlein's beer included an image of Rip Van Winkle, with the caption, "No wonder Rip would go away, / And in the mountains roam. / For without Moerlein's Lager Beer / There is no joy at home."[63] An advertisement for Louis Zierngibl California Wines and Brandies quoted a booklet on wine use that advised "Let every woman cook a good meal, and put a bottle of good Claret wine on the table, and she will see, that her husband and sons will have no desire to go out evenings and spend their time in saloons."[64]

In her recent book, *Domesticating Drink,* Catherine Murdock has discussed the many ways in which alcohol use was integrated into domestic life in the late nineteenth and early twentieth centuries.[65] This was particularly true among European immigrants, many of whom were accustomed to consuming alcohol, particularly beer, in their homes with their families and considered it an important, traditional, and stabilizing part of family life. As a Norwegian civil damage act plaintiff testified, "The old country and this country is not alike, there is not so much temperance there."[66] Civil damage law defendants often pointed out that it was hypocritical for plaintiffs, many of whom were European immigrants, to sue saloonkeepers for providing alcohol to their husbands when they themselves served and consumed it in the home.[67] Antitemperance writers often portrayed temperance reformers as disrupting immigrants' domesticity. E. N. Chapin's 1893 novel, *Iowa Cranks,* depicts overzealous prohibition agents invading "a neat little cottage owned by a Swede named Ole Oleson" and taking Mrs. Oleson's medicinal beer and then breaking up the "home-like scene" of the "little frame house" of a German immigrant family.[68]

In temperance narratives, though, the drinker's home was never "cozy." A pamphlet distributed in New Orleans in 1841 described alcohol as producing a "sad change in the domestic circle, from peace and happiness to continued bickering and boisterous strife" and "rudely wither[ing] that sympathy which was wont to entwine itself around the domestic alter, and alleviate family afflictions."[69] A Washingtonian tune in an 1843 songbook, "Sweet Home," contained the lines, "The drunkard abandoned was once left to roam / His fam'ly neglected, deserted his home / Home, home, sweet sweet home / Oh what drunkard's dwelling was ever a home."[70] Drunkard narratives throughout the century invariably describe drinkers' homes as cold, stripped of furnishings, filled with disease, and insufficiently stocked with food. Because of this neglect and because of the drunkards' own violent and unpredictable behavior, the family home became a place of want and insecurity. One antebellum temperance play described alcohol as "the pest of the humble home . . . the withering curse of the happy circle."[71] This staple of antebellum temperance discourse remained equally pervasive into the Gilded Age. A drunkard in an 1882 temperance play put the same sentiment more directly, exclaiming "Home! Oh the hollow mockery of the word!"[72] Two of the Woman's Christian Temperance Union's favorite mottoes were "Home Protection" and "For God and Home and Native Land." In a 1903 allegorical temperance play, "Rye" and "Barley" tell King Alcohol that, as wholesome grains, they "filled the lab'rer's cottage / With sweet content and joy." Once he made them into liquor, however, "thou, O robber of the poor / Dost all this peace destroy."[73] Once the home was no longer home-like, temperance reformers throughout the century feared, it was only a matter of time before family members dispersed.

Picking up this theme, civil damage plaintiffs frequently complained that their husbands or sons rendered their homes uncomfortable, even uninhabitable. (Remember Clara Cramer's implausible case at the beginning of the chapter.) Plaintiff Martha Johnson, in an 1889 case, argued that alcohol made her husband "ugly and disagreeable in the house, scolding and jawing in the house, nobody could stay there very well, everybody hated the house. Of course, those that had to stay there, me and the children, had to, and sometimes we would clear out."[74] Stories of domestic violence and abuse pervaded the testimony. Ann Wilson's lawyer, in an 1885 case, described a domestic scene in which a drunken husband "beat his wife down with a chair and severely wounded her. . . . he then was about to seize another chair when his young son interfered to protect his mother from further outrage, and he fell upon the floor. . . . the children cried and were terrified."[75] Thirteen-year-old Anna Peters, in her 1879 testimony, similarly described her father's destruction of her home. "He broke the dishes and everything in the house." As a consequence of his drunken behavior, Anna continued, "Mother went out washing, and my sisters went to work to make our living." Anna's sister Margaret added that, in addition to driving other family members from the home, their father sometimes "could not find his way home because he was drunk."[76] Plaintiffs like Hester Worley recounted the nights they spent hiding out of doors, the times they were forced to take shelter with neighbors or relatives, the weeks for which their husbands disappeared.[77] Alcohol, in these accounts, destroyed homes and scattered family members. Temperance crusader Mother Stewart, arguing on behalf of a civil damage act plaintiff in 1872, told the jury how glad she was that now "our women might come into the courts and prosecute the rum-seller for the destruction of their husbands and homes."[78] Regina Bellison's attorney argued, in 1899, that his client was "entitled to a house to shelter [her family and] to the comforts and surroundings of a home."[79]

Both reformers and their opponents claimed that they were working to uphold and solidify the home and community. Drunkards dispersed households, temperance advocates argued, which made for unstable communities. Many of those who supported saloons, however, suggested that public drinking could build community spirit. In fact, saloons did frequently serve as "workingmen's clubs" and community centers. Drinking songs, particularly German beer songs, often nostalgically evoked home and homeland. Some songs suggested that through drinking German beers, homesick Germans could imagine themselves sitting contentedly by the Rhine.

For their part, temperance reformers often portrayed drinkers and their families as drifters, evicted from their homes, estranged from friends and extended families. Antebellum temperance stories like Sarah Josepha Hale's 1839 *My Cousin Mary* imagined drunkards' families wandering the world "never stay-[ing] long enough in one place to feel at home."[80] One popular melodramatic convention in temperance drama was to reveal that a mysterious drifter who had just come to town was actually a relative, friend, or business partner of the main characters, missing for years because of drink.[81] In a play from the 1850s, the character who has been so displaced and found has adopted the alias "Speculation."[82] Later plays like S. N. Cook's 1870s *Out in the Street* and Charles Babcock's 1880 *Adrift*, as their titles suggest, are filled with refugees from alcohol, displaced and anonymous, wandering the country.[83] Reformers sang songs like "Where is My Wandering Boy Tonight," and "Redeemed," in which a reformed drunkard recalled, "Up and down the streets I wandered, / Oh how utterly alone / Ties of home and love all sundered."[84]

Civil damage law plaintiffs frequently took up this theme, claiming that drink had caused their separation from community life and security. When Jennie Franklin, in 1894, complained that she had been "obliged to leave her home and deprive herself of the ordinary necessities and pleasures of life, and go among strangers to work as a servant," she was talking about social dislocation as much as economic decline.[85] A few years earlier, Eugenia Peacock, from a considerably higher class position, declared that she had "been driven from society and its enjoyments and comforts, she has been deprived of the society and comfort of friends and relatives, and . . . her feelings and sensibilities have been injured, wronged and outraged beyond the power of expression."[86] Jennie Franklin, Eugenia Peacock, and their lawyers believed that the court would recognize a responsibility to compensate them for being not simply econom-ically uprooted but also cut off from the comforts of familiar society.

As concerned as they were with contentment as a means to strengthen indi-vidual ties to family, community, and class, drink debaters also saw the feeling of contentment as an end in itself. They worried that discontent and social dislocation fed into one another, creating a dangerous spiral. Just as a stable social order could only be preserved if people were willing to accept their situa-tions within it, people could only know the pleasures of contentment if the order was stable enough to allow them to chose stasis.

Temperance advocates were particularly interested in what it meant to be truly "content." As reformers, however, they had to constantly ask themselves whether this state of acceptance was always desirable. Though they vocally advocated an aesthetic of contentment, reformers were openly working to transform, rather than to accept passively, their places in homes, communities, and the nation. Though temperance reformers called for everyone to be con-tent with their situation in life, they were not oblivious to the fact that some situations could be quite difficult to endure. They were all too aware, as one 1854 novel put it, that "the ways of the world are not always as pleasant as they might be."[87] To be content was to accept what reformers frequently referred to as life's "stern realities." Life could, at times, seem unfair, unstable, dull, even unbearable. The author of an 1880 temperance monograph wrote, "in this world men are often the mere foot-balls of circumstances over which they have no control."[88] Yet, reformers insisted, it was imperative that people prudently face reality rather than try to avoid or escape it, whether through drink or other means.

Civil damage plaintiffs often testified that their husbands' drinking had robbed them of psychological contentment. In most jurisdictions, juries were not allowed to award damages for emotional pain and suffering, but they occa-sionally did so anyway, and judges frequently allowed plaintiffs to introduce testimony about their mental anguish and distress even when juries were not supposed to be factoring it into their decisions. The breadwinners' drinking disrupted the plaintiffs' economic security and their comfortable relationships to friends and family, and it threatened to throw the plaintiffs into a state of perpetual distress, robbing them of their "peace of mind." Some plaintiffs even suggested that they were in danger of going completely insane. Iowa's Narinah Ennis claimed in 1877 that she was "constantly filled with alarm and fearful forebodings for the future."[89] Martha Johnson complained twelve years later that her husband's drunken comportment had caused her "great distress in mind."[90] Louise Faivre said that since her husband Andrew's accident, the "work and worry and loss of sleep and anxiety . . . injured her greatly in person, for that it has broken down her health."[91] Of course, these claims have to be understood as part of a strategy to win damages from a jury, but it is significant that, just as Eugenia Peacock and Jennie Franklin predicted that judges and juries would want to compensate them for their social alienation, so Narinah Ennis, Martha Johnson, and Louise Faivre believed that the court would be compelled to action by their claims of mental unrest.

Many drink debaters imagined that discontent like that of inebriates and their wives was spreading so ominously as to be a major social problem in itself. As more and more people grew discontented and set off in search of quick profit, it became difficult for a person who wanted to choose contentment to find a place sheltered from the chaotic forces of risk. Both widespread land speculation and the unpredictable fluctuations of agricultural commodity prices were very much on the minds of nineteenth-century farmers. At the same time, the portion of the population living in urban areas increased noticeably. Improved transportation and communication and other ever-larger businesses brought urban money-chasers into closer relationships to those who had prudently chosen to stay on the farm. While it would be easy to overemphasize the extent to which the Midwest before this period had been composed of pastoral island communities, many drink debaters experienced their world as increasingly integrated, fast-paced, and out of control. It seemed to many as though urban forces dangerously threatened spaces of contentment.[92]

In a peculiar passage at the beginning of her novel, *The Worst Foe* (1886), Grace Strong describes the farm of a prudent, contented, and temperate family, the Denesmores. "John Denesmore has for twenty-five years occupied this coveted home. Here he and his wife began their married life together. Here their children were born and grew to maturity. He has seen the little village grow to a thriving town, approaching nearer and nearer to his home, devouring bit by bit his once extensive farm, converting his field lots into town lots and streets, greatly enhancing the value of the land and increasing Mr. Denesmore's wealth."[93] This passage sounds almost idyllic until we reach the word *devouring*. Though John Denesmore has lived a sober, stable, agricultural life, choosing contentment over risk, risk has come to him, in the form of both urbanization and land speculation. Much of the remainder of the novel traces the temptation and fall of the house of Denesmore. Denesmore's son, Guy, in an obviously allegorical move, is seduced by a manipulative town girl into taking his fatal first drink. Soon he manages to lose the farm. As spaces of risk devour spaces of contentment, reformers believed, it became increasingly more difficult to opt for stability.

Saloonkeepers' counsel liked to make this point in civil damage defenses. While they conceded that drunkards' families' situations had indeed worsened, drink was not to blame. Rather, they argued, such unpredictable economic mobility was the nature of life in the late-nineteenth-century United States. As one attorney said, the plaintiff's husband "was doing well in 1871, not so well in 1873. Cannot this be said of a greater part of men in business during this time? Men whose habits are of the best . . . can say the same."[94] An attorney in an 1878 case, probably referring to the same economic depression of 1873, claimed that he might have found the plaintiff's story that rum ruined her home more compelling "if a thousand and one things, and among them unfortunate business transactions, had not occurred (as was, in fact, true) during the intervening ten years, to have changed their condition in life and society."[95] It was a mistake, these lawyers insisted, to make alcohol the scapegoat for widespread social instability. In these cases and others, saloonkeepers' attorneys questioned the assumption at the heart of the civil damage acts—that, were it not for drink, families would comfortably occupy some stable position within the economic structure. In depicting drinkers and their wives as grasping speculators and drinkers' families' fates as dependent on boom and bust cycles and unfortunate business transactions, these lawyers questioned the possibility and justice of restoring them to some supposed rightful class position.

In many formats—novels, plays, tracts, and courtroom testimony—nineteenth-century drink debaters used the language of contentment to describe how individuals ought to carve out spaces of relative autonomy (such as the home) to protect them from the uncontrollable forces of their environment. At the same time, through the drunkard narrative, they expressed concern that finding such shelter was becoming increasingly difficult, perhaps even impossible. Just beneath the surface of the drink debate was the question of whether American culture itself was stable enough to allow the choice of contentment.

The space in which individuals could, through the exercise of virtue, lay claim to some control over the course of their lives seemed to be shrinking as the forces of chance gradually but ineluctably encroached on its domain. To temperance reformers, alcohol represented, encompassed, or inspired the social forces that increasingly rendered it impossible to be content. Alcohol caused men to leave their homes and to adopt many other risky activities. As they abandoned their homes and communities, they left destruction in their wake.

One key to understanding the significance of contentment in the drink debate may be found in the writings of a decidedly unusual figure, Edgar Watson Howe. Like other moderates, Howe, a novelist and newspaperman from Atchison, Kansas, distinguished between liquor, and wine and beer. He accepted beer and wine advertisements for his paper and considered drinking these beverages less odious than the consumption of hard liquor. Yet he was himself a teetotaler. In his autobiography, he referred to himself as "a tiresome preacher of temperance."[96] He called whiskey drinking "dangerous, disgusting, and a crime against self and society,"[97] and he told drunkard narratives in his newspaper columns and in his fiction.[98] Nevertheless, Howe was a hostile opponent of the temperance movement, and considered the civil damage acts unjust. He questioned the practicality of prohibition and had contempt for reformers.[99] There was an alcohol-related double murder outside a brewery in Atchison in 1900 in which one man killed two others.[100] The wives and children of the murdered men and of the murderer (who was captured and imprisoned for life) all sued the local brewery under the civil damage law. The brewery settled with the families of the victims, and the wife of the murderer went to trial and was awarded $5,000 in damages.[101] Howe was incensed at the injustice of blaming the brewery for the violence and commented frequently on the progress of the cases.[102]

Howe, who lived only about fifty miles from Charles Sheldon, constantly mocked Sheldon's *In His Steps* and the larger Social Gospel movement Sheldon promoted. After the novel's publication, Sheldon decided that he would take over a local newspaper for a week and attempt to run it "as Jesus would," promoting causes like prohibition and omitting sensationalist and violent articles. Howe countered, offering to preach a series of sermons "like a newspaper editor would" while Sheldon was otherwise occupied.[103]

Much, though not all, of Howe's opposition to temperance reformers seems to have arisen out of his notable misogyny. He noted at one point that a nearby liquor crusade "has reached the mass meeting stage, when old girls of forty get up and sing 'Father, dear father, come home with me now.' "[104] His novels were not temperance novels in any conventional sense; in fact, he used them to ridicule the predictable and sentimental plots of conventional temperance fiction. Nevertheless, though they refuse to fit tidily into either the temperance or pro-drink camps, his writings were very much part of the drink debate. Drunkard and reformer characters pervaded them, and he frequently evoked alcohol and temperance as central metaphors.

At the psychological center of Howe's fiction—from his acclaimed *Story of a Country Town* to his less successful *A Moonlight Boy*, *A Man Story*, and *The Mystery of the Locks*—is the realization that contentment is unattainable for men.[105] In Howe's small-town Midwest, men were tragically unable to make either their families or themselves happy, and dreamed only of escape. In real life, Howe's father had abandoned him and his mother, claiming that he was too discontented to remain.[106] Yet Howe's father himself knew that leaving was not a solution; he "had always said that temptation assailed those who went out in the world."[107] All of Howe's novels include accounts of men failing to find contentment with their families and leaving home to wander alone. In *A Moonlight Boy*, one man explains, "when I discovered . . . that I was not altogether content myself, it seemed such a monstrous offence that I resolved to devote my life to overcoming it. But in spite of everything I could do, the discontent grew upon me."[108] Similarly, in *A Man Story*, Mr. Tom can never fully enjoy his passionate love for his second wife because he knows that he will eventually become as dissatisfied with her as he did with his first.

Howe equated discontent with drinking. In his fiction, he compared men's inability to find permanent satisfaction in their wives with men who "ha[ve] a taste for liquor, [who after] drinking it all the time, [find] fault with [their] tipple after [they] had tired of its taste and effect."[109] Mr. Tom, unable to stay away from his second wife even though he feels certain his love for her will one day wane, responds to her forgiveness, "It is the draught that intoxicates . . . poor drunkard that I am, let me forget my sorrow in dissipation; pass the cup again." Again, at the end of the novel, he tells her "after you are gone, my sober sense will tell me that I drank the draught that intoxicated me, and then praised it. I believe that it is for the best that we never live together again."[110]

Howe disliked both alcohol and women because they inspired desires that they could never satisfy. Men fell in love for the same reasons that they became drunk—to escape from the loneliness and banality of life. This assertion was decidedly out of line with the temperance mainstream, and it posed a problem to their argument. Temperance writers acknowledged that there was a certain class of giddy and risk-taking young women who seduced men into taking their fatal first drink. Falling under the spell of such a seductress was parallel to entering the dangerous space of the saloon. However, these women were exceptions; the bad influence of such women differed in kind from the wholesome influence of mothers, sisters, wives, aunts, right-thinking sweethearts, and other reforming women. To imagine, as Howe did, that yielding to the influence of a women was structurally identical to yielding to the influence of drink was to fundamentally challenge the temperance movement. There is little doubt that Howe wanted to make precisely that point. In his *Story of a Country Town,* the woman for whom the discontented man leaves his family just happens to be the local temperance reformer.

Howe, then, also associated discontent with social reform. To Howe, discontent was central to the problem of the individual drinker who drank to imagine an escape from his situation in life, and to the problem of the reformer (particularly the temperance reformer) who was discontented with the state of society and believed it could be changed drastically, immediately, and through her own agency. Though Kansas was a prohibition state, Howe lived in Atchison, located in the heavily German northeastern region, on the Missouri border. This area was notorious for its failure even to make a pretense of enforcing liquor laws. Howe opposed both drink and temperance reformers chiefly because they served as an illegitimate and ultimately unsuccessful means of escape from discontent. He accused reformers of being ineffective (which, in Atchison, they clearly were); he accused them of hypocrisy, suggesting that they drank at home or that they indulged in other equally vicious activities; and he believed that their conviction that it was possible to change the world through idealistic legislation was sheer folly.[111] Howe agreed with reformers' aims; he simply did not believe that people could be reformed, particularly not immediately or through legislation. One ought to be content with the way one is, rather than imagining the possibility of self-transformation. The reformer, in turn, ought to be content with society as it is, rather than imagining that it can be improved.[112]

CHAPTER FOUR

Seduction

Here is the danger: the poison creating such a craving in the drinker that he longs to be poisoned again. It is not so with most other poisons. A boy swollen up with poison ivy or nettles, or one who has taken lobelia or deadly nightshade, is very careful to avoid these poisonous plants ever after. To see him poison himself again and again until he became a mass of rottenness and corruption would be strange indeed, but that is exactly what happens to thousands of men who take alcoholic poison.

JULIA COLMAN, *Alcohol and Hygiene;*
An Elementary Lesson Book for Schools, 1880

"I have been so intoxicated that I was hardly conscious of what passed around me. Never but once." . . . She covered her face with her hands, as if to shut out some fearful sight. Yet still it rose before her. Brilliantly-lighted rooms; the flashing of jewels, and the gleaming of white arms; music, and the fragrance of flowers; the subtle fumes of wine, and whispered words of passion she but half comprehended.

MARY DWINELL CHELLIS, *Wealth and Wine,* 1874

In 1879, a nineteen-year-old native of New York named Eugenia married Thomas Peacock, a thirty-one-year-old English-born businessman. Eugenia and Thomas's household was a full one from the start; Thomas brought with him two sons from a previous marriage and his parents.[1] At first, according to Eugenia, Thomas was "in all respects a good, kind and indulgent husband . . . [who] remained home evenings with his family, attended well to his business, was industrious and sober and temperate, and was prosperous and successful in his business." In every way, in those early years, Thomas "conducted himself as a good and faithful husband should do."[2] He was also a wealthy man; he ran and operated a planing mill, a sash and door factory, and a lumberyard in Reed City, Michigan.

Though Thomas Peacock was considerably more prosperous than most subjects of civil damage suits, like them he struggled with a drinking habit. After about four years of marriage, according to his wife, he began to drink heavily, squandering money and property, becoming "cross, peevish, ugly, and quarrel-some," and causing his wife Eugenia "great annoyance, trouble, vexation, an-guish and sorrow."[3] For a while, under the influence of a revivalist minister, he sobered up. For a few months he again became a model husband and business-man, but his reform was brief. Within half a year he returned to his heavy drinking, "grossly abus[ing] and ill-treat[ing]" Eugenia "to such an extent that she could bear it no longer."[4] The situation came to a head on May 1, 1889, when, by Eugenia's account, Thomas attacked her violently, "struck, pulled, jerked and hauled" her around their home, "smashed and broke up the house-hold goods," and caused her "great bodily and mental suffering."[5]

Finally, Eugenia Peacock brought a civil damage suit for $5,000 against Thomas's regular saloonkeeper, Daniel Oaks,[6] who she claimed had violated Michigan law by ignoring her earlier order to cease selling liquor to her hus-band and by serving liquor on Sundays and after official closing time at night. Yet to win her case, Eugenia Peacock and her lawyers would have to surmount two major obstacles. First, Oaks's lawyer could prove that Eugenia herself on at least one occasion had drunk with her husband, Oaks, and Mrs. Oaks, which was likely to make the jury less sympathetic to her. Second, despite temperance reformers' assurances that drink brought speedy and inevitable economic fail-ure, Thomas continued to prosper in business and to provide generously for his older son's education and for Eugenia's wardrobe in addition to covering their regular household expenses. Eugenia could certainly claim physical abuse and emotional distress, but she could not make the case that was usually the most powerful in a civil damage suit: economic loss.

To win a large judgment in the face of Eugenia's embarrassing tippling inci-dent and the family's continued prosperity, Eugenia Peacock and her lawyers downplayed Eugenia's suffering and emphasized Oaks's dastardly conduct even more than was standard in civil damage trials. To do this, they fully mobilized an important element of temperance discourse: the language of seduction. That is, they presented Oaks and his saloon as a treacherous rival for Thomas's atten-tions. As a result, the case played out rather like an "alienation of affection" suit. According to Eugenia, Thomas has first begun to drink to excess due to Oaks's undue "influence," which he "wrongfully exercised" over Thomas.[7] When Thomas reformed, Oaks felt the loss of business and "wrongfully, wickedly, and stealthily planned and sought to again ruin" Thomas by "inducing" him to violate his abstinence pledge. He succeeded in luring Thomas back to his sa-loon, and once there, he made "sport" of Thomas's new religious friends, "used all and every wicked device possible to overcome [his] scruples," and "by the expression of strong friendship" for Thomas, persuaded him to accept his treat of a glass of liquor which, as Oaks had calculated, led to many more.[8]

As Eugenia told her drunkard narrative, Oaks knew well that he was her competitor for her husband's affections. When she went to the saloon to bring her husband home, Oaks frequently refused to allow her to enter. She recalled standing on the street outside the saloon, where she would "see [Thomas] stand right to the bar and drink drink after drink."[9] On two occasions, Eugenia Peacock claimed, she and Oaks had rather dramatic confrontations. Once, they both arrived at Thomas's office to escort him away at the dinner hour. Eugenia beseeched her husband to come home to eat with the family. Peacock, however, chose to go with Oaks. When he later arrived home, he was intoxicated.[10] At another time, Eugenia paid a visit to Mr. Oaks to "implore him" to stop selling alcohol to her husband. He merely "cursed" her and told her that her husband knew his "own business and knew when he had enough."[11] In view of the sexual undercurrents of this competition for Thomas, it is interesting that Burt Peacock, Thomas's adult son, said that when his father was intoxicated, he did "not treat [Eugenia] like a woman."[12]

Eugenia's special circumstances forced her lawyers to focus much more than was usually the case on a concept at the core of the civil damage laws and of temperance thought generally—that it was fair for saloonkeepers to compensate those who suffered from others' drinking because they actually, deliberately and often treacherously, seduced men into drink in order to increase their own profits. The jury awarded Eugenia $500, which, while only a tenth of the amount she had requested, was still a substantial sum. The supreme court, however, overturned the jury's judgment. There were various technical grounds on which they did so, but the biggest reason was that Eugenia and her counsel had not submitted their argument. Perhaps Eugenia did not find the $500 worth fighting for, but it seems more likely either that Eugenia and Thomas had reached some sort of understanding or that Thomas had managed—perhaps by sobering up—to assert his patriarchal role and suppress Eugenia's rebellion.

Civil damage laws functionally assumed that saloonkeepers and the alcohol they served bore at least partial responsibility for the actions of their clients. As this idea was controversial, one of the questions hovering over cases like the Peacocks' was how, exactly, to imagine that the saloonkeeper had come to be so responsible for the actions of his clients. Many people tried to explain this process by evoking the trope of seduction that was so popular in nineteenth-century culture.

These efforts to describe the process through which the forces of alcohol appropriated the drinker's will opened up the still wider question of the relationship between the individual and the environment with which he interacted. If it was possible, that is, for Daniel Oaks to cause Thomas Peacock to behave otherwise than he himself desired, what did that say more generally about the coercive power of the external influences over individuals? The case of the drunkard seemed to manifest this issue with a particular directness because alcohol was an external substance that men took into their bodies. As Karen Sánchez-Eppler has argued, many nineteenth-century Americans were "acutely aware of the dependence of personhood on the condition of the human body."[13] To them, few single acts illustrated the influence of the external environment on the internal self better than the consumption of food or drink. One temperance reformer in 1835 quoted Shakespeare: "Oh that men should put an enemy into their mouths to steal away their brains."[14] To contemplate putting a bit of one's environment into one's mouth; to imagine that consumed object altering one's mind and perhaps becoming part of one's body was acutely disturbing. To further believe that one's body might contain an inherited proclivity toward that substance, rendering one unable to resist it; or that the substance itself might create in the mind and body such an inability to resist, was to confront directly the relationship between self and environment. Consumption blurred the line between the self and the environment; temperance reformers would mobilize the metaphors of invasion and seduction to draw a newer—and they hoped more sustainable—boundary of the self. Rather than continuing to maintain that the self began with the boundaries of the body, they would try to distinguish strictly between the elements of self and the external forces that had violated those boundaries.

The implications of consumption, and the desire to distinguish between the consuming subject and the consumed object, fed into one of the more striking debates within the drink discourse: the argument over whether alcohol was a food.[15] Those who supported alcohol use made expansive claims about alcohol's usefulness in sustaining the body. Advertisements for alcoholic products depicted their consumers as healthy, strong, well-nourished folks. The image of the buxom woman bearing beer steins, already present in late-nineteenth-century advertisements, was meant to express sexuality and a fleshiness to which, presumably, the beer had contributed. An 1894 ad for The Genuine

Johann Hoff's Malt Extract featured an image of muscleman Eugene Sandow, claiming that the product had helped him to achieve his body.[16] Another ad for the product labeled it a "FLESH AND BLOOD MAKER"[17] (fig. 5). A 1904 ad for Schlitz beer insisted that there were "no wasted, fatless men" among regular beer drinkers.[18] Alcohol manufacturers made their strongest claims about alcohol's "food value" when advertising products intended for medicinal use. Malt Nutrine's producers, for instance, insisted that it possessed "blood-making properties," provided "cell-creating elements essential for the development of blood, bone and tissue," and was "Flesh Restoring."[19]

Temperance reformers, however, weren't buying. Alcohol, they insisted, "undergoes no digestion or assimilative change in the digestive organs and is not converted into any elements capable of contributing to the growth or repair of the organized structure of the human body."[20] They argued that alcohol was fundamentally and unalterably external, and could never become a part of the body. It was not a food; it was a poison. Rather than being incorporated, it rushed through the body wreaking havoc until the body managed to expel it. Reformers' passionate insistence that alcohol could never *become* flesh is illustrated in their careful explanation of the notable girth of some heavy drinkers. Rather than characterize it as "fleshiness," they labeled it "bloating."[21] To them, drinkers' beer bellies were mere parodies of flesh—artificial or full of nothing.

Of course, any consumption, even that of food, could have the same disturbing implications to the independence of the volitional self. It is no coincidence that temperance reformers tended to be drawn to dietary reforms such as vegetarianism, spice-free diets, avoidance of overly hot or cold food or beverages, and the like. Temperance reformers understood that consumption of food was an inescapable necessity, however troubling its implications. They were so passionate that alcohol, unlike other foods, remained fundamentally separate from the constitution of the physical self because they believed that it most powerfully and treacherously affected individual volition. Though they observed that alcohol altered the character and desires of the drinker, they wanted to believe that the character and desires inspired by drink were of an entirely different nature than the true character and desires of the sober individual. Desires produced by alcohol, like beer bellies, were artificial.[22] If alcoholic desires were artificial, however, their power over the drinker was all too real. Precisely because it was difficult to distinguish in practice between the individual's own desires and those inspired by drink, temperance advocates were careful to maintain a theoretical distinction. Reformers in the early years of the

Fig. 5. Advertisement for "The Genuine Johann Hoff's Malt Extract," 1894 (Photo courtesy of the Warshaw Collection, Archives Center, National Museum of American History, Smithsonian Institution)

movement sought ways to describe the relationship between the drinker's "real" and "artificial" characters and desires.

To describe the relationship between the drinker and his drink, then, was to describe the process by which the individual consumed his environment. Temperance reformers were in nearly unanimous agreement that drunkards were not entirely responsible for their fates. The vast majority went further and argued that drunkards were not chiefly responsible for their fallen state. Rather, the blame for the drunkard's plight rested upon alcohol itself, the men who sold it, the churches who refused to take a sufficiently strong stance against it, the politicians who supported it, and the society that kept these politicians in power. Where temperance reformers disagreed with one another was in describing the technology of the process through which these forces exerted their baneful influence. Precisely how did environment exert sufficient pressure on a sober young man to cause him to become a drunkard? Sometimes reformers described this process with the languages of corruption, pollution, or deterioration;[23] sometimes they spoke of liquor and its supporters as "poisoning" the drinker.[24] At other times they saw drink as desiccating him,[25] or they imagined that drink and its supporters ate away at the drinker like a disease or a cancer.[26]

As we will see, they often spoke of this relationship in terms of invasion, imagining that drink conquered the drinker's will.

One of the most common ways in which reformers described how pro-alcohol social forces operated on potential drunkards, however, was through the language of seduction. The seduction analogy imagined that alcohol and its supporters created new desires in the bosom of the drinker. Temperance reformers understood alcohol as an object of desire. To understand the movement, one must appreciate why reformers loathed alcohol but also why they feared drinkers' (and their own) fascination with it.[27] Through their temperance writings and particularly through their drunkard narratives, they explored the nature of desire and the power of external forces in creating them.

Seduction, as understood in the nineteenth-century United States, was a highly unstable term. It fell awkwardly between choice and coercion, and usually implied an overdetermined mixture of both. It was the process through which one person (the seducer) caused another person (the victim) not simply to act, but even to *want* to act, as the seducer desired. Because the actual mechanism of seduction was quite vague (and, in the case of sexual seduction, because drink debaters were reluctant to be too explicitly descriptive), writers usually described seductions metaphorically. For instance, they often described the seducer as enticing, alluring, enthralling, fascinating, or charming the victim. Generally, though, a seduction involved the displacement—through a deliberate process of deception—of an individual's native set of values, customs, and desires by a foreign and artificial one.

Though many historians have been skeptical about the psychoanalytic idea that temperance reformers harbored a desire for the substance they strove to destroy, some scholars have recently begun to more closely analyze problems of desire in the temperance movement. Since reformers themselves frequently dwelt quite explicitly and at length on the seductiveness of drink, there is no need to attempt to descend into their subconscious minds to make such a claim. Temperance advocates used the seduction metaphor much more than did their pro-drink opponents. Furthermore, they imagined that their opponents were using the language of seduction against them.[28] Saloon supporters did occasionally argue in terms of seduction; at least one very early temperance opponent, drawing on anti-Catholic tropes, accused male temperance reformers of using their cause to win entry into women's homes and confidences in order to seduce them from husbands and fathers. After women became dominant in the movement, temperance critics began to argue that the movement itself alienated members' affections from husbands.[29] On the whole, however, drink defenders' rare attempts to portray reformers as seducers seem to have fallen flat.

There are various reasons that seduction language appealed to reformers more than it did to their opponents. To begin with, the seduction metaphor challenged saloon supporters' generally more confident views about individual agency. Perhaps most importantly, however, the imbalance certainly was closely intertwined with the different genres in which members of each group chose to work. Saloon supporters tended to participate in the drink debate by publishing pamphlets and periodicals, giving speeches, and accumulating facts to dispute those produced by the temperance movement. The two creative genres within which they most frequently worked were advertisements and songs; there was relatively little explicitly antitemperance fiction, drama, and poetry. Comparatively, temperance reformers produced a much greater body of fictional literature, and one of their favorite modes of creative expression was the novel. The history of the novel itself was intricately interconnected with narratives of seduction. For these and other reasons, the theme of seduction was central to nineteenth-century reformers' explanation of the drunkard's fall.

When Americans told, wrote, read, or heard the story of the drinker as a story of seduction, they connected it with two other types of tales common in the early-national and antebellum United States: stories of seductions by gentlemen ("rakes") and by priests. In fact, the novel form in which so many temperance writers embedded their drunkard narratives emerged largely out of rake seduction narratives. Some literary critics consider Samuel Richardson's novels *Pamela* and *Clarissa* to be the first fully modern examples of the genre. Written in the middle of the eighteenth century, these English epistolary novels center around notorious rakes ruthlessly pursuing and imprisoning moralistic young women. Though both Pamela and Clarissa proved remarkably adept at thwarting their seducers' intentions, their counterparts in novels modeled after Richardson's were often less successful. Susanna Rowson's *Charlotte Temple* (1791/4) and Hannah Foster's *The Coquette* (1797) were the most prominent of the early seduction novels in the United States. Each tells the story of a young woman who allows herself to be seduced by a rake and thus severs ties to family and community, is abandoned, and pays with her life. In the United States, the late 1700s and early 1800s saw the publication and circulation of numerous stories of women who had met similar fates, along with sermons delivered on the occasion of the deaths of seduced women and lengthy accounts and partial transcripts of seduction trials.[30] Tales of sexual seduction permeated early national culture much as the drunkard narrative would in later decades.

While the seducers were the villains of these narratives, the victims generally were not blameless and were often depicted as complicit.[31] They may have been tricked by fake marriage ceremonies, may have been so young as to have been easily misled, may have been poorly or treacherously supervised by parents or guardians, may even have fainted and been carried off to their elopement; nevertheless, they were attracted to their handsome seducers and had unwisely consented to exchange correspondence with them or to meet them in private. They often agreed to these intimacies through a too-trusting nature and a desire to please those around them—as well as a desire for adventure and romance. However limited and understandable their attraction and consent was, it made them vulnerable to seduction. Even if they never made another mistake, their doom was sealed.

Recently, literary critics and historians have taken a close look at the broader implications of the novels of the early republic, including Foster's and Rowson's. They have argued that despite their domestic orientation, these works had important political content. Early American authors and readers used stories about romantic love and deceit to work through their recent separation from England and to imagine how a democracy might work.[32] These novels and earlier novels of seduction like Richardson's may have been so popular in the new republic precisely because they explored the disturbing possibility that an individual could irretrievably lose virtue through the smallest misstep and thereby come under the power of a manipulative charmer.

While the political implications of the stories were veiled by the fact that the all-too-easily seduced characters were female, contemporaries did not have to work hard to consider the male corollary to this story of female seduction. A young man (or an entire young nation) could all too easily come under the political sway of a member of the social elite. The sexual purity of young women closely paralleled the volitional integrity of their male counterparts. Though the story of political corruption was hardly repressed in the early republic, the increasing prominence of the literature of female seduction shaped that discourse while writing women, though only in an allegorical capacity, into the story of American democracy.

Another type of seduction narrative emerged simultaneously with temperance fiction, though it flourished earlier and for a briefer time. As Irish Catholic immigration assumed huge proportions in antebellum years, some Protestants began to see the Catholic presence as a real threat to their nation. Many of them mobilized an already widespread antiprofessional and anti-elitist rhetoric to suggest that Catholic priests exercised dangerous levels of authority over believers. Catholics, in this view, lacked the autonomy necessary for participants in a democracy. Politically, the threat was that the Jesuits would control male Catholic voters and ultimately install the pope as a tyrant. This fear became a major issue in the 1840s and 1850s—particularly in northeastern cities like Boston, Philadelphia, and New York—giving birth to secret orders and political parties like the American Republicans and the Know-Nothings.[33]

Just as early-national seduction fiction offered a feminized parallel to fears about the potentially corrupting power of the political elite on male citizens, so anti-Catholic fiction alluded to the political corruption of Catholic men when it told the story of how priests could seduce and sexually corrupt young women. In the 1830s, anti-Catholics produced a number of books, pamphlets, and short stories recounting instances of priestly seduction, most famously Maria Monk's *Awful Disclosures of the Hotel Dieu Nunnery* (1836). Many of these sources described a young, usually Protestant, woman lured or deceived by priests into converting to Catholicism and entering a convent. Once in the priests' power, she realizes that far from having entered a life of religious purity she has become an inmate of an institution maintained for the purpose of providing sexual partners for priests. Other anti-Catholic tales of seduction told of priests bewitching young women into becoming members of the Catholic church, often with the intention of luring them into the privacy of the confessional.

Though the victims of priestly seduction in these stories were almost exclusively female, Jenny Franchot points out in her analysis of anti-Catholicism in the early United States that the few male victims offer "an intriguing masculine counterpart to Susanna Rowson's *Charlotte Temple*."[34] Indeed, the anti-Catholic press did occasionally describe the sexual seduction of males. An Iowa temperance newspaper, in 1869, reprinted a story that had been a standard among antebellum anti-Catholics. According to the story, during the Inquisition, one of the torture devices was a painted figure of an incredibly beautiful woman. This painted woman was so beautiful that victims would spontaneously and predictably attempt to embrace her. In so doing, they triggered a mechanism that caused a knife to spring out, stabbing them in the heart.[35] Anti-Catholic seduction fiction of all varieties declined quickly after anti-Catholicism's heyday in the 1850s.

The novel of seduction in its classic "rake" form began to disappear around the 1840s. According to Nina Baym's classic work on domestic fiction, "the disappearance of the novel of seduction is a crucial event in woman's fiction, and perhaps in woman's psyche as well."[36] More recently, Elizabeth Barnes has argued that "the decline of seduction fiction and the rise of the domestic novel in the early decades of the nineteenth century signals a radical shift in the representation of affective bonds."[37] Yet the novel of seduction did not really disappear. Rather, rake and priest seduction narratives first coexisted with and then finally gave way to increasingly popular narratives of the drunkard's seduction. Both types of seduction narratives were very much on the minds of producers and consumers of drunkard narratives. In 1855, for instance, the Massachusetts legislature, which considered one of the earliest civil damage laws, was concurrently involved in a scandalous investigation of a local convent.[38] Though drunkard narratives differed in some important ways from narratives of rake and priest seduction—most obviously, the victims were male—drunkard narratives were inextricably interconnected with them.[39] Civil damage law juries, writers of temperance dramas, and readers of short stories in temperance newspapers came to drunkard narratives with well-developed expectations and associations. In turn, drunkard narratives, whether they conformed to, challenged, or tweaked these older seduction narratives, resonated far beyond the sphere of the drink debate.

It is not surprising, given the genre from which they emerged, that drunkard narratives emphasized the role of the seducer. The language that these accounts used to describe seducers remained notably consistent from the 1840s through the end of the century. Because they did not have to conform closely to specific facts and events, writers of fiction often had more freedom in characterizing these figures than did, for example, civil damage act plaintiffs. The classic fictional seduction scene began when a young potential drinker met up with a person or group of people who encouraged him to drink, overcoming his objections and emphasizing alcohol's attractions. When this seducer was female, this scene of seduction was often a minor variation of Eve's offer of the apple: a young woman offered a young man a glass of wine, and took his initial reluctance as an offense to her beauty or hospitality.[40] Occasionally, she (and an inevitable crowd that formed around them) mocked his temperance principles or issued him an ultimatum: if he did not drink, she would have to believe that he was not interested in her favor.[41] The seductress was always beautiful, always desirable, always "bejeweled," and the sexual connotations of her extension of a glass of wine to the young man were hardly subtle.

Just as often, however, the seducer was a treacherous young man or a group of peers. Temperance authors often described these young men, who were inevitably middle-class Anglo-Saxons, as "slick" or "fast." Seducers were often interested in gambling or speculative investments, or were scheming to separate the drinker from either his wife or his property. They persuaded a temperate acquaintance to enter a saloon, then mocked his devotion to home principles and extolled alcohol or claimed that they would be offended if their friend would not accept their hospitality.[42] Sometimes their powers of persuasion were even greater; one male seducer required an abstainer to drink in order to seal an important financial deal between the two. If writers of temperance fiction depicted young seductresses as Eve, they often associated young male tempters with the serpent. The role of the seducer was well established even in the earliest years of temperance fiction. One drunkard in an 1858 work accosts his seducer: "Behold in me the remnant of that man you once, serpent-like, tempted and called friend."[43] Another synopsis of an 1847 temperance play describes a seduction scene: "the Tempter, in the shape of Dognose, a low *sport,* leads [the future drunkard] off to the public house."[44]

Frequently, the seducer was the saloonkeeper himself. Temperance writers portrayed saloonkeepers as plotting and conspiring to make young men into drunkards to replace the customers rapidly lost to drunkards' graves. To do so, they arranged and furnished their bars so as to associate alcohol with prosperity and luxury, and then lured young men under false pretenses.[45] In particular, they deliberately created a deceptive environment by using shiny, bright, and gilded furnishings that seemed to be of more value than they were. The saloonkeeper narrator in T. S. Arthur's *Three Years in a Mantrap* (1872) compared his saloon to a sand trap for ants: "I never saw one poor ant escape."[46] In describing saloonkeepers as seducers, particularly in the later years of the nineteenth century, temperance reformers were also able to mobilize anti–big business rhetoric.[47]

Once the young man had consumed his first drink, alcohol itself became his irresistible seducer. An 1859 Tennessee treatise quotes nationally known temperance reformer Jesse Torrey referring to "the fascinating *charm* and twining gripe, with which that cunning *Serpent,* Alcohol, inveigles its prey."[48] The Reverend Robert Bigham, in his 1879 *Wine and Blood,* evoked Circe, the serpent, witchery, and charming to mark drink as an agent of seduction: "the Circean cup seemed wreathed in flowers of good manners and good feeling until he scarcely dreamed of the poisoned thorns lying hid in the beautiful foliage. . . . The wine-serpent's gleamy eye witched with its charm of ruin."[49] In Elizabeth Avery Meriwether's 1886 temperance play *Devil's Dance,* anthropomorphic (male) liquors conspire to seduce young men to drink.[50] Temperance writers used some of the same language to characterize liquor's power over the drinker that they did to characterize human seducers'. Yet authors tended to use stronger metaphors, like "slavery," "monstrous grasp," or "iron grip" more frequently to describe alcohol's power than they had to describe that of human seducers.

Civil damage law plaintiffs and their lawyers described seducers similarly, though in such accounts the seducers were almost always saloonkeepers. One of the central purposes of civil damage laws, after all, was to make saloonkeepers, whom reformers already considered morally responsible for customers' drinking, legally responsible as well. Though civil damage laws could be used against saloonkeepers even when there was no evidence that they had actively recruited the drinkers involved, plaintiffs like Eugenia Peacock relied heavily on these accounts of seduction. As legal reference writer R. Vashon Rogers explained in 1881, in some states, drinkers' wives who showed that a saloonkeeper had deliberately "placed temptations in the way of one to seduce him from the paths of sobriety" made themselves eligible for exemplary damages.[51] Margaret Dunlavey, for instance, claimed in an 1874 case that a saloonkeeper "did use said liquors and other means to allure said [Thomas] Dunlavey to the said saloon, thereby rendering the said Dunlavey drunken."[52] Remember, too, Eugenia Peacock's more detailed declaration that Oaks "wrongfully, craftily and wickedly sought" her husband and "coaxed and invited [him] to go to [his] saloon and came often and several times each day to [his] office . . . for the sole purpose and intent of inducing [him]" to drink at Oaks's saloon.[53] Plaintiffs like Margaret Dunlavey and Eugenia Peacock often portrayed their husbands as well-meaning but weak, vulnerable to saloonkeepers' manipulations. They strove to prove that saloonkeepers had beckoned to their husbands on the street or mocked their husbands' attempts to reform.

Medical literature tended to be more cautious in its use of metaphor than did temperance fiction and civil damage declarations, but it, too, often described companions, saloonkeepers, or drink itself as seducers. Even an 1890 article in the *Quarterly Journal of Inebriety,* which was usually careful to maintain its scientific tone, referred to "the wiles of the champion enchanter—alcohol."[54] Moral literature, not surprisingly, made repeated references to human tempters (as well as to the allure of alcohol), commonly describing them in biblical terms. By using the language of fictional accounts of seduction, these nonfiction sources threw a blanket of professional authority over their largely metaphorical arguments.

The figure of the seducer, then, was often fairly straightforward. Lacking moral scruples, he or she attempted, out of greed, folly, or general viciousness, to cause others to abandon their principles. Drunkard narratives held these seducers—whether saloonkeepers, beautiful young women, or devious "fast friends"—largely responsible for the drinker's downfall.[55] Were it not for the seducers who encouraged him on his path, who deliberately took advantage of his weaknesses, he might well have avoided alcohol. The same was true for those men who had once become drunkards and had struggled valiantly to reform. If they were not constantly faced with alcohol and its agents—"tempted by ruinous, seductive demons on every hand"—they could, perhaps, lead sober lives.[56] This logic supported placing inebriates in asylums far from such sites of seduction, and prohibition, which aimed to turn the nation into an inebriate asylum. Given that men's wills were weak, the state should act either to remove them from the path of temptation or to remove the path of temptation from them.

Ultimately, seduction—whether by a rake, a priest, or a saloonkeeper—was a problem of desire. Narrators shook their fists against those "fiends in human form" who led others to their destruction, but the slippery question of the victim's complicity bore the real weight of the narrative and gave it its psychological power. Richardson's prototypical victim of seduction, Clarissa, was attracted to her seducer Lovelace, and later accounts of sexual seduction often suggested that victims had invited or at least enabled their victimization.[57] Catholic priests, similarly, had persuaded their future victims that they offered a world of faith, love, and meaning in place of banal secular existence. Did seducers create desires in their prey or just invite them to reveal desires that they already felt? To tell the story of the drunkard as a story of seduction was to ask whether the drinker's innermost longings were responsible for his decline. Every person who told a drunkard narrative gave an account of desire. Temperance reformers, who immersed themselves in all varieties of drunkard narratives, seem to have had an endless appetite for these accounts.

Narrators, particularly those who were temperance reformers, often gave elaborate explanations of how a young man came to take his first drink. Generally he believed that, by drinking, he could establish himself as mature, manly, and unafraid of the warnings of parents, wives, sisters, and reformers. His decision to drink represented an attempt to escape the constraints of family and community opinion and to establish some degree of independence. Often, he combined this desire to escape family and communal restraints with an overly optimistic assessment of his own willpower, as he assured himself that he was in no danger of becoming a slave to alcohol, though he knew that others had.

Of course, temperance thinkers knew that once he took this first drink, the young man would have within him a growing desire for alcohol. In an 1880 temperance hygiene book for children, Julia Colman warned her readers that the danger of alcohol lay in its ability to "creat[e] such a craving in the drinker that he longs to be poisoned again."[58] A female character in a temperance novel feared that while she herself had "no desire for [alcohol] . . . it may be that a single glass might arouse a demon in my breast which would not down at my bidding."[59] Alcohol had the ability to create (or, more terrifyingly, arouse) a desire for itself within the drinker. However, if human seducers and alcohol itself were able to reshape, transform, and even create the (future) drinker's desires, it became very unclear to what extent those desires belonged to the drinker at all. Like accounts of sexual seduction and rape, and priestly seduction and abduction, stories of the drunkard's seduction and coercion blended easily into one another.

David Reynolds has argued that writers in the nineteenth-century United States frequently used "fictions about faraway peoples or about angelic visitations as a safe means of airing liberal, sometimes quite skeptical notions."[60] T. J. Jackson Lears has similarly shown how antimodernists in the late nineteenth century did the same with the "Oriental."[61] Of course, a huge literature on "Orientalism" and imperialist discourse has demonstrated how the same dynamic has been at work throughout this century. The saloon served as a sort of distant land for temperance reformers, who were naturally more comfortable talking about drunkards' "feebleness of the will" than in baldly discussing their own. But this attempt to distance discussions of will from their own lives was not very successful. Perhaps such attempts were never more than half-hearted. The saloon was too close to be foreign, the drunkard too immediate to be "other." Temperance reformers' doubts about the will inevitably came home to roost.

The drinker's real problem, the seduction metaphor implied, was that he had become alienated from his own desires. Because the drinker's desires were wound up in the fantastic images created by his seducers, they were, in an important sense, no longer even expressions of his self, but rather of that of his seducers. Although they took care to establish the illegitimacy of the drinker's desires, drunkard narrators, and particularly the authors of temperance fiction, often seemed simultaneously to empathize with those desires.[62] Some of the temperance reformers' more astute contemporary critics noted their seemingly paradoxical tendency to glamorize alcohol. In 1888, Edgar Watson Howe charged that temperance reformers made drink and the saloon appear exciting, talking "too much about the allurements and pleasure of drink: of the gilded palaces where drink is sold, and of its pleasing effects," when in fact "the 'gilded palaces' in which [drink] is sold are low dens kept by men whose company is not desirable . . . the reputed pleasure in the cup is a myth . . . drinking is an evidence of depravity as plainly marked as idleness and viciousness."[63] Howe found it strange that professed opponents of alcohol so often dwelled at such length upon alcohol's attractions.[64]

Howe was on to something important. Temperance reformers often described the pleasures of alcohol with striking enthusiasm or even longing. In the second quotation beginning this chapter, for instance, Mary Dwinell Chellis has a rare female drunkard character explain her own former fascination with drink. Though, significantly, she tries to block the memory, she cannot. A collage of images come back to her: "brilliantly-lighted rooms; the flashing of jewels, and the gleaming of white arms; music, and the fragrance of flowers; the subtle fumes of wine, and whispered words of passion she but half comprehended."[65] In another novel, Chellis has her temperance-reformer character acknowledge that "people sometimes crave sparkling stimulants that foam and flash before them; and when imbibed, quicken all the pulses of their lives."[66] The rather implausible description of a working-class saloon from an 1887 poem called "The Drunkard's Wife" is another good example:

> Ah, soon they beheld the door opened wide
> That led to a tapestried palace inside,
> Where chandeliers shone like jewels ablaze
> And electric lights flashed like the sun's bright rays.
> How bewitching the sight! Grand mirrors were there,
> Bright pictures adorning the walls everywhere
> And the noted works of sculpture and art
> Were gleaming with beauty to ravish the heart.[67]

It is interesting to contemplate what must have gone on in the minds of temperance advocates writing and reading these sorts of passages. Surely, such descriptions did not inspire a shudder and a sense of unmixed relief that one was, and always would be, safe from such places and experiences. Nor were these examples anomalous. Drunkard narrators often employed powerful images, such as jewels, bright lights, gilding, music, warmth, and mirrors, to signal the saloon's sensual attractiveness.[68] Producers and consumers of drunkard narratives were often more than willing to concede that, however illusory and dangerous it was, the realm of drink had an unmistakable attraction. As one temperance leader and poet wrote in 1895, "I know that experience teaches us well / But O, what bright visions dissolve neath her spell."[69]

Drunkard narrative producers' and consumers' willingness to go this far with the drinker suggests that their relationship to the drinker was more complex than a simple "othering" of him. Indeed, these texts give many indications that drunkard narrators identified with the drinker as much as they differentiated him from themselves. In civil damage cases, for instance, the most common plaintiffs were drunkards' wives. They almost invariably shared race, class, region, history, ethnicity, and religion with the drunkard husbands whose stories they told. Significantly, they often also shared habits. One of the most common defenses against civil damage suits was that the plaintiffs were themselves drinkers and had encouraged their husbands or even purchased them liquor, until they decided they could make money by bringing suits. Particularly among recent European immigrants, who did not have the same cultural taboos against female drinking, drinkers' wives often admitted to being occasional drinkers. Even beyond that, however, many witnesses in these suits faulted the plaintiffs for having married such men in the first place. These women, like their husbands, were often considered fast; defendants frequently called witnesses to impeach their characters. When a drinker's wife told the story of her husband's seduction by drink, she was endangering her own character as well.

Not only did drunkard narrators in civil damage cases tend to resemble their subject, but also they tended, quite noticeably, to sympathize with him. To attempt to exonerate him from blame for his poor behavior was both legally necessary and expedient. According to most interpretations of civil damage laws, a dependent could win a suit against a saloonkeeper only if there was good reason to believe that the drinker would have supported that dependent if he had not been damaged by drink. If the defendants could demonstrate that the drinker was a shiftless, lazy, and irresponsible person who had never been a reliable provider, the plaintiff could not recover. Furthermore, the better the degraded man had been before becoming a drunkard, the more sympathy the jury and judge would be likely to have and the more damages they were likely to award. The accused drunkard himself was often present at the proceedings and had often changed his ways since the bringing of the lawsuit (either because he had seen the light or because any saloonkeeper would be a fool to sell to him). Dependants may well have seen it as in their interest to be as positive about him as the nature of the suit would allow. Naturally, then, most plaintiffs went to great lengths to assert the excellent qualities their providers displayed when sober. Though they had clear strategic reasons for making these arguments, they were able to make them plausibly because of the cultural popularity of a drunkard narrative that allowed for such a sympathetic and positive presentation. By participating in this narrative when telling their stories, they themselves added to its cogency and penetration.

Even some of the science of the day gave authority to temperance writers' sympathetic or positive depictions of drunkards. Medical experts identified chronic inebriety as one possible manifestation of neurasthenia, a disease to which only those with particularly refined constitutions were susceptible.[70] Doctors writing about the causes of inebriety emphasized that people who worked hard, either mentally or physically, were tempted by alcohol's promise of relaxation and release. In their own moments of identification, they often pointed out that doctors themselves, whose work called for great physical and mental effort, were especially susceptible to inebriety.[71] Harry Levine has pointed out that temperance rhetoric often imagined that alcohol could "destroy the lives of even the finest citizens."[72] Edgar Watson Howe, who criticized temperance reformers' glorification of the saloon, also argued that they glorified drinkers themselves. Whereas most people had a multitude of character failings, these reformers considered drunkards to be perfect but for their addiction to drink.[73]

Countless tellings of drunkard narratives back up this claim. In Metta Fuller's antebellum novel, *Fashionable Dissipation,* a drunkard's sister defends him as "affectionate and yielding as a child, and as pure-hearted, his tastes are only too delicately fastidious, his nature too refined; but he has not physical nor moral strength to resist the tempests of feeling and passion which sometimes shake him."[74] John Gough similarly thundered: "Take a . . . young man and he shall be full of fire and poetry. He shall be of a nervous temperament and a generous heart; fond of society and open and manly in everything he does. Everyone loves him. That is the man most liable to become intemperate."[75] Grace Strong, in *The Worst Foe* (1886), likewise describes future drunkard Guy Denesmore as "all a fond parent might ask . . . obedient, kind, with no ignoble qualities, and enough ambition to stimulate him to action, yet not enough to trample under foot the rights of others." His one flaw is "an overweening confidence in his friends and a tendency to have his actions directed by their desires. This weakness, if it was a weakness, was more the outpouring of a generous heart than a real fault."[76] The only failings temperance writers commonly ascribed to men who would become drunkards, in fact, were the possession of "too trusting natures," overactive imaginations, and excessive ambition to transcend their station in life.

Some writers further suggested that people with active imaginations—particularly, literary people—were likely to become drunkards. The idea that alcohol could inspire art and that many great artists were also great drinkers was widespread throughout the century. In Mary Dwinell Chellis's *From Father to Son*, for instance, the reader first learns that Caspar is in danger when he is overly enthusiastic about books, preferring them to farm chores.[77] This excitement foreshadows his later euphoria upon taking his first drink. The potential relationship between literary and artistic imagination and the dangerous delusions of the drunkard may well explain why many temperance writers insisted that their works were not the products of their own imagination but transcriptions of real events they themselves had witnessed. Even so, writers and readers of temperance fiction clearly felt a certain sympathy for the young man brought to his decline through a heightened imagination and artistic sensibility.

The typical drunkard-narrative protagonist closely resembled many reformers' self-perceptions in other ways. In temperance fiction, he was usually Anglo-Saxon, Protestant, and middle-class. Anglo-Saxon characters like Charles Thornton, Guy Denesmore, Hastings Warland, Dick Wilson, Charles Lennard, Harry Drayton, and Colonel Bertram outnumbered the ethnic characters like Teddy O'Rafferty by a huge margin. The temperance-fiction drunkard was also particularly handsome, particularly affable, and usually "good" before his decline. From the antebellum years to the century's end, temperance-fiction drunkards tended to be vocal temperance advocates. As they drank, they cursed the saloonkeepers who took their money and the government that failed to prohibit saloons and remove them from the temptation they were unable to resist. Though they were slaves to the bottle, they did rattle their chains.[78] If the votes of temperance-novel drunkards decided local option elections, the saloons would be long gone—recall Jack London's vote for woman suffrage. Frequently, temperance authors chose the drunkards themselves to deliver their most concentrated temperance messages.[79] In this sense, drunkards stood as figures for the authors rather than as alien and threatening others. Despite the fact that, as both medical writers and writers of temperance fiction were well aware, many problem drinkers were immigrants, poor, black, Catholic, or in other ways socially distinct from them, writers chose to tell of drunkards ethnically, socioeconomically, and religiously like themselves. As awkward as it made their position, they sympathized, even identified with, the drinker.

Most tellers of drunkard narratives, at least after the heyday of the autobiographical narrative in the antebellum years, differed from their subjects in one obvious way: gender. Civil damage narrators were very much aware of this difference and placed great significance in it. Drunkards depicted in temperance fiction and nonfiction, and the subjects of civil damage act suits, were almost always men. A clear majority of writers of temperance fiction and plaintiffs in civil damage suits, and probably a majority of writers of nonfiction drunkard narratives, were women. Because of this gender difference, the identification between narrators and drunkards could not be a simple one. Temperance women would not have been the first to project their fears onto a gendered other: this is precisely what recent literary critics have suggested about the use of domestic seduction fiction to contain concerns about early American political life.

Though, ultimately, it was in gender difference that reformers found their resolution to the problem the drunkard narrative posed to moral autonomy, their path was not an easy one and would lead them outside the boundaries of the drunkard narrative itself. The gender difference between narrators and subjects was far from clear and was often undermined by the reformers themselves. For instance, civil damage narrators were aware of the existence of female drunkards and occasionally made reference to them, treating them very differently, and often with much less sympathy, than male drunkards.[80] In fact, they rarely evoked a "drunkard narrative" in their accounts of female inebriates. The drunkard narrative simply did not work as well with female subjects. First, the central tension of the narrative depended on the immense consequences that followed one brief and understandable choice, and a young woman's choice to take a drink was considerably less understandable in nineteenth-century culture than a young man's. Second, as we have seen, the space of the saloon and its sharp differentiation from the home became quite important to the temperance narrative. When temperance reformers did mention drinking women, they were generally women who drank at home or at social events. Those women who drank in saloons were much further beyond the pale than were men who did the same, and tellers of drunkard narratives tended to ignore them entirely.

Of course, there were also plenty of male tellers of drunkard narratives, such as Lucius Manlius Sargent, Walt Whitman, John Gough, occasional male plaintiffs in civil damage suits, and male writers of medically oriented temperance nonfiction. It is generally true that male fiction writers were more interested in the economic plight of their characters, male plaintiffs tended to be less melodramatic and to lose their cases, and male medical writers generally placed more explicit stress on the free-will issue. Their drunkard tales, however, did not differ much from those of their female peers; they were clearly working within the same genre and employing the same conventions.

Although the presence of male narrators and female drunkards may have modified the distance between narrators and the subjects, what really bridged the gap was the gender ambiguity of male drunkards. The central figures of seduction tales, whether rake narratives, anti-Catholic narratives, or drunkard narratives, had always been somewhat gender-ambiguous. Seduced women, from Clarissa on, tended to be headstrong and adventurous, and they chafed against the subordinate position of their sex. Anti-Catholic seduction narratives portrayed gender relations between supposedly "chaste" and feminized priests and their female victims as perverse as well. Given the genre's relationship to the larger body of seduction fiction, drunkard narratives could hardly avoid continuing the convention that the victim of seduction was of uncertain gender. Those familiar with seduction narratives would have understood that the male drunkard bore a striking resemblance to the rake's potential (female) victim. In particular, they both fell for the same reasons. Future drunkards, like female victims, were often described as possessing generally excellent characters but as being too vulnerable to suggestion, too eager to please friends, too socially ambitious, and too willing to indulge in romantic notions and to leave home ties behind in pursuit of these notions. In all of these senses, drunkards were depicted in the tradition of sexual seduction victims like Charlotte Temple.

Temperance novelist Mary Dwinell Chellis, in an 1874 novel (quoted at the head of this chapter), described a female former drinker trying to repress the memory of a drunken spree.[81] If Chellis's description doesn't sound all bad, it was in line with how many temperance advocates imagined inebriates' experience. Temperance advocates had opted not to enter the whirl and bright lights of the saloon. Rather, they followed the advice of a matron in another Chellis novel, "I think it would be better not to drink . . . at all, only do the best you can without them."[82] Temperance reformers like Chellis and her readers fully believed that the pleasures of drink promised only danger and destruction, and therefore it was necessary to protect men from drink's enticements. Yet many of them clearly had a strong, even exaggerated, sense of what the pleasures of drink might be. As their writings reveal, on some level, they felt the allure of the saloon, and of the world of imagination and transformation with which they associated it.

The nature of temperance reformers' fascination with the saloon is complex, but it clearly had much to do with the possibility of self-transformation, mobility, and freedom from the home. Reformers constructed the saloon as the antithesis of the home. To step into it was not only to leave the home but also to forget it. The nature of the drunkard narrators' desire for the saloon and for freedom from the home begins to become clearer when one fits it into a larger social and political context: the suffrage movement, and various women's rights initiatives with which temperance women, and others, involved themselves. In drunkard narratives, these reformers expressed their desire for such freedom and transformation, and their fear of the consequences that such changes might bring.

Considered in a still larger context, the drunkard narrative was a story of an individual who left his home and family behind in favor of an artificial and imaginary realm. It questioned whether he acted of his own will or was merely a victim of seducers who would determine his fate. In endlessly telling and retelling this story, drunkard narrators explored the extent to which it was possible to leave behind the family and community into which one was born, and the extent to which any choices one might make were ultimately determined by environmental and social influences. Drunkard narrators, in other words, sought to locate between the protective home and the invasive environment a space in which an individual could truly be said to be exercising volitional freedom.

By understanding alcohol as seductive and then by understanding and sympathizing with the drunkard's desires, temperance reformers caused themselves several problems. Most importantly, the "seduction" trope made alcohol's corrupting allure resemble female "influence" all too closely. The wife and the saloonkeeper labored to create cozy and stimulating environments to attract the drinking husband's attention in the evenings, and each at times had to resort to wiles and deceptions in their competition. Both argued that they were merely serving the drinking man's wants, but at the same time worked to introduce in him new desires and needs, or to awaken dormant ones. Temperance reformers, saloonkeepers, and drinkers' wives often understood this competition between home and saloon quite clearly. The Woman's Christian Temperance Union's *Union Signal* printed fictional accounts of drunkards' wives setting up "home saloons" replete with saloon amusements and selling whiskey to their husbands by the nickel, so that at least some of the liquor money could be kept in the family. Reformers chastised saloonkeepers for deliberately imitating the home in constructing their dens of vice.

This rivalry between the spaces of the saloon and the home manifested the competition between the saloonkeeper and the drinker's wife for the drinker's affections. Temperance-novel saloonkeepers were forever attempting to make their saloons more attractive, more alluring, than men's own homes. In T. S. Arthur's popular 1872 novel, *Three Years in a Mantrap*, for instance, saloonkeepers saw themselves as engaging in a direct competition with the home: "We had many new attractions now in our place . . . mirrors and pictures, bits of statuary and other things to please the taste of our customers and to make our saloon pleasanter to them, if possible, than their homes."[83] Once inside the door of the saloon, the drinker invariably forgot about the home. Since one of the primary contributions of men to their family lives in the nineteenth century was financial support, temperance reformers often argued that, in giving his wages to the saloonkeeper rather than the wife, the drinking husband was signifying a domestic alliance with him. The suggestion that the drinker must love the saloonkeeper's family better than his own—because he buys the saloonkeeper's family fine clothes while he leaves his own in rags—is a commonplace in temperance literature.[84] At some points, the almost sexual competition between the wife and the saloonkeeper for the allegiance and affections of drinking husbands became all too obvious. Remember, for instance, the many tense encounters between Eugenia Peacock and her husband's saloonkeeper, Daniel Oaks, discussed at the beginning of this chapter. When, in 1879, Della Welch complained to William Jugenheimer that her husband was drinking excessively, Jugenheimer apparently "told her that he knowed her husband better than she did, as far as that was concerned."[85] Upon entering the saloon, the drinker, as so many wives complained both in temperance novels and civil damage cases, was transformed and his domestic allegiances cast in doubt.

As disturbing as it was for temperance reformers to imagine that their own exercise of "influence" resembled the saloonkeeper's seductions, it was equally disturbing to contemplate that the saloonkeeper's power was stronger. If the wife and the saloonkeeper were both attempting to seduce or influence the drinking husband into a certain pattern of behavior, temperance advocates were increasingly convinced that the deck was stacked against the wife. The wife was selling contentment and the domestic sphere, while the saloonkeeper was selling risk and the public sphere. Risk would always be bright, gilded, and exciting in a way contentment never could be.

In the mid-1860s, Louisa May Alcott dealt uniquely with this issue in a manuscript entitled "Fair Rosamond," which included many elements of the standard drunkard narrative. Its main character, however, was a woman, and instead of becoming a drunkard, she allowed herself to be lured into a false marriage. "Fair Rosamond" is a fascinating combination of the conventions of the drunkard novel and the novel of seduction. The story's name, and some elements of its plot, come from accounts of a young noblewoman, Rosamond Clifford, who allegedly was seduced by Henry II of England, became his mistress, and was murdered (by being forced to drink a bowl of poison) by his queen, Eleanor of Aquitaine. Popular accounts of "Fair Rosamond" abounded in the early-nineteenth-century English press, where they circulated as chapbooks.[86]

Alcott's "Fair Rosamond," however, differed greatly from the earlier story. The seducer in her account is not King Henry II but rather Phillip Tempest, a wealthy and handsome man bearing a striking resemblance to Mephistopheles. Tempest meets the secluded young Rosamond and is attracted to her combination of innocence and adventurousness. Rosamond is bored with her bleak life with her grandfather, and "comfort[s her]self with hopes and dreams."[87] Fascinated by Tempest and his "freedom" to travel the seas, she willingly accompanies Tempest on a visit to his private yacht, "Circe." Once there, the satanic Tempest lures Rosamond into "the [yacht's] luxurious little saloon," where she drinks "her host's health in choice wine from a slender stemmed Venetian glass."[88] (Alcott used "saloon" in a technical sense, to describe a luxurious cabin in a yacht. It was around this time that American popular drinking places appropriated the word "saloon" to suggest the luxury and taste of their establishments.) When Rosamond emerges from the saloon, she finds that Tempest has ordered the yacht to leave shore and that they are headed out to sea. While Rosamond is enticed by Tempest, she is too strong willed to allow herself to be abducted. By threatening suicide, she persuades Tempest to bring her home to gain her guardian's consent to their marriage. After winning (literally, at the gaming table) this consent and staging a false marriage ceremony, Tempest leaves with Rosamond again.

Life with Tempest is initially all that Rosamond has hoped for, and they experience a year of happiness. Yet Tempest refuses to be content. To explain his melancholy, he despairs that love can make men and women into slaves. In response, she insists "It will Never have power to make a slave of me," and "lift[s] her handsome head with the defiant air of some wild, free thing indignant at the thought of bonds."[89] Soon after this exchange, however, Rosamond discovers that Tempest is already married and has abandoned his first wife and kidnapped their son. At this point Rosamond flees, and the rest of the novel follows Tempest's pursuit of her across the continent.[90] Ultimately, as Rosamond attempts to return to her childhood home, Tempest unintentionally kills her.

This manuscript's many parallels to temperance fiction can hardly have been accidental; Alcott was quite familiar with the genre and with its use of the theme of seduction. Alcott always occupied an uncomfortably ambiguous position toward the use of alcohol.[91] Although her stories often endorse the social use of wine, she also wrote some fairly conventional temperance fiction. A decade after she wrote "Fair Rosamond," she published her temperance short story, "Silver Pitchers," and included a drunkard narrative prominently in her novel, *Rose in Bloom*. She also depicted a female opium addict in her pseudonymous 1865 short story, "The Marble Woman: or, The Mysterious Model."[92]

It is unlikely that Alcott failed to appreciate the extent to which "Fair Rosamond" mirrored the temperance fiction so pervasive at the time and in her social circles. She was not the sort of writer to be wedded to generic conventions, and as a story of vice and decline, "Fair Rosamond" is a hybrid of a novel of seduction and a drunkard narrative. One very significant way in which Rosamond differs from other female victims of seduction and drunkard-narrative drunkards is in her behavior after her fall. Whereas standard victims of seduction generally show remarkably little resilience, Rosamond resists her false husband's entreaties to return to him and manages, through stealth, cunning, and impressive athletic feats, to evade his pursuit throughout most of the book. Classic seduction narratives depict the death of drunkards and seducees (as they progressively poison themselves or waste away from neglect and shame) as the natural consequence of their "fall." Rosamond, in contrast, appears to exercise a quite healthy volition after her fall and summons up all of her impressive inner resources to escape the clutches of her seducer. Her death is an accident, as Tempest, pursuing her over the sea, unknowingly rams her ship. She is destined to die by the logic of the situation, but death does not come from a seed of destruction planted within her. Rather, an external agent executes her fate. Significantly, Rosamond (and Alcott) blames Tempest's treachery for her fall, rather than her own desire for adventure. Her false marriage has not been a seduction but an outright attack on Rosamond's virtue.

The ways in which Alcott plays with the genres of the seduction and drunk-ard narratives are self-contradictory. On the one hand, the message of "Fair Rosamond" is an optimistic one. Rosamond falls from virtue but refuses to develop a fatal case of consumption or jump off a cliff. Rather, she impressively clings to her life and dramatically asserts her freedom from her would-be se-ducer. On the other hand, the fact that Alcott invites the reader to celebrate Rosamond's many escapes makes it all the harder when she ultimately meets the death that is inevitable within the genre. The tenacity of Rosamond's voli-tion after her seduction makes it seem all the more unfair that it should finally catch up with her. It is as if Alcott rejected the logic of seduction fiction and the drunkard narrative, but could not quite fix on a plan of how to replace it. Yet even as Alcott wrote "Fair Rosamond," there were those who were beginning to piece together just such a plan.

CHAPTER FIVE

Invasion

Some ass, who never possessed brains at all, perhaps died a drunkard, and
he is straightway, by *supposition,* made a saint of. O, but if it had not been
for rum, he might have been such a great man, such a wise man, such a
wonderful man! He had a brilliant intellect, they say, but what a vast pity
that *rum* ruined him! He could have been any thing, and done any thing he
chose, but for accursed *rum!* That destroyed him, and the bright hopes of
his friends along with him! O, if only this *rum* could be banished from the
world, then, perhaps, every man of bright parts might shine as he was born
to shine. . . . [Rum] is a capital scape-goat to bear the mortification of his
friends at his own natural lack of mother-wit.

"A New England Journalist," *The Ramrod Broken,* 1859

There is no nobler sight on earth than the triumph of such weighted ones
over their lurking and implacable foe—a foe the more terrible that it lies
concealed within their own bosom.

NORMAN KERR, "The Heredity of Alcohol," 1882

Before his troubles began, John Sankey, a tailor in Chicago in the 1880s, quite
probably saw his alcohol use as harmonious with his domestic and social contentment. According to his wife, Rose Ann, John had "an attraction" to his
regular saloon, run by Daniel McMahon. He liked to spend time there, Rose
Ann said, because it had "men all his own class of people." As an Irishman, he
never went to the two other nearby saloons, which were run by "a Dutchman"
and a Norwegian, respectively.[1] McMahon's saloon was right down the street
from John and Rose Ann's home on Halsted Street, and John sometimes bought
beer there to bring back in a tin pail for home consumption.[2] Rose Ann, a
Scottish immigrant, was not opposed in principle to her husband's drinking.
Indeed, she herself fetched beer from McMahon's saloon and sometimes sent
her teenaged sons to do so.[3] She also drank a bit of beer and allowed her husband to give "a little to the children."[4] Immigrant urban dwellers, the Sankeys
were just the sort of people who formed the core of the opposition to the
temperance movement.

Yet even in the pro-drink Chicago immigrant community in which he lived, John Sankey found that his excessive alcohol use led others to intervene in his business, cast doubt upon his manhood, and disrupted the very domestic and social contentment in which it played a part. To begin with, John sometimes drank so much it interfered with his work. According to Rose Ann, "He could not measure right and made mistakes all the time . . . he couldn't do nice work, nothing for to suit the customer."[5] John's fellow tailor, Michael Kerns, disagreed, claiming that, while John was sometimes "feeling pretty good" at work, he was never "past work."[6] Yet there was evidence to show that John's wages had fallen to half what they had been before he became a regular drinker.[7] Concerned, Rose Ann approached John's saloonkeeper, Daniel McMahon, and asked him not to sell her husband any more alcohol. McMahon apparently responded that if Rose Ann did not want her husband to go out, she should "keep [her] man to home" and that he did not "like to refuse a neighbor a drink."[8]

There were other signs that John's drinking was getting the best of him. His neighbor Daniel Lavin once saw him falling drunk on the street, surrounded by about a dozen boys "hollering 'Oh, Sankey, where is Moody?'" referring to an evangelical musician with whom Sankey shared a last name.[9] Another neighbor, Italian immigrant Frank Dasso, noticed that Sankey "would get on a little 'Hurrah' once in a while," sometimes for days at a time.[10] While Dasso did not consider Sankey's drinking any of his business, he was angered to learn that Sankey was abusing Rose Ann during his drinking bouts. He decidedly invaded Sankey's business when he punched Sankey for mistreating Rose Ann.[11]

In 1887, John spent Christmas Eve at McMahon's saloon, which was doing excellent business. After a sleepless night, he headed back to McMahon's when it opened very early Christmas morning, around 4 A.M. He returned home from time to time, but when his family had their midday Christmas dinner he was so drunk that he could not properly sit at the table.[12] Later that day, visibly intoxicated, he dangerously tried to board a moving streetcar in front of his house. Although passengers managed to pull him safely onto the streetcar, he soon fell from the car, which ran over and crushed his leg. Two weeks later, John died of his injuries.[13]

It is not clear how Rose Ann got the idea to sue McMahon for damages after her husband's death. When McMahon asked Rose Ann who told her to bring the suit, he was no doubt insinuating, perhaps correctly, that temperance reformers had encouraged her.[14] However the idea of bringing the suit had come to her, the logic behind the civil damage laws must have been foreign to Rose

Ann Sankey. Indeed, if there was one type of person who should have been resistant to the logic of the civil damage laws, it was a drinking urban immigrant like her. Perhaps she saw an opportunity to raise some much needed money to support her family after John's death. Perhaps she herself had come to interpret her husband's failures in light of the drunkard narrative which—even solidly ensconced as she was in urban, immigrant Chicago—she could hardly have avoided. At any rate, Rose Ann was fortunate as a civil damage plaintiff. Not only did she win her case in the first instance, the judgment was affirmed by the supreme court.

To describe the drunkard's relationship to his drink as an invasion was to suggest that alcohol, an alien power, forcefully entered the drinker's body. Of course, the seduction metaphor, as used by temperance reformers, often emphasized the power of external influences to such a great extent that the drunkard bore little of the blame. Yet the choice to use a metaphor of invasion rather than the metaphor of seduction with which it competed was more than a shift of emphasis. Neither metaphor was empty. Much as the metaphor of seduction carried its generic history within it, so the metaphor of invasion suggested the martial and the medical. Though the seduction story remained largely the same as the invasion story—an external force gained entry into the body, internal elements took the part of the external force, and the body was transformed—it fit into different contexts and solicited different responses.

Like the seduction metaphor, the invasion metaphor was present in temperance rhetoric from its beginnings. Yet, while the metaphor of seduction was at its peak in the antebellum years and receded somewhat after the war, the invasion metaphor emerged within the context of prewar reform and became increasingly popular as the century progressed. The valence of "invasion" would change over the decades, particularly in response to the Civil War in the 1860s and the growth of imperialist ventures toward the end of the century. While reformers, as the century progressed, came increasingly to doubt the power of individual volition in the face of external forces, the invasion metaphor began to make more sense to them. Indeed, by the 1870s, the most radical of the temperance reformers looked to the language of invasion for a potential solution to the crisis of the drunkard.

The antebellum reformism out of which the invasion metaphor emerged was a highly interconnected system. As activists moved promiscuously from one cause to another and back again, temperance, women's rights, antislavery, anti-Catholicism, and numerous other reform causes inevitably shared the same vocabulary. The invasion trope, at least by the 1840s, was important to many parts of this integrated reform community. In particular, it was important to the anti-Catholic nativist movement, which had come to prominence in the 1830s. Nativists used invasion metaphors to distinguish between "native" citizens and institutions on the one hand, and dangerous European transplants on the other. When antebellum nativists used metaphors of invasion, they often were not describing the immigrants themselves. A key characteristic of antebellum nativism was that many nativists accepted that immigration was inevitable, even desirable. The immigrants themselves would be assimilated into the national body like nourishing food was assimilated into the human body. Rather, nativists objected to transplanted foreign institutions and practices like the Catholic church and demagoguery. Carefully distinguishing between the immigrant "food" and the institutional "poison," nativists designated foreign institutions and practices as "transplanted" or "artificial."

Antebellum temperance reformers frequently embraced nativism, but it would be a mistake to interpret their acceptance as proof that temperance was fundamentally a movement of Anglo-Saxons determined to preserve their power and values against the "teeming masses."[15] Like many other nativists at the time, temperance reformers were generally not as concerned about the immigrants themselves as about the larger institutional bodies of which they seemed to be a part. Just as anti-Catholics primarily objected to the fact that immigrants increased the power and influence of the Catholic church, so temperance reformers primarily feared the alcohol businesses immigrants would support. Just as the nativist American Republican party of the 1840s warned Protestants to arm in preparation for a violent uprising of Catholics in favor of a papal invasion, temperance activists imagined that immigrants were ready to throw their support behind a government led by the liquor trust.[16]

Some interpreters have used temperance reformers' repeated references to immigrants as invaders to document their arguments that the temperance movement was inspired largely by a deep-seated hatred for the immigrant and a paranoid fear of the new. However, temperance reformers often used the metaphor of invasion in surprising, even inconsistent ways.[17] Consider, for example, an 1854 novel called *Uncle Sam's Farm Fence*. This very odd book is premised on the metaphor of building a fence around the nation to keep alcohol out. What is unusual about the novel is that, while immigration is one of its central themes, it is decidedly not an anti-immigrant work. In fact, the fence is explicitly meant to protect immigrants and their children, as well as native-born Americans, from the forces of alcohol.[18] While temperance reformers used the language of the nativist movement, they did not always do so as an attack on immigrants themselves.

To explain alcohol's effects on the drinker in terms of the language of invasion was to emphasize alcohol's externality and to attribute to it an independent agency. Within the drunkard narrative, the language of invasion removed much or all of the responsibility for the drunkard's fall from the drunkard himself. It enabled narrators to imagine the potential drunkard as an upstanding young man, defeated and changed by nefarious but external forces. It allowed them to refer to the drinker's unified self—before the consumption of alcohol and the corruption it introduced—as a "pure" body.

It is impossible to appreciate the stakes of the discourse of drink without considering the importance of the idea of "purity" to reformers. In the 1820s and 1830s, this concept had not been particularly important to the movement. The earliest American temperance organizations, appearing in these decades, had (as the term "temperance" suggests) advocated moderation in alcohol consumption, though some had suggested that certain types of alcohol—"ardent spirits"—should not be consumed at all. This moderate form of temperance, however, was short-lived. By the 1840s, teetotalism was replacing the moderation arguments of earlier decades, and the shift from moderation to abstinence was part of a more general trend in the reform tradition towards perfectionism.[19] Religious perfectionism—that is, the belief that it is possible to achieve a sinless state in this world—gained credence as religious revivalism spread through America. The idea inspired such familiar mid-nineteenth-century historical episodes as the rise of communitarian societies like the Oneida community and Brook Farm, and Henry David Thoreau's and John Brown's dramatic attempts to remove themselves from even indirect participation in social evils.

The perfectionist impulse had two major impacts on reform. First, some individuals imagined that if they properly regulated their bodies, they could eliminate sinful desires. The temperance movement, food reform, and the physical culture movement were just three among many reforms that grew in response to this idea. Second, as reformers became increasingly convinced of the "contagion" of sin, and hence of the moral dangers of living in a community in which others were sinning, other people's vices came to seem as spiritually dangerous as their own. Strategically, these changes led to a radicalization of reformers' agendas and to a move towards what Joseph Gusfield has referred to as "coercive" reform. Discursively, they brought the language of purity and the invasion metaphor to the center of reform thought.[20]

The trope of purity was closely related to the "cult of sincerity" described by Karen Halttunen, who has argued that antebellum Americans had a profound commitment to visibility. They wanted to believe that surface appearance expressed underlying reality. To be pure was to be uncorrupted, to be entirely oneself rather than a composite of external influences, to be homogenous; if a person or object was truly pure, its appearance would always accurately reflect its inner reality.[21] Like other nineteenth-century reformers, temperance advocates were deeply concerned with misrepresentation and counterfeit.[22] Drunkard narratives often featured counterfeiters and forgers, and the saloons' inevitable thinly gilded fixtures almost invariably signified impurity.[23]

If to be pure was to be entirely oneself, free of external intrusions, then the concept of purity was quite similar to the concept of volitional independence. Both purity and freedom required the preservation of an unassailable core of selfhood. Just as the sexually pure woman (or man) had been protected from vicious situations as well as from the potentially corrupting knowledge, so the free man (or woman) had been shielded from dangerous spaces such as the saloon and from the risky cultural ideas that would make them vulnerable to corruption. Because such people had been shielded both from dangerous external forces and from the planting of insidious internal ones, their desires and wills would always be of native origin and therefore consistent with their situations in life.

Reformers' obsession with purity is one reason they evoked the image of water so frequently. Clear and clean, water represented both purity and self-consistent homogeneity. Temperance reformers were often as passionate about advocating water as they were about condemning alcohol. They elevated water to an almost sacred stature with standards like "The Old Oaken Bucket" and "Drink from the Crystal Stream," campaigns to improve city water supplies and provide convenient public access, and frequent rhapsodies on the health-giving, natural, and sparkling qualities of water.

The language of invasion allowed temperance advocates to understand people and spaces that alcohol had corrupted as initially "pure." At the same time, by distinguishing between "internal" and "external," the language of invasion posited a unified "internal." This tactic in temperance discourse described the body of the drinker as unified and natural. Scholars have often noted the perfectionist commitment to casting off all corruption. It has been less emphasized that this commitment was based on the assumption that there was a consistent and perfect body to be preserved from corruption in the first place. Discussing a problem, whether disease or social unrest, in terms of bodily invasion is often at least potentially comforting. Almost half a century ago, Richard Hofstadter argued that progressive-era American reform emerged precisely out of an unsinkable and widespread conviction that "some technique can be found" that would restore America to a mythical perfection.[24] If a problem can be seen as the result of an invasion, then one can imagine a healthy body that, though invaded, has a separate existence. If only one could expel the invaders, one would be left with this still-sound body. The most obvious alternative explanation of a problem, an explanation that seems to leave less hope for recovery, would be that somehow the body itself has become corrupt. In that case the best that could be done would be to attempt to slow the inevitable progress of corruption, an exhausting and thankless task calling for constant vigilance and promising only ultimate failure.[25]

To some extent, the metaphor of invasion frequently adopted in the discourse of drink does seem to have provided participants precisely this kind of comfort. For some temperance reformers, all the United States' problems could be laid at the door of alcohol. If only the nation could rid itself of the essentially Old World vice of alcohol, it would reveal its near-millennial perfection. An 1854 Iowa temperance newspaper, for instance, described social ills caused by alcohol as "attach[ing] like a plague spot, to our otherwise great and happy nation." Given the huge damage that "this cancer" was doing to the national body, the writer asked, why is it "suffered to eat into and destroy the vitals of the body politic . . . why is it not cut out and destroyed, root and branch, that health may once more come back to the diseased body?"[26] In depicting alcohol as an external substance to be cut out of or driven from the body, temperance reformers performed a task of segregation. Daphne Giles's *East and West,* an antebellum temperance novel, works in a similar way. The novel tells the story of a stable and pleasant village ultimately ruined by the entry of a stranger who sets up a tavern. The village is a transparent metaphor for the nation. When a reformer declares her desire "to rid my country, and especially this little village, from an evil that is calculated to ruin our young men, and to blunt the sensibilities of those who have been hitherto pillars in society," she is imagining a prelapsarian United States invaded by external agents bearing alcohol.[27]

One sign of the central importance of the invasion metaphor to temperance thought is temperance opponents' urgent efforts to counter it. As did foes of other perfectionist movements, they mocked reformers' claims as unrealistic. As one antebellum antitemperance commentator expressed his objections to the perfectionist temperance movement, "I believe not only that we must *permit* evil to grow up with the good, even as tares will grow with the wheat,—but that, even if we try ever so much we cannot *prevent* it."[28] Temperance reformers' insistence on the possibility of purity and their opponents' equally passionate insistence on its impossibility constituted one of the most pervasive themes in both groups' writings.

Even before the Civil War, some temperance advocates thought of the relationship between alcohol and the drinker in military terms. The "Washingtonians" chose Revolutionary War general George Washington as their icon and referred to the war quite frequently in their songs. From "The Temperance Revolution," to "The Two Revolutions," to numerous "temperance" versions of national patriotic tunes, the Washingtonians were tireless in their efforts to equate the temperance struggle with the American Revolution.[29] In 1841, a New Orleans temperance lecturer compared victims of drink to those who died defending that city in the War of 1812. Intemperance, he insisted, was more harmful to the city than the British attack had been—partially because intemperance, over the years, had claimed more victims than had the battle. Intemperance was also "an enemy more insidious, more cruel, more inexorable than a foreign foe" because of the demeaning way in which alcohol claimed its victims. It "meets his intended victim in the high-way, binds him in sight of his wife, children, and friends; thus manacled, carries him into bondage, and there makes him the slave of a cruel tyrant . . . the slave of a bottle." When foreign enemies had forced Americans into servitude a few decades earlier, it had contributed to our entry into the War of 1812. Yet somehow Americans would not rally in the same way to save their brethren from slavery to liquor. "Who hears the loud complaint of an indignant nation; the groans of the mighty moral lever, the public press? does it sound the tocsin? does the mighty nation beat to arms to rescue the captive? No—no!"[30] Some other antebellum military metaphors had less specific references. In 1829, a preacher in Knoxville, Tennessee claimed that alcohol was "a greater scourge to the United States, than the sword of an invading army."[31]

Many temperance reformers, particularly those affiliated with the Whig party, deplored that the United States had gotten itself involved in the Mexican War. Yet some also used military themes to publicize their war against liquor. In the 1840s and 1850s, it was common for temperance organizations to march on or around July 4th, combining a patriotic display with a call for temperance measures. In 1847, for instance, Memphis temperance reformers gathered boys together into a "Cold Water Army." The "army" paraded around the city carrying a large banner with the words *Liberty* and *Temperance* upon it and an American flag. These boys were not, like many of their older brothers, fighting the war in Mexico, but they were taking enlistments in their own temperance army.[32]

The Civil War changed the resonance of the invasion metaphor. It is also striking, at times, to what extent contemporaries drew upon temperance rhetoric such as the drunkard narrative to describe the causes of the war. Take, for instance, one Northern writer's description of how a noble young Southerner (who happened to be a nephew of Davy Crockett) came to support the Confederacy:

> [He was] naturally a noble man, of generous impulses and warm sympathies, of hopeful soul and patriotic heart, but in the worst company that could have been selected for him. . . . In short he seemed as "a strong man bound," without the power of escaping from those who were applying to him the excoriating lash of disunion, and forcing him to utter *their* sentiments, not his. He had been taught by his mother to love the country and the flag for which his father had died; he had been taught by her to respect the truth and acknowledge the superior claims of justice; he had been taught to avoid evil and keep out of the way of evil doers. But the insidious serpent of secession had coiled itself about his soul, fastened its poisonous fangs upon his heart, and destroyed his manhood.[33]

This passage comes from a long tract exposing the "Knights of the Golden Circle," a pro-Southern secret society thought by contemporary conspiracy theorists to be responsible for secession. The tract explains how the group recruited its members. "An honestly disposed man is picked up in the street, and is hardly aware of it before he has taken the most binding oaths to violate the constitution of his country."[34] This passage, too, closely parallels the drunkard narrative. Northerners, particularly those steeped in reform tradition, had come to understand the South much as they understood the drunkard—as a fundamentally sound body that had been invaded and permeated by the corrupting force of pro-slavery fanaticism. Good, patriotic Southerners like Crockett had been temporarily whipped into a frenzy by a small handful of demagogues, but actually they were true-hearted Americans. They would gladly return to the fold if they could be released from the fire-eaters' spell. They were not rebels as much as misguided victims. Though the Civil War complicated the invasion metaphor, it did not fundamentally transform its structure. If "invasion" in the 1840s raised the specter of teeming immigrant masses in Boston harbor, in the Civil War era it often provoked a quite different image. One antebellum pamphlet comparing inebriety with slavery, for instance, argued that alcohol "not only excites all the passions to fierce insurrection against God and man, but kindles a deadly civil war in the very heart of their own empire."[35]

In the years during and after the Civil War, reformers commonly spoke of alcohol in terms that evoked the conflict.[36] A northern temperance broadsheet printed by the Good Templars in March of 1865 insisted that the war against alcohol was "a still more terrible warfare" than the war against the Confederacy. It was worse not only because of its allegedly greater magnitude but also because of the way in which it defeated its victims. "Its conquests are so *secret,* that before the victim is aware he is bound hand and foot." Because the drinker consumed his enemy and allowed it to pervert his will, death by alcohol "has the power to destroy both soul and body in hell." Another pamphlet warned former Union soldiers, "Rum is a rebel, a guerilla, an assassin." Even the bravest must beware of the "subtle and wary" ways of alcohol and its servants. "The hero of the battle . . . is in great danger of falling entangled in the meshes woven in secret and spread in the dark." The real difference between the Union's battle with the Confederacy and the drinker's battle with his drink was that the drinker did not know he was being attacked.[37]

Alcohol, as one booklet explained in 1868, "creates a rebellion, and is rejected from the system as an intruder."[38] Some references were less explicit and perhaps less deliberate but must have been read through the lens of the war. When an Iowa temperance newspaper, in 1869, described alcohol as "the great canker worm of our nation," its readers would no doubt have realized the indirect reference to the recent war. The cancer imagery had been a staple of the antislavery discourse, and by imagining the cancer as a worm eating out the nation's vitals the metaphor evoked the invading armies of both North and South cutting through the countryside a mere four years earlier.[39]

Southern temperance advocates similarly tried to explain the movement in terms of the war. One of the most ingenious attempts was in a sermon by Samuel W. Small, published in 1890. In a masterful piece of wish fulfillment, he tells southern reformers, "to-day, in a holier and grander cause [than that of the Confederacy] by the approving smile of God, old Georgia has fired a gun upon the Sumter of sin and intemperance in this country that will arouse the whole nation; and we will batter down these forts of intemperance, whether they are in Cincinnati, Chicago, or New York."[40]

An excerpt from an 1872 Midwestern temperance monograph and a map from a weighty 1888 Bostonian tome show the impact of the Civil War on the meanings (if not on the structure) of the invasion analogy. The first is an only partially successful attempt to update the language of invasion. It explicitly, though inconsistently, evoked the new valence of "invasion" in the wake of the war and in light of America's new, more confident position on the world stage. In this account, as alcohol approaches the stomach, it "sends forth its fiery threats, crisping and searing that sensitive organ. Then it rides, like Jehu, along the highways of nature. Its fiery chariot wheels burn deep ruts in their passage." In response, the body mounts its defense: "all the forces of life and health rally like Sherman's Bummers, at the signal gun or bugle note, and swarm around the intruder till they have expelled it from the system."[41] Though there certainly had been Confederate raids of northern territory, northern readers must have noted the awkwardness of characterizing Sherman's bummers as home defenders driving out intruders—particularly intruders who were riding along highways, "crisping and searing" their surroundings. The Northern author appreciates that the old temperance analogy of invasion had a new, much more specific resonance, but has not adjusted his imagery to accommodate this new usage. Though the writer must have felt the instability of his analogy, he, like many temperance reformers, struggled to continue to understand his political community as a subject rather than a perpetrator of invasion.

The second text is a foldout map in a massive 1888 temperance volume, Henry Blair's *The Temperance Movement.* The book made something of a splash in temperance circles, perhaps because its author was a senator. The map represents the location of saloons of New York City.[42] All of the natural features, place names, and streets are drawn in black on the white page, but nine thousand small bright red dots, each representing a saloon, cover the map; it almost looks as if New York has the measles. Significantly, it also bears a distinctly military look. The saloons are indeed everywhere on the map, but underneath this covering of red remains a New York in black and white, a pristine and saloon-free New York. New York in this case stood in for the entire nation: the volume to which the map was appended was devoted to wiping away those red dots and recovering the United States they temporarily obscured.[43]

One of the most striking things about the message of the map is how consistent it is with the discourse of the antebellum era. By 1888, there was little prospect of an actual military invasion of New York. The literal level of the metaphor had lost the plausibility that it had sixty years earlier, but it continued—as it would for many decades to come—as part of a powerful discursive pattern. One reason that the metaphor of invasion may have remained as stable as it did despite the changes in America's military situation was that it operated on so many levels. Reformers used "invasion" language not only to describe foreign attacks on the nation, but also to describe "invasions" of small communities by strangers, of homes by drunken men, and of drinkers' bodies by alcohol itself. When temperance reformer John Wooley used the metaphor of liquor invading the national body in an 1892 article called the "New Declaration of Independence," he imagined the nation's enemy as already within its borders, besetting its communities and homes: "The cardiac artery of the municipal body politic is the liquor traffic pulsing with the rhythm and resistless might of law, pumping torpor into the industries, poverty into the home, paralysis into the spine, and insanity, vice and crime into the brain of the citizenship."[44] As invasions of the nation became less literally plausible, the metaphor came to refer almost purely to the community, home, and the individual. Since "invasion" is primarily a political term, though, the description of invasions of the national body continued to serve as a master trope through which invasions of smaller entities such as communities, homes, and human bodies could be understood. Whether it was intended or not, any author explaining the technology of foreign invasion of the nation, of a stranger's invasion of a town, of a drinker's invasion of his home, or of alcohol's invasion of the human body would often be read as making a statement about each of the others.

In the era of the trust, it made cultural sense to think about outside forces impinging on and transforming small American communities. Particularly in the agricultural Midwest, which was both heavily dependent upon the railroad system and directly interested in the unfathomable machinations at the Chicago Board of Trade, people were increasingly concerned that the forces of big business were menacing their communities. Temperance reformers understood alcohol, sometimes in the form of the "Liquor Trust," to be prominent among the external forces that were invading their communities.[45] While dedicated local reformers fought to rid their communities of alcohol, the liquor power was busy in Washington and in state capitals, influencing government leaders to oppose prohibition and local option legislation. Where reformers managed to pass state or local prohibition, the federal government enforced the right of delivery companies to ship alcohol to individuals within ostensibly dry communities and states.[46] Temperance advocates imagined organizations of the manufacturers of alcohol to be far more powerful and organized than they actually were, and believed them to be plotting together to infiltrate even the smallest hamlets.[47] By the last years of the century, with the rise of the tied-house system, the local saloon must have seemed to reformers and progressives like a more threatening version of today's chain restaurants—colorless and homogenous, distantly owned and utterly unrepresentative of the local community.[48]

Though helpful to the understanding of alcohol as invader, the antitrust argument was by no means necessary. Often, in their fiction, reformers portrayed alcohol as being brought into a community not by big business or by corrupt government but rather by seemingly independent "strangers." One classic type of temperance story begins with a fairly prosperous and saloon-free town. A stranger or (less often) a local worker determined to climb in social status decides to set up a saloon. This outsider, designated as such either by geography or class origins, goes into business. Just as the United States welcomed alcohol-bearing immigrants as necessary additions to the labor force, and hence contributors to national prosperity, so temperance-fiction communities welcomed saloon-building strangers as heralds of municipal growth: "One day there came into town a wandering tramp. . . . He said if Sweet William could be made a 'wet town,' . . . that it would soon become a very great wealthy city . . . and that all its small storekeepers would become rich merchant princes."[49] Gradually, the saloon attracts the promising men from the town, who yield to its enticements, spending more and more time there and less and less in the community.[50]

In temperance fiction, the saloon is not part of the community but rather an outside force at odds with the community.[51] Established by an outsider, the saloon pulls the most promising young men out of the community, takes their money out of circulation within it, and often takes over their property. It transforms those who otherwise would become the pillars of the community into drunkards, all of whose resources are then dedicated to propping up the saloon itself. These formerly promising young men become servants of their community's invaders. Similarly, the saloon transforms those young men who have begun families into invaders of their own homes. Rather than feed and clothe their wives and children, they pawn their families' garments or take their wives' hard-earned money to hand over to the saloonkeeper.[52] Two drunkard narratives told in civil damage courtrooms gave extreme versions of this story. In the first, a drinker actually laid the raw steak intended for his family dinner on the bar as payment for a drink. In the second, a drinker brought a fish home for his family dinner, asked his wife to prepare it, then took it and gave it to the saloonkeeper![53] Rather than protecting their wives and children, drinkers exposed them to public insult, and beat, abused, and sometimes killed them. The drinker became an invader of his own home.[54]

When they spoke in the language of invasion rather than in that of seduction, tellers of drunkard narratives sometimes presented the moment of the first drink as a clear-cut scene of coercion, describing a scene that eerily mirrored gang rape. In one temperance novel, a group of young men lure a reformed drunkard into a clubroom, lock the door, and attempt to pour alcohol into him by force.[55] A temperance newspaper writer, in 1884, claimed to have a friend who had recently had a similar experience. When his friend had refused to drink at an exclusive young men's club, "a pistol, loaded and cocked, and aimed at his head, added its persuasive force. They proposed to hold his hands, open his mouth, and pour it down his throat, but he was wise and full of nerve and finally argued them out of it."[56] Other fictional and nonfiction accounts told the same sort of story.[57] Sometimes a saloonkeeper would covertly pour strong liquor into what was purportedly only lemonade or small beer, or drug a customer's glass of liquor, or even serve liquor to a customer who thought he was drinking soda water.[58] One saloonkeeper in an 1897 play actually imprisons a drunkard attempting to escape his clutches, feeds him nothing but salt herring, and allows him nothing but alcohol to quench his thirst. A 1903 temperance novel goes so far as to depict three of a town's four saloonkeepers chasing a drinker-turned-reformer through the town's main street in broad daylight and gunning him down.[59]

These extreme depictions of first drinks as physically coerced, however, were fairly rare. Almost always, even those drunkard narrators using the language of invasion imagined that the future drinker, through a somewhat voluntary act, opened himself to alcohol's attack. Once a young man had entered the space of the saloon and had taken that fatal first drink, however, he was, in the logic of many drunkard narratives, absolutely powerless to resist future drink. One temperance physician wrote in 1882 of the sons of hereditary drinkers, "The smallest sip of the weakest form of fermented or distilled liquor has power to set in a blaze the hidden unhallowed fire." In most temperance fiction, the power of the first sip was equally strong even for those with "untainted" heritage.[60]

By taking his first drink, the drinker put himself in the power of saloonkeepers and evil companions, and, perhaps even more importantly, allowed alcohol to enter his body and begin to transform it. The alcohol coursed through his veins, unseating his reason and inspiring in him a thirst for more. It pervaded him entirely and wiped away whatever positive resolutions he may have had. In fact, ultimately, it wiped away the drinker himself. As one author described a drunkard, there was "not much left of him." A villain said of another temperance drama drunkard, "All his thoughts, feelings, and actions begin and end in the bottle."[61]

An 1876 temperance volume contains an illustration that resembles in interesting ways the map of Manhattan discussed above. A chart entitled "External Symptoms" shows three drawings of the same man entitled, respectively, "Wine at 21," "Whiskey and Brandy at 28," and "All Kinds at 35." As the young man progresses through years of drinking, his face becomes wider, his moustache and lamb-chop sideburns grow thicker and more unkempt, and his eyebrows seem to change shape. The most striking difference between the first and third figure in the progression is that the face of the third is covered with red spots.[62] A number of temperance reformers saw the redness of drinkers' faces, along with other marks and spots on the drinker's person, as signs of impurity. Julia Colman, for instance, explained in her children's hygiene textbook that the redness of drunkards' faces "is truly a 'Danger Signal.' On railway trains a red flag or a red lantern is a sign of danger; so here nature hangs out, on the very face of the drinker, this red signal." The temperate person's blood, in contrast, "flows calmly and evenly in his veins" and his "brow bears aloft the white flag of purity, peace and safety."[63] A second set of images displayed on the same page as the three images of the drinker's face also bears mention. Like the first set, it depicts alcohol as marking and deforming the body. Instead of showing the face, however, it shows the stomach's progression from purity to impurity, from a homogenous pink to a splotchy black melange of colors. As an 1849 alcohol foe maintained, "the doggery keeper [has] cloaked [the drunkard's] character with clouds and blotches quite as deep and dark as he has his stomach with ulcerations."[64]

It could be argued that to the extent that drink debaters read the red dots on the surface of the drunkard's face or on the map of New York as erasable, they imagined them not as "invasions" of the body but rather as "marks" on the body's surface. In a sense, drunkard narrators wanted to have it both ways. On the one hand, they liked to use metaphors of marking to express what they believed to be deeper impurities precisely because they could then imagine them as separable from the body. On the other hand, they wanted very much to believe that it was possible to read the true nature of a body from its visible surface. They wanted to read the drinker's face like they read the map of New York City. Red dots, like the other external markings temperance reformers imagined on the bodies of drinkers, were "flags" or signs of the underlying corruption of the drinker's body. By mapping bodily corruption and invasions onto a surface, they could manipulate and reimagine the nature of the threat and the possibility of defeating it. Temperance reformers mobilized the language of invasion to depict alcohol as something fundamentally separate from the nation, communities, homes, and bodies it endangered. Like red dots on a black-and-white map or on a drawing of a young drinker's face, they often depicted drink as something that alcohol's opponents, given enough power, could wipe away to reveal a pure object beneath. Drink was an outsider, a stranger, that insinuated itself into a pure body by fraud or force, only to turn immediately and dramatically against its host. While this language showed remarkable endurance throughout the century, however, it never achieved true dominance in the discourse. Instead, reformers seemed to question and undermine it as frequently as they evoked it.

Most temperance opponents insisted that nothing was either perfectly pure or perfectly evil. Alcohol, like the rest of God's creation, was in itself neither good nor evil, and could be used or abused. Similarly, no person was either entirely evil or entirely pure. God had ordained that the wheat and tares would grow up together in this imperfect world.[65] Man's sinful nature was the root cause of social imperfection, and reformers who believed that they had found a panacea for them did not understand this nature. If some men did drink to excess, they were not innocents confronted with a deceptive but evil product or lured into a den of vice. They had chosen, of their free will, to drink to excess. As one antiprohibitionist wrote in 1901, "drinking is, usually, the drinker's *voluntary* act. *All* drinkers *begin* voluntarily. Moreover, in most cases, they never lose the ability to stop, if they really try to—and this last fact is almost as important as the first."[66] For every man who became a besotted drunkard, there were many more who chose to drink moderately. The surest way to improve society was not to engage in the hopeless task of combating all evil but to assure that each individual (and in particular each man) had the widest possible degree of latitude to work out his own salvation. It was only by continually making decisions, whether right or wrong, and overcoming or yielding to temptations, that a man exercised his freedom.[67]

Temperance foes often challenged purity rhetoric by evoking hypocrisy. Often, they claimed, those who talked loudest about purity were themselves actually indulging in excessive drinking or in far more sinful pursuits. Temperance opponents took great pleasure in the frequent downfalls of "reformed drunkard" lecturers, temperance pledge-signers, and pious religious leaders. Making use of the same rhetoric of illusion that was so prominent in temperance depictions, they suggested that, in this imperfect world, people who appear pure on the surface are inevitably morally corrupt underneath.[68] Temperance reformers frequently heard and responded to these attacks, which posed a serious challenge to their imagination of the pure and unified body. Just as damaging to the image, though, was the logic of some reformers' own rhetoric.

Temperance activists appropriated language of "invasion" in their attempts to resolve the tensions of the drunkard narrative. Still, the account of the drunkard's decline as an invasion was so slippery and compromised that it rarely provided reformers with a comfortable space. The metaphor of invasion failed most dramatically when temperance reformers tried to imagine national politics in its terms—casting America as a fundamentally temperate body besieged by immigrants bearing alcohol. First, if immigrants were invaders, and the carriers of the old-world evil of drink, even the most sanguine nativist or prohibitionist could see that they were invaders who were here to stay. Unlike red dots on a black-and-white map or on an image of a drinker's face, they could not be wiped away. Nor were they neatly geographically limited or otherwise clearly separable from native-born Americans. Second, temperance reformers' use of metaphors of alcoholic invasion on the national level competed with their understanding of alcohol as encroaching upon the community, the home, and the individual. If alcohol was an invader, it was difficult to imagine a location that had not already been invaded.

Furthermore, the physical bodies invaded by alcohol often were seen in a double character as both the victims and the perpetrators of invasion. That is, invasion language all too frequently slid into seduction language. The seeming omnipresence of alcohol and the shifting of position between invader and invaded within the discourse of drink made the metaphor of invasion considerably more disturbing than comforting. As on the other levels of metaphorical invasion (and like the vampire, a close thematic relative), alcohol first had to be voluntarily admitted by its victim.[69] He might choose to take a first drink because of social pressure, a desire for excitement, or overconfidence in his own powers of self-control. Joel Dorman Steele, in an 1872 textbook, described alcohol as "So seductive in its advances, so insidious in its influence, and so terrible in its triumph."[70] Only after it had gained a foothold in an individual body did it reveal its true nature.

While some temperance reformers called passionately for Americans to build a metaphorical fence around the nation's borders to exclude encroaching drink, others did not see this as a solution. To them, the enemy was already within. The liquor trust was more difficult to portray as a foreign potentate than was the pope because temperance forces never succeeded in identifying a single individual (other than allegorical individuals like King Bacchus or King Gambrinus) as its leader and because many key figures in liquor production and distribution were based within the country.[71] Unlike anti-Catholics and even abolitionists, temperance reformers tended to slip into metaphor and allegory when discussing the threatened tyranny of alcohol. As one temperance play for schoolchildren warned, "these Germans . . . are trying to seize the government of this country, and put over us a King Beer that shall tax us enormously and grind us down in a thousand ways."[72]

Furthermore, the story of an America invaded and threatened by Europeans bearing alcohol had another, more troubling valence in the late nineteenth century. In this time of Custer's last stand, the Dawes Act, and the Battle of Wounded Knee, American reformers were aware of both the history and the almost certain future of Native Americans. Figures of what we would today call imperial subjects continually troubled temperance writers and their story of a nineteenth-century America invaded by Europeans bearing alcohol. This invasion had happened before in the history of the continent, with results that were not only disastrous for the Native Americans but also foundational for the very nation that the reformers sought to protect. Moreover, such scenes were daily being repeated around the world and Americans could not divorce themselves from culpability in them. Ian Tyrrell has exposed the ambiguities in temperance activists' position toward imperialism; although they loudly protested the treatment of imperialism's victims, their own attitude toward world reform was at times deeply patronizing and intrusive.[73]

Looking around at a world that they understood to be, as an 1892 *Union Signal* article put it, "a sheol of doomed nations," temperance advocates were obsessed with the American Indians as the example of failed nationhood closest to home.[74] Though they looked at the history of white-Indian relations with widely varying degrees of sophistication, they tended to agree that Indians had fallen so quickly before the white man's advance largely because the white man had treacherously introduced an enemy into the Indians' camp: fire water. As one 1891 temperance encyclopedia summarized, "In every stage of the sad history of the Indians, whiskey has been probably the chief agent in the work of corruption and extermination."[75] Temperance fiction was replete with stories of noble Indian warriors, invincible against all human foes, who were struck down by the white man's drink. Often in these tales Indian drunkards' daughters warned their unheeding people of the doom that awaited if they continued to drink.[76] Additionally, temperance advocates took an active interest in the treatment of contemporary American Indians, regularly reporting Indian-related news in their papers, condemning the government for mistreating them, reprinting Indians' temperance addresses, and inviting their representatives to temperance conventions. The disturbing implications of the parallel between the defeated Indian civilization and their own troubled nation was not lost on temperance advocates. They often explicitly compared the fate of the two civilizations, suggesting that it was perhaps not too late for the United States to heed the warning of its predecessor.[77]

One particularly striking representation of Native Americans and drink comes from *The Doom of King Alcohol,* a 1903 play distributed for ten cents a copy by the Workman's Temperance Publishing Association. At the beginning of the play, Tellus (mother earth) wanders around her ruined land, while in the distance a triumphant King Alcohol has established himself as ruler. A group of fruits and grains approach King Alcohol to tell of the evils of drink and to request that they no longer be used to produce alcoholic beverages. Each of the fruits and grains represents an ethnic group; barley and rye, for instance, are Eastern European. After the apples, peaches, grapes, barley, and rye have told their melancholy stories, and even hops has pleaded eloquently to be used in the making of bread, Corn approaches the throne. Dressed as Indian princess, Corn first describes how important she was to pre-contact Indian culture.

> But alas! The pale face cometh
>
> .   .   .   .
>
> And the sweet maize cake that nourished
> THOU hast turned to Fire Water
> Burning out the Indian's soul.

Corn is immediately followed by the final supplicant, Wheat, a "golden haired [European-American] maiden," who demands,

> Turn not my glorious golden crown
> To hue of bloody red
> I tremble not at thy fierce frown
> Give back the people's bread![78]

It is no easy task to disentangle the strands of allegory in this play, but three points bear notice. First, the author is suggesting that alcohol's destruction of the Indian people is parallel to the fate of the United States. Second, the assembled fruits and grains are ultimately saved only by a premillennial *deus ex machina* in the form of the Angel of Prohibition leading the heavenly host—an allegorical solution providing no clear direction to any workingman inspired to action by the play's message. Third, both Corn's and Wheat's stories (and the stories of the other fruits and grains) center on alcohol's capacity to transform something naturally wholesome and pure into something dangerous and evil. Their complaint is not simply that King Alcohol has destroyed them or impoverished them or abused them, but that alcohol has turned them into agents of their own destruction.[79]

The story of alcohol's role in the destruction of Native Americans worked to destabilize whatever was comforting about the invasion analogy by reminding readers that alcohol had won the last battle and that the existence of the United States was predicated on the invasion of Europeans and their alcohol. Some might have found brief comfort in the notion that it was only in the early years of the nineteenth century that the inhabitants of the United States began to realize the dangers of drink. It was possible to make the argument that their European ancestors did not have access to the scientific information their descendants now possessed. If alcohol was central in colonial America and in the early national United States, it was because their predecessors did not know its destructive power and did not bother to exclude it. In the enlightened days of the nineteenth century, however, Americans realized alcohol's dangers and were increasingly willing to confront it and cast it out. Now Americans saw that alcohol was not really part of the nation; though it was not new, it was nevertheless an alien to be expunged. Though alcohol had threatened the nation for a long time and though the land on which the nation now existed had been won through the agency of alcohol, the nation was now ready to cast away alcohol and reveal its still-sound sober body.

Temperance advocates' intense interest in the fate of the American Indians was matched, perhaps even exceeded, by their interest in the contemporary liquor trade in Africa. They reported continually on African affairs, sent missionaries, attempted to influence American foreign policy, and even wrote fiction, poetry, and songs about alcohol and the African plight.[80] Opponents of drink were appalled at Americans' and Europeans' enthusiastic exportation of rum to Africa and the devastation that inevitably followed. They claimed that the Hottentots had been wiped off the face of the earth due primarily to imported rum.[81] According to temperance accounts, alcohol was distributed with a free hand by Westerners who hoped to take Africans' land. As Senator Henry Blair wrote in his 1888 book (the book that contained the red-dotted map of New York), "Everywhere the heathen nations and barbarous tribes are giving way before the demands of the western powers, which, with gunpowder and opium and rum, proceed at once to 'develop' their destruction."[82] Ida M. Budd made the same point in her 1903 temperance song, "Bibles and Beer": "Mustn't the heathen consider us queer / Sending them cargoes of Bibles and beer?"[83]

Belle Brain, in her 1897 handbook *Weapons for Temperance Warfare*, suggested that local organizations hold "African Palavars" focused on the rum trade. Among the excerpts to be read aloud was: "We have opened the rivers of Africa to commerce, only to pour down them that 'raging Phlegethon of alcohol,' than which no river of the Inferno is more blood-red or more accursed."[84] Here is a familiar pattern: invaders have entered Africa on false pretenses, and instead of helping to build it, they are set to transform it. Just as "Wheat" and "Corn" had been transformed "to hue of bloody red" and into agents of alcohol and destroyers of their own people, so the very rivers of Africa had become "blood-red" carriers of destruction.[85] Western invaders intended to take control of and change the fundamental nature of Africa and its people. Africa was not to be an invaded body but a transformed body. The *Cyclopedia of Temperance and Prohibition* quoted Kama, "a chief of Bechuanaland," as saying: "I fear Lo Bengula [a great warrior] less than I fear brandy. . . . I dread the white man's drink more than . . . the Matebele, which kill men's bodies, and it is quickly over; but drink [?] devils into men, and destroys both their souls and their bodies forever. Its wounds never heal."[86] Drink was worse than other devils because it was, as one 1894 pamphlet put it, a "liquid devil," polluting and transforming the bodies that consumed it. It "permeated" bodies, introducing the disturbing possibility that it could no longer be separated from them.[87]

Just as drink's opponents saw a parallel between the destruction of Native

American civilization and the danger faced by the nineteenth-century United States, so too they saw a parallel with Africa. Henry Blair suggested that the "civilized" world was even more vulnerable to alcohol than were Africans "because those advanced nations have more brain and nerve upon which the poison works."[88] Africa, in temperance accounts, had its own Neil Dow, its own "Heathen John Gough."[89] Like the United States, Africa was struggling mightily to cast off, or cut out, alcohol. Some even suggested that African battles against alcohol should be seen as a model or an inspiration for U.S. temperance reformers. The story of America's role in the alcoholic invasion of Africa, like the story of Europeans' role in the alcoholic invasion of Indian lands, destabilized the image of the United States as a sober republic, a fundamentally sound body that liquor might be, for the time being, "in" but that it would never be "of."

Awkwardly, America was simultaneously invaded and invader. One of the most striking extended uses of the invasion metaphor can be found in an 1894 booklet entitled *The Stars and Stripes Insulted* by temperance reformer Isaac Naylor. Only an extensive quotation can convey the feel of this work, bizarre even by the standards of temperance literature:

> Hark! through the States of America's Union, and through the towns and cities and hamlets of Britain's dominions there rings out a trumpet cry of Treason! Treason!! Treason!!! A powerful enemy has invaded these lands, and from carefully hidden forts and battlements, and from powerfully entrenched positions, by their powerful cannon they are . . . killing tens of thousands of citizens. . . . Against this foe the nations now are incited. . . . Amid the darkness and gloom, amid the lightning's glare and the thunder's boom, there suddenly appears a gigantic throne, reaching far up in mid-air, upon whose summit sits an object wrapped in fiery garments; a giant of giants, whose brow is wreathed with an iron crown, his gigantic hand waves a scepter of tyranny. . . . Every sword is unsheathed and flashes in the air. The arms of every man are raised, the gun of every ship is pointed. . . . "Let thy name be known, monster!" . . . "Hast thou not yet discovered my name? My name shall be written on my brow, so that all shall see it," and like lightning flash in letters of livid fire there is written on his dark brow the word "Bacchus." "You ask where my army is? Ha! ha! ha! why most of ye men with drawn swords are my army. . . . At that moment every sheathed sword, every gun and every weapon are cast at the feet of the tyrant.[90]

In a sense, in this excerpt, America and Britain have been invaded and conquered by the monstrous King Alcohol. In another sense, they are both invaded and invader, conquered and conqueror. As with "Corn" and "Wheat," as with the blood-red rivers of Africa, the "liquid devil" alcohol has not so much invaded but entirely transformed America.

Alcohol, however, was a particular type of transforming agent. Just as Dracula could not enter a home unless voluntarily admitted, so alcohol could not invade any body without some degree of consent. Nations allowed alcohol to enter because they did not appreciate its true nature and because it seemed to come in a package with other things necessary for material prosperity, like cheap workers or glass beads. However, communities also allowed alcohol to enter—out of ignorance, apathy, and a desire to become as wealthy and prosperous as Chicago or New York.[91] Even victimized families of drunkards could be seen as having invited alcoholic invasion; commonly, in temperance fiction, the wives of drinkers had known before marriage that their fiancés "drank a bit" and had failed to heed the warnings of the wise. Some wives allowed alcohol to be served at their table or kept in their homes.[92] Often, drunkards' wives had themselves caused their husbands to take the "fatal first drink" that launched them on their drunkard's progress.[93]

Of course, the individual did, almost always, make a choice to take his "fatal first drink." In temperance novels, he often made the choice because of a desire for excitement and an insufficient respect for the advice of his betters. Even before he drank, the drinker—always carefully and repeatedly described as pure, perfect, and ideal—possessed that one aspect of his character congenial to alcohol. Once he drank, of course, alcohol worked to weaken his will, particularly his will to cease drinking. If alcohol was an invader, one of the first things it did inside the body was to foment an insurrection. It transformed the will, creating an appetite for itself in the invaded body. Drinking, it was common to say in temperance circles, "dethroned reason." As the drinker drank more and more, he became "not himself." He behaved entirely differently than he would have behaved if he had been sober. Yet if he was "not himself," who was he?

The phrase "dethroned reason" was potentially unsettling, for it suggested that reason was a monarch ruling over the rest of the body: an old metaphor but one not quite appropriate in a democratic republic. As one temperance physiologist put it, alcohol released the "brutish part of human nature. . . . The beasts of the menagerie may be no fiercer than before but they rage more violently and are more dangerous because the cages are open and the keepers are gone." He followed this animal analogy to a thinly veiled analogy to class: "The lower passions being thus left without a master, the tendency to evil of every sort is greatly augmented."[94] Put this way, intoxication begins to sound less like invasion and more like insurrection.[95] Alcohol is not exactly causing the drinker to be something other than "himself"; it is enabling one part of him to break out of its cage or revolt against its betters. As another physiology text explained, when one becomes intoxicated, "the hidden nature comes to the surface. All the gloss of education and social restraint falls off, and the lower nature stands revealed."[96] In the late-nineteenth-century United States, poised between the faculty psychology of the early century and the Freudianism soon to come, the status of this repressed hidden nature, this beast within, had become increasingly uncertain. On one level, drink was an external force attacking a body that could be imagined as being somehow sound underneath the attack. That is, one could imagine extracting or driving out the invader to reveal a pure and whole body. On another level, though, drink was an infiltrating force not so much itself attacking the body as revealing the body's preexisting fissures and corruption.

Temperance advocates' metaphor of invasion, then, was decidedly complicated. Certainly they continued, in many formats, to insist that America, the community, the home, and the body, were essentially pure though temporarily invaded. However, they interspersed these repeated assertions with other narratives with which the invasion metaphor was in tension. America might be a pure body invaded by alcohol, but it was also, at times, an ally of alcohol or a carrier of alcohol into other bodies. Drinkers, homes, communities, and nations were pure, yet there was something within them that caused them to allow alcohol to enter, and some part of their putatively pure bodies acted as a fifth column on behalf of invading alcohol.

Temperance reformers complicated their metaphorical invasion still further, imagining that the invader alcohol was itself a victim of invasion. The model of complete transformation from a pure body to a servant of drink was central to temperance thinkers' understanding of the production of alcohol. As one temperance physiologist put it, "The effect . . . of fermentation is to change entirely the character of the substance upon which it acts." He claimed that any substance that has gone through fermentation "loses its innocence."[97] As one character in an antebellum temperance novel insisted, " '*The pure juice of the grape!* Kate, there is not a more systematic counterfeiting organization in the world than belongs to the rumselling business' "[98]

To reformers, the process of creating alcohol itself was premised upon a form of invasion, and once the alcohol was produced, it continued to be invaded repeatedly in its turn. It is striking, in both fictional and nonfiction temperance literature, how often temperance writers mention the adulteration of alcoholic beverages. Alcohol, they claim, is a poison. As if that were not enough, merchants add even more disgusting and dangerous items to it: "Among the most common," according to one temperance physiologist, "is *coccolus indicus*, a very poisonous vegetable substance which produces a kind of intoxication which is more injurious than that produced by alcohol."[99] Temperance sources overflow with discussions of adulteration and horrifying lists of common adulterants. A drinker who thought he was having fine liquor also might be ingesting arsenic, wormwood, red peppers, or bootblack. According to one writer, who actually opposed prohibition, dishonest merchants were known to attempt to impart a "fruity flavor" to inferior wine by adding "burned cockroaches."[100] The idea of adulterated liquor was not confined to the pages of temperance novels and physiology textbooks. At the end of the century, Mickey Finn was busily immortalizing his name in a Chicago saloon.[101] One reformer, in 1869, took the process of imagining impurity one step further: not only did alcohol invade the pure body, not only was alcohol itself corrupted by adulterants, but the adulterants themselves, he claimed, were impure![102]

The trope of purity was resonant enough throughout the culture that manufacturers of beer and liquor took great pains to respond to these temperance charges. In fact, "pure" is one of the most common adjectives in nineteenth-century advertisements for alcoholic beverages.[103] An 1864 advertisement for a new liquor store, for instance, insisted that its wares were "perfectly pure and free from all drugs and adulterations."[104] A two-page pamphlet for Meadville Rye Whiskey, printed in 1890, included variants of the word "pure" eleven times.[105] In the same year, "Old Maryland Dutch Whiskies" advertised itself as "The Purist Stimulant in Existence."[106] "Old Continental Whiskey" claimed to be "Famous for its Absolute Purity."[107] At around the same time, Tilforo and Company advertised its wine as "A Wine Which is the Pure Juice of the Grape."[108] The Rochester Brewery, like many of its competitors, reprinted an "Affidavit on the Purity of our Beer" on an advertising pamphlet, in which its brewing manager swore that "the Beer as manufactured by said Company is a pecfectly [sic] pure and unadulterated article."[109] An 1896 booklet produced by the Schlitz brewery included a huge female personification of "Purity" hovering over a drawing of the brewery. The slogan was "Purity Built it." Page after page elaborated on the extreme efforts the brewery took to ensure the absolute purity of its product. Like many other late-nineteenth-century brewery and winery advertising booklets,

Schlitz's included drawings of each of its production rooms, emphasizing the orderliness and cleanliness of each phase of production. The text on the page illustrating the bottling room insists, "Our Bottling Department is a Glittering example of absolute scrupulous cleanliness.[110] The common use in alcohol advertising of images of virginal little girls and cherubs in natural scenes was part of the same attempt to associate alcohol with purity.[111]

The most extreme consequence of temperance reformers' elaborate discourse of purity and impurity is the imaginary substitution of bodily fluids for alcohol. If alcohol operated by transforming the invaded into the invader, it made sense that reformers would figuratively depict alcohol as a bodily fluid such as blood or tears. As a temperance newspaper put it in 1869, "each drop" is "the bloody sweat of human torture."[112] In one temperance novel, reformers created a banner with a picture of a man holding "a barrel," while from the bung-hole issued a red stream, lettered *"The Blood of Hearts!"*[113] Many other works of temperance fiction similarly imagined alcohol bottles full of blood or tears.[114] With this imagery, reformers had moved as far as possible from the idea of the invaded body that was still pure underneath it all. The invaded and the invader were finally indistinguishable.

Temperance reformers are not usually thought of as having been intellectually courageous. While most historians of reform acknowledge that they broke new ground for women and paved the way for suffrage, many have maintained or implied that temperance itself was more of an evasion than a confrontation of real social and intellectual issues. According to this interpretation, in attributing all of America's woes to the demon rum, reformers sought a simple answer to complex social problems. At times, particularly when they insisted upon the metaphor of the perfect body, this characterization seems fairly accurate—both for temperance reformers and for their opponents. Taken as a whole, however, the discourse of drink was not a comforting discourse. Often it was too inconsistent and self-questioning to provide any answers, and often the implications of the invasion metaphor were deeply unsettling. Temperance reformers wrestled with the question of purity. They mobilized the potentially comforting metaphor of the pure body beset by external invaders, but they also insistently and continually undermined whatever might be comforting about that metaphor by telling stories in which the United States was invader rather than invaded, in which the invaded body was in some way identical with or sympathetic to the invader, and in which alcohol itself was invaded rather than invader. Certainly it would have been possible for them to refuse to give much attention to the history of the American Indians or to the plight of the Africans, to focus on hoary nativist arguments, and to insist upon America's pristine purity. By and large, however, temperance reformers did not take that path. If anything, they seem to have dwelled most upon those things that rendered the metaphor of the invaded body most problematic, rejecting again and again the comfort it offered.

Temperance reformers were engaged in a process of constructing and destroying a metaphorical pure body. One of the most surprising things about the nineteenth-century discourse of drink is how subtly it changed from its early days as a mass discourse in the 1830s through the end of the century. To the casual observer, it did not seem so much to move forward as to go around in circles, with each individual and each generation treading the same discursive ground. As one temperance novelist perceptively introduced her work, "In presenting this book to the public, no apology is offered for selecting, as my themes, subjects that have been used over and over again."[115] The discourse of drink, in many ways, was not so much about resolving participants' fears as it was about providing a forum in which they could repeatedly express them. Yet even as they repeatedly told the drunkard narrative, drink debaters slowly reformulated it, negotiated its terms, and sought solutions to the problems it posed. After the Civil War, as reformers began to tell the story using the language of invasion rather than that of seduction, they drew lessons from their own invasion accounts that they would apply to their reform tactics. If alcohol won men over not through its seductive influence but through its invasive coercion, and if it did so by storming through their bodies replacing their native desires and tendencies with artificial ones, then perhaps reforming women could win men back in a similar manner. Perhaps it was time for women to change their tactics. Rather than attempting to influence men to remain in domestic spaces, more and more reformers, inspired by invasion language, called for women to leave the home, invade the male domain, and reclaim drunkards by force.

Elizabeth Avery Meriwether, a Memphis resident, was one of the women who called for such invasive action.[116] She and her husband, Minor, were intellectually sophisticated and eclectic (indeed, they were avowed atheists), fundamentally committed to the economic development of the South and its adoption of a more northern-style commercial economy, and, by most measures, considerably more cosmopolitan and forward-looking than the average residents of prewar Memphis.[117] Both Elizabeth and Minor seem to have voiced some moral objections to slavery before the war, though they at times owned household slaves. Minor claimed to have emancipated some of his father's slaves and colonized them to Liberia.[118]

After the war, Elizabeth poured a good deal of energy into various social reforms. Her passionate beliefs on many political and social issues became increasingly radical and public; in particular, she threw herself into temperance and women's rights. She defiantly refused to allow gender conventions to get in the way of her participation in the public sphere. On many occasions, she challenged gender norms by giving public lectures and writing political editorials. In a play and a novel she wrote in the mid-1880s, while president of a Woman's Christian Temperance Union chapter, Meriwether illustrated some of the dilemmas the invasion metaphor could pose in her political and gendered position, and some unexpected ways in which the same metaphor could be deployed to deal with some of those problems.

The play, *A Devil's Dance* (1886), begins with a stag party. A young wife, in her innocence, has allowed her husband to attend the party. Later that evening, a leering stagecoach driver deposits the husband's unconscious body in her front hall. Immediately, the wife knows the stakes and springs into action. Understanding that this is a scene straight out of a drunkard narrative and knowing that she can never truly be her husband's wife if he continues to drink, she takes extreme measures. Pretending that she thinks that he is suffering from a fainting spell, she applies home remedies. She rips his clothing, blisters his body and the soles of his feet, calls in a sympathetic doctor to bandage him, shaves his head, gives him castor oil, and—when he awakens in his new helpless condition—refuses to feed him anything but watered-down gruel for the weeks she has determined that he is to remain in bed to recover. Unwilling to confess the true cause of his unconscious condition to his wife, the husband has no choice but to submit. Her intervention successfully arrests her husband's seemingly inevitable course. Kept away from his drinking associates and in the confines of the home, and having learned the consequences of drink, he is more than happy to sign the temperance pledge. The final act is set ten years later. By then, the other young men at the stag party have proceeded through the narrative, dying terrible drinker's deaths, one of them murdering his children with a bottle. Our former invalid, in contrast, is the sober, successful and happy head of a family consisting of two healthy, intelligent sons and one sweet and docile wife.[119]

Meriwether's story illustrates the extent to which the drunkard narrative could ultimately be more about restoring the patriarch than about questioning him. Stories like Meriwether's suggested that at times it was necessary for women to coercively assume men's prerogatives briefly, in order to make men fit to exercise them permanently. The epigraph to *The Devil's Dance* suggests that Meriwether wrote with such a strategy in mind. "Books are not absolutely dead things, but do contain a potency of life in them to be as active as that soul was whose progeny they are. . . . I know they are as lively and as vigorously productive, as those fabulous dragon's teeth, and being sown up and down may chance to spring up living men."[120] Meriwether took this role of creating and maintaining "living men" upon herself throughout her life. Through her fiction, she suggested that other women do likewise.

The *Devil's Dance* was neither Meriwether's first nor her most extensive consideration of how reformers could use coercive power to restore drunkards. In 1883, she had addressed the same issue in *Black and White*. While this novel deals with many issues, including reconstruction politics, racial violence, and women's rights, one of its central story lines concerns a man who has found a way to restore drunkards to perfect physical and moral health. This man, Calyx, is a mesmerist. He bases his treatment on the theory that since the drunkard's body is "a citadel in which the dreadful spirit of Drink was entrenched, every part and atom of that body, every nerve and tissue and muscle was permeated, and pervaded, and ruled by the Spirit of Alcohol," he can be cured only by sending some other force to invade his body and drive alcohol out. Meriwether makes two unusual choices in the novel. First, she focuses on the story of a female drunkard who has descended into drink after being seduced by an immoral "gentleman" and driven out of respectable society. In making this choice, Meriwether, like Alcott, reunites the drunkard narrative with the seduction narrative out of which it emerged. Second, Meriwether begins the story after the drunkard/seducee's fall. Her story, significantly, is one of reconstruction rather than decline.

Calyx subjects the drunkard/seducee to a regimen of steam baths and hot water beverages. "I shall send my cohorts through every nerve and tissue of her body," he says, "to drive out the demons; the molecules of her blood, brain, muscles, nerves, and glands shall be purified."[121] He causes his reluctant patient to consume cup after cup of steaming hot water by using his mesmerizing powers to make her believe that the water is liquor. The water cure succeeds. The woman's reddened and blotchy complexion returns to ivory. Her external appearance gives no sign of her previous dissipation. Indeed, every trace of the liquor has been driven from within as well, and her natural modesty, integrity, and moral purity has returned. She is no longer even particularly susceptible to drink's or the seducer's allurements; she has been entirely restored to her pre-lapsarian state, and, incidentally, to her rightful place in society. In restoring her, however, Calyx has not made her his slave.[122] Rather, he beseeches her to "make an effort, bring your WILL to life, your will lies dormant, drowned and drunk in alcohol, wake it up . . . and you will regain your freedom from the despotism of drink." The pure water he has sent coursing through her system has not become a new master but rather has restored her to her rightful self.

One of the novelties of this drunkard/seduction narrative, of course, is the gender inversion of the drunkard and reformer. Meriwether chose to make the drunkard female because she was distressed at the common double standard that drinking men were tragic whereas drinking women were "beyond the pale," and because it gave her an opportunity to advance her social purity message along with her temperance views. But why did she make the savior of the drunkard male? As a temperance reformer and women's rights advocate, Meriwether was committed to the gender implications of the drunkard narrative and so was hardly likely to give a man credit for temperance reform work that actually was predominantly performed by women. Rather, she summons an archetypal image of female power to insist that it *is* ultimately women who have done the saving. As Calyx first begins his work of purifying the drunkard, he suddenly remembers one of his ancestors who had been burned as a witch. "It had often been observed that our young student strongly resembled his witch ancestress. Since Calyx had discovered himself to possess that mysterious power over others, called mesmeric, thoughts of the witch-woman continually haunted his mind."[123] Meriwether never further develops this startling revelation. Its sole purpose appears to be to establish, in the strongest possible terms, that Calyx's power to invade bodies and drive out the enslaving forces of alcohol is ultimately a female power.

In a sense, Elizabeth Meriwether was taking up Louisa May Alcott's project where she left off. Both women saw the parallel between the seduction and drunkard narratives and united elements of each in one character. Both, to some extent, bought into the logic of these stories and worked them into their own writings. Yet both seem to have been profoundly disturbed by the idea that once people fell only death could free them from the clasps of those who, by seductive or invasive means, had penetrated into the very core or their selfhood. Louisa May Alcott's "Fair Rosamond" was unfinished; she never got it to the place where she was ready to see it published, and she never resolved the problem that she had posed by challenging the conventions of seduction and drunkard narratives. While Elizabeth Meriwether lacked Alcott's skill as a writer, she at least made an effort, through the imagined medical discovery of Calyx, to find a way through which Rosamond might have been allowed to live. By imagining a way in which purity itself could aggress against impurity, invading the spaces it had corrupted and restoring them to their pristine state, Meriwether proposed an alternative to the depressing logic of the drunkard narrative.

CHAPTER SIX

Resolution

> [Carry Nation] said she couldn't get a church [to lecture in], so she got a sa-
> loon, that it was more to her liking anyway, as it was where Christ would
> preach if he were on earth. Her next play was to jolly the saloon men. She
> [said that she] didn't care what business a man was in if he had manhood
> about him. "Mrs. Nation in Atchison,"
> *Atchison Daily Globe,* March 25, 1901

> An Atchison [Kansas] woman says one of her kin is a woman who weighs
> 400 pounds. The woman's husband only weighs 125 pounds. He drinks to
> such an extent that he has been known to have *delirium tremens* for three
> weeks at a time. When the woman hears that he is dead drunk somewhere,
> she hunts him up, and picks him up by the back of his trousers, and carries
> him home. *Atchison Daily Globe,* 1904

The troubled marriage of Harriet and William Ferman illustrates how the tensions among drink, gender, and family authority could come to a head in
nineteenth-century families. Born in Lancaster, Pennsylvania, in 1843, William
moved west with his parents to Illinois as a child. When the war came, he
served as a fife-player for a Union regiment.[1] During his service, William sustained an injury that would trouble though not incapacitate him throughout
his life: he injured his "testicle chord." After the war, William returned to take
up farming, and in 1869, at the age of twenty-five, he married a seventeen-year-
old native of Illinois named Harriet, called Hattie. According to Hattie's later
testimony, at the time of their marriage William "was a nice, decent man."[2] Ten
months later, Hattie gave birth to the first of their nine children. William soon
left farming to move to town, where he opened a drug store. When the drug
store burned down in 1882, William became a barber, working out of his home.
By the early 1890s, by his own account, William was "a little of everything . . .
barber, plasterer, paper hanger." He had also become a frequent heavy drinker.
Hattie testified that he would "come in weeks in and weeks out to his bed
staggering drunk and not to go to bed sober and be so drunk that he has gone to

bed with his clothes on." According to his neighbors, William was often too intoxicated to work. As one of his customers put it, "There was times when I went there to be shaved that he . . . wasn't in a fit condition to shave a man."[3] A Mrs. Philena Black testified that he once was so intoxicated that he could not remember the name of his own son.[4]

Hattie Ferman was not the sort of woman to submit quietly to the consequences of William's behavior. She made many efforts to save William from drink, imploring him not to drink and sending their children to the saloon to bring him home. On at least one occasion, she claimed to have gone herself on such an errand. As she remembered it, "There was a customer wanted to be waited on in the shop. . . . I walked in the saloon after him. . . . I asked him to come home. He said I should go and attend to my own business. I says, 'Come home and attend to your business.' "[5] Hattie also tried more coercive measures. In an effort to cut off William's supply of liquor, she frequently gave local saloonkeepers notice not to serve to her husband. In the early 1890s she filed a suit against one of his saloonkeepers, Charles Hanewacker, to compensate her for William's lack of support.

Even as Hattie attempted to restore William to sobriety through these means, however, she worked to fill the roles that he had abandoned. To make money to support the family, she did various domestic chores for their neighbors, including washing, ironing, and general housekeeping. Finding this income insufficient, she persuaded her brother to hire her for the traditionally male part-time job of steering a skiff down the river and lighting lamps on government piers at nightfall. She even supplemented her earnings with winnings from cockfighting. When asked in his trial why he allowed his wife to take on this male provider role, William replied, "I could not stop her."[6] It came to be understood in the community that Hattie, not William, was running the Ferman household. Their physician, Warren Hunter, for instance, acknowledged that it was Hattie who paid the family's bills. Yet, he insisted, "I always charge all bills to him, not to her, he should be the head of the family."[7]

William's drinking, the family's destitution, and Hattie's efforts caused a good deal of trouble in the Ferman household. As their neighbor Henrietta Heagy put it, "their house is anything but a house of comfort I can tell you that."[8] Some nights William would go to play his fife in a saloon and would stay away from home until the next morning, which would frequently start a family quarrel.[9] On those occasions Hattie would frequently "shut down on" William by telling saloonkeepers not to sell to him. In a candid moment, William revealed that Hattie had shut down on him in other ways as well. "I came home from work now for the last three years and she never makes my bed. . . . Not until about the last Fourth of July, did she make friends with me."[10] For her part, Hattie divulged that William had physically abused her when he was intoxicated, pushing her around and choking her.

William was probably intoxicated throughout his testimony in his wife's civil damage suit. Yet even in his drunken state, he appreciated that his manhood was at stake. He claimed that he had consented to become involved in the case only because he "wanted to see if I am an inebriate drunkard or not and if I can prove to the contrary I am going to do so. . . . Yes sir, I am going to clear myself."[11] He insisted that he had never drank so much "but what I knew what I was doing and could attend to business."[12] In his eagerness to help his saloonkeeper, Hanewacker, win the case, William went farther still, insisting that he had never purchased alcohol in Hanewacker's saloon. Though he admitted to frequenting Hanewacker's establishment, he insisted that he did not buy alcohol from him. If anyone had witnessed him drinking liquor at Hanewacker's saloon, he implausibly insisted, it was liquor that he had brought to the saloon from his own home.[13]

The relationship among gender, alcohol, and power in the marriage of Hattie and William Ferman was complex. Hattie exercised many roles that their neighbors considered to be male responsibilities. Obviously, she was not happy with many aspects of her husband's abdication of responsibility. She, the children, and William himself all suffered financially and emotionally, and she suffered from his physical abuse, in part because William did not properly play the protecting manly role traditionally assigned to him. William seems to have enjoyed his release from his socially assigned role as head of household, even if he was somewhat ashamed to see his failure as patriarch so publicly discussed. It is harder to tell from the transcript whether Hattie enjoyed some aspects of her unconventional position within her family. Some things about her behavior, however, suggest that she may have. The fact that she was a cockfighter and that she agreed to take the physically challenging job of rowing the skiff, for instance, suggest that she was not deeply invested in traditional notions of womanhood. In any case, William's alcohol use and his social designation as a "drunkard" provided a way in which those within and without the family could understand the unconventional gender roles in the Ferman home.

Hattie Ferman won her civil damage suit at the circuit court level. The jury awarded her a generous $1,200. The appeals court upheld the jury's decision, though it acknowledged that there had been some irregularities at the trial. The supreme court, however, reversed the judgment on technical grounds and remanded it back to the circuit court. It is unclear whether Hattie pursued her case any further. It is likely that she, like many civil damage law plaintiffs, never received any settlement. In any case, the experience of going through their civil damage case almost certainly had a permanent impact on Hattie and William's domestic life. By ultimately bringing the matter to court, Hattie destabilized what family structure she and her husband had developed. Harriet also became a public figure of sorts, having enlisted friends and local temperance advocates in her cause and having brought a case all the way from the local to the state court. This no doubt widened her sphere of familiarity and her sense of empowerment. William was publicly ridiculed, which must have stung once he was sober. Shortly after the civil damage trial, as the case was making its way to the state supreme court, Hattie and William's marriage collapsed entirely. In 1892, William moved out. For a while, Hattie had a taste of independence, though surely a difficult one; during part of their separation, the children temporarily lived with William while Hattie went to the city to work as a dishwasher. In 1904, Hattie finally brought and won a suit for divorce and custody of the two children who were still minors. William, who had apparently been at least partially supporting himself as a musician, died a few years later when an ingrown toenail became infected and gangrenous.[14]

The Fermans' situation was no more ambiguous than that of many men and women trying to come to terms with the meaning of alcohol use. William and Hattie, like other male heavy drinkers and their wives, found themselves in distinctly nontraditional gender roles. However, it is unclear whether, in bringing the civil damage suit, Harriet sought to further increase her power and independence or to force William to assume his proper patriarchal role. In a sense, she was trying to do both—to exercise temporarily a level of power truly unusual for a woman and restore William to his proper position. Ultimately, the tactic failed but situations like theirs still raised a difficult question: Could women like Harriet, by temporarily assuming new roles, restore drinking men to manhood? The civil damage laws and much of the rhetoric of the post–Civil War temperance movement were based on the premise that they could. The reality, evidently, was much less certain.

Like Hattie Ferman, many wives of heavy drinkers challenged traditional gender roles in dealing with their husbands. Indeed, it was a common perception that drunkards' wives wielded unnatural levels of authority within their house-holds and over their husbands. The inversion of gender roles in the drunkard's household became a comic staple in the nineteenth century. An 1872 Mardi Gras parade in Memphis, Tennessee, for instance, featured a "fat, red-faced old dame" (almost certainly a cross-dressed young man) pushing her "helpless" drunkard husband in a wheelbarrow while "launch[ing] invectives" at him.[15] An advertisement for Yuengling beer featured four young men drinking behind a fence; they have not yet noticed the arrival of a woman shaking her fist at them. What is fascinating about this image is that the woman is noticeably disproportionate in size to the drinkers. To many male drinkers, females intent on challenging them no doubt loomed large (fig. 6).

Although even the most radical temperance reformers did not endorse fe-male domination of men in general, and although many were highly uncom-fortable witnessing the skewed relationships between couples like William and Hattie, many people—both within and without the movement—agreed that drunkards' wives had little choice but to move beyond traditional female roles. They needed to do so both to protect their families from violence and want, and to save their husbands from themselves. For instance, the *Iowa Temperance Standard,* in 1869, chastised a woman who claimed that her husband's drinking habits were "none of my business." It advised women to make men's drinking their business.[16] Increasingly, as nineteenth-century reformers came to doubt the power of women's quiet influence, they acknowledged that in some cases drinkers' wives would have to move radically beyond their traditional spheres and use coercion.

Some drunkards' wives challenged their husbands with surprising fierceness. Sometimes these wives responded to their husbands' violence with some of their own. One man breaking up a fist fight between a saloongoer and his wife in the early 1880s found, to his surprise, that restraining the husband was not sufficient to stop the fight; another man claimed that his wife had chased him from their home with a knife.[17] Testimony of plaintiffs in civil damage law suits further shows how strong some drunkards' wives became. One wife said in 1898, "I have taken the jug full [of my husband's liquor] and slammed it out in the yard right before him. I have disguised it [that is, adulterated it] in every way to sicken him." Examples of such passionate and direct defiance abound in civil damage transcripts.[18]

These women, and others who were more conventionally proper, often took up the family responsibilities they felt their husbands had abandoned. Defense

Fig. 6. Advertisement for Yuengling Beer (n.d.) (Photo courtesy of the Warshaw Collection, Archives Center, National Museum of American History, Smithsonian Institution)

lawyers in civil damage cases often suggested that the women plaintiffs had taken over their households. One drinker in an 1875 suit had apparently taken to regular saloongoing to escape the constant criticism of the other three residents of his home: his wife, sister, and mother. A lawyer in another case in 1877 referred to the drinker's wife as the "captain of the family"; a third, in an 1873 case, suggested that a drinker's wife was "the head man of the house."[19] The wives in these cases generally denied the defense's characterization of their home lives. Indeed, the lawyer for one drinker's wife emphasized the degree to which she had submitted to her husband's authority even though he was a drunkard. While "we may not be able to understand the power of a drunken husband over a patient, broken-spirited wife," he continued, "the sad fact" is that drinkers' wives like his client often endure "griefs and outrages" from their husband with "submission and silence." He reminded his audience that usually a woman's desire to "subordinate her will to" her husband's "reasonable wishes" was one of the "highest adornments of female character."[20] Yet it is clear from the testimony of drinkers and drinkers' wives that many wives of saloongoers did exercise what was perceived as an unusually great amount of power within the home. Drinkers complained that their wives would not "let" them have any money for drink; would not (as in the case of Andrew Faivre) tell them family financial information, such as the wages of their children; or, as one put it in 1873, were trying to "drive [them] off."[21]

Also, of course, drinkers' wives extended their activities beyond the confines of the home. Despite the consensus that it was a man's responsibility to support his family, some saloongoers were unable or unwilling to provide support. Many drinkers' wives who brought civil damage suits found alternate means of supporting themselves and their families. Some performed traditionally female tasks such as working as domestics, sewing, or taking in washing; some seem to have practiced prostitution. Some women took over the management of family farms. One was in the real-estate business. Others appear to have sought alternative male protection, whether from a father or from a boarder or neighbor. In any case, their husbands' failure to fulfil their manly roles within the family either allowed or forced their wives to move into the vacuum.[22]

The drunkard's home, then, in the minds of many nineteenth-century Americans, was a space in which gender roles were perversely inverted. In the face of this perception, it is significant that state governments, particularly in the 1870s and 1880s, specifically designed legislation to support (rather than to limit) drunkards' wives ability to assume the roles their husbands had abandoned and to give women certain coercive powers over their husbands. The civil damage laws are the prime example of this, but they were only one of many weapons state legislators added to drunkards' wives' arsenals. States passed an array of laws that either were specifically aimed at empowering drunkards' wives or were touted as having that consequence among others. A frequent argument for the married women's property acts that swept the nation at midcentury, for instance, was that they would allow women to protect their earnings and inheritances from the grasp of inebriate husbands. The same was true of legislation liberalizing divorce laws.[23] Some legislatures contemplated giving drunkards' wives even more power. As the 1872 Illinois Senate debated the civil damage act, a temperance member went so far as to propose an amendment that would actually have required all married men to present their wives' written permission before purchasing liquor.[24] Many states with civil damage laws—and even some without them—passed legislation requiring saloonkeepers to honor drinkers' wives requests not to serve their husbands. In Georgia, after 1883, for instance, a saloonkeeper had to stop selling alcohol to a known drunkard if he received a notice from the man's "wife, father, mother, brother, or sister."[25] Wives, therefore, had the authority to "shut down" on their husbands.[26] One reformed drunkard claimed that his wife had sent such a notice to every saloon in Atlanta.[27] A number of drinkers' wives used this power and gave notice to saloonkeepers not to allow their husbands to purchase alcohol. Emma Rush, the wife of blacksmith James Rush, claimed to have warned a saloonkeeper, "Well, don't sell him any more, for if you do, I will put the law in operation against you."[28] Some husbands, through violence or persuasion, convinced their wives to rescind their orders, but courts frequently held that saloonkeepers could not accept such retractions if they had any reason to suspect undue coercion on the part of the husband.

State legislators and their constituents had become increasingly convinced both that drunkards posed an extreme social problem and that giving drunkards' wives unprecedented coercive powers was one of the most promising solutions. Officials were willing to allow drunkards' wives these new powers over their failed husbands even though it meant overturning time-honored gender norms. Already, by midcentury, the logic of the drunkard narrative had significantly contributed to a widespread sense that drunkards' wives—and women generally—ought to have more control over their property. Already, by the postwar years, legislatures were giving individual women coercive control over their husbands' social behavior. It was only a matter of time before the logic of the drunkard narrative would contribute to still more radical changes in women's roles.

As radical as it in some ways was, government-sponsored coercion such as civil damage litigation did not always seem sufficient to temperance reformers. Particularly in the 1870s, public confidence in the legitimacy, integrity, and effectiveness of government was low throughout the United States. In particular, the many reformers who understood the drink problem as gendered feared that harnessing the coercive power of the existing government was a fatally flawed solution. The government was, after all, male. The very failure of moral suasion that made coercive legislation necessary as much as guaranteed that women's influence would fail to convince voting men to pass it or enforce it. Of course, just as reformers never ceased trying moral suasion tactics, they continued to put a great deal of energy into convincing men to pass and support prohibitory laws. Yet they also adopted a new strategy that brought together their concerns about gender and volition and suggested a solution to both: they increasingly turned to vigilante-style efforts to take on the saloons themselves.

Temperance reformers' most dramatic early attempt to put this technique of female invasion into practice was the Women's Crusades of 1873–74.[29] The

Women's Crusades began in Fredonia, New York, when a group of women took seriously a traveling temperance preacher's call for woman-powered prohibition. In a sermon he had given countless times, Reverend Diocletian Lewis recounted an instance years earlier when his own mother had gotten together with other temperance-minded women, marched on saloons, and persuaded their proprietors to close down. Just as Lewis had told the story dozens of times, so these temperance women had almost certainly heard similar stories before. Many other, localized instances of such female invasion of saloons had occurred at least since the 1850s and had been covered in temperance-sympathetic newspapers, pamphlets, and speeches.[30] In 1873, such actions moved from being a trope to being a powerful social movement.

Lewis' account of his mother's boldness inspired the women of Fredonia. They determined to march upon local businesses that sold alcohol and to persuade or coerce their proprietors to close them down. When they met with some initial success, others adopted their tactics. Lewis proceeded to Ohio, where he sparked more crusades. Accounts of the crusades spread rapidly through the nation; within months, more than 56,000 reformers throughout the East and in the Midwest, especially, had formed bands and descended upon saloonkeepers, grocers, and druggists.[31] When they approached these corrupt male spaces, crusaders generally sang hymns and prayed for Christ to soften the heart of the drink purveyor. Whether they convened their prayer meeting just outside the door to the establishment or actually entered it, crusaders deliberately installed themselves in spaces of corruption, transforming them temporarily into female spaces of moral purity and religious piety. If their crusade succeeded, the women would retreat back to their homes, and public spaces would become morally neutral—creating "dry" dry goods stores, temperance tea houses, or the like.

The crusades rested on an unusual strategy of female power combining moral suasion and coercion. This approach emerged out of the widespread perception that conventional forms of women's influence were fruitless; attempts to protect their male family members from drink and attempts to persuade a male-controlled legal system to provide sufficient safeguards against alcohol's power often failed.[32] An 1874 *Harper's Weekly* article described the crusades as the "cry of mothers, wives, daughters, and sisters against a desolating evil with which the law and all other influences apparently wrestle in vain."[33] One southern woman, frustrated by the failure of a neighbor to reform her husband, told her sister that "the woman's crusade is needed in Raleigh."[34]

Through their "invasion" of male spaces, crusading women engaged alcohol in its own space and with its own tactics. The female saloon invasion—more than any other idea, narrative, event, or action—encapsulated and provided a solution for many of the central ideas and problems the movement had struggled with through the decades.

The ideas behind the crusades and even their mode of operation had much in common with those of the civil damage laws. Both responded to the perceived failure of private female moral suasion and public governmental regulations by attempting to find some sort of amalgam of or compromise between the two. "Mother" Eliza Stewart, an Ohio temperance reformer, actively participated in both. In the years before the crusades, Stewart had been an active supporter of Ohio's civil damage law. She encouraged drunkards' wives to bring suits under the law, protectively shepherded them in and out of courtrooms, encouraged temperance-minded women to attend the trials in a show of moral force, and even went so far, on at least two occasions, as to herself deliver the plaintiff's opening argument to the jury.[35] After working so hard to see civil damage and other temperance legislation pass, Stewart was disgusted at the failure of male law enforcement officers and courts to give the laws teeth. She became convinced that women needed to take even more aggressive steps. To Stewart, the crusades represented just such an opportunity, and she became one of their most prominent leaders.[36] In the crusades, as in civil damage suits, women stepped well out of their proper spheres to attack saloons that they felt were destroying manhood. However, the crusades were even more public and political than the civil damage laws. Although the government, in passing civil damage acts, leant its coercive power to private women, the crusaders seized public coercive powers from a startled government.

The women's crusades receded almost as quickly as they had spread, lasting less than a year. Nevertheless, they encouraged thousands of temperance women to act as drunkards' wives did in civil damage suits—to temporarily enter forbidden, impure, male spaces, and to appropriate coercive powers normally reserved for men, in hopes of saving endangered patriarchs. These temperance advocates had largely given up on the idea that women could exercise sufficient power through influence; influence alone could not compete with the invasive power of drink, the saloon, or the public environment more generally. Still, temperance women saw their invasions into male spaces and prerogatives as fundamentally different from those of their foes, the forces of alcohol. They entered men's spaces and appropriated their powers not to establish permanent rights for themselves but to liberate enslaved men and restore them to their proper spaces.

The idea of female invasion was sufficiently resonant for the women's crusades to inspire a good deal of literature. Autobiographical accounts of crusade leaders proliferated in the years following the crusades, and there were also numerous fictional accounts. One of the best-known of these, *Women to the Rescue: A Story of the New Crusade,* was written in 1874 by temperance stalwart T. S. Arthur. One temperance play—which approvingly depicts drinkers' wives heroically bursting into a saloon, setting the liquor and saloon on fire, and *beating their husbands with clubs* until, as the stage directions say, "men are on their knees, crying 'mercy' "—was actually written a year before the major wave of the crusades began.[37] The story of female invasion, like that of the drunkard's decline, was powerful. Nineteenth-century Americans wanted to hear it again and again.

One reason that the crusade narrative was so powerful and versatile was that by entering saloons temperance women appropriated and reconfigured the account of invasion so central to the drunkard narrative. Instead of alcohol or the forces of the saloon entering and destroying the home, the forces of the home were entering and destroying the saloon. Though reformers never seem to have discussed it explicitly, they were taking the structural position held by alcohol itself in the drunkard narrative. Rather than identifying with the invaded bodies, the reformers had become part of the encroaching environment. In shifting their position within the narrative of invasion, temperance reformers could imagine the self, the home, and the sphere of contentment pushing back against the chaotic and powerful forces that had threatened them. The male drunkard, in this account, of course, was helplessly trapped in the space of the saloon, dependant upon his female saviors to burst through the door and liberate him from the grasp of the saloonkeeper.

The inverted logic of female invasion was not confined to the crusades and the civil damage laws. The crusades led directly to the formation of and heavily influenced the ideology of the Woman's Christian Temperance Union. Many of the organization's founders were supporters of the civil damage acts, and the organization continued to give the acts their time and support. The pattern of female invasion—the idea that women should emerge from appropriate feminine spaces, invade and rectify corrupt spaces, then withdraw back into their own domestic sphere—would characterize the WCTU for decades. Though the organization's leadership quickly moved away from actual invasions of saloons, the organization, in many ways, remained true to the movement that gave it birth. The *Union Signal* from time to time printed fictional stories praising women who dared to enter saloons to challenge saloonkeepers and save husbands. More importantly, however, much of the WCTU's work explicitly involved pure women who—voluntarily and temporarily—immersed themselves in sinful, filthy, and unwholesome environments in order to transform such places.[38] Not only were members asked to befriend and visit poor neighbors, they were to bring flowers to prison inmates and operate homes for fallen women. The organization supported and eagerly read the reports of "round the world missionaries" who spread the temperance message among people whom they believed to be unwashed and unenlightened. Frances Willard and many others in the WCTU became highly interested in the opium dens and white slave trade of the West Coast. At the same time, as many historians have argued, it was precisely reformers' insistence that their ultimate goal was to return to the home that made the WCTU so successful in convincing moderate women to embrace their radical, invasive tactics.[39]

A small incident perfectly exposes the theory that underlies this seemingly contradictory dream of saving domesticity and conventional female roles by temporarily leaving them. In 1893, Frances Willard received a letter from an English seamstress in need of advice. The young woman complained to Willard that, as a female, she could not "raise herself to any position of importance" either inside the temperance movement or in the world of business. Willard's open reply to her letter, which she published in 1895, began rather as one would expect. She spoke generally, suggesting that it was her "firm conviction" that someday soon women would "have conquered a firm foothold in the trades and professions." What followed, however, is rather surprising. After having fully entered men's world, Willard believed that "women will gradually withdraw from mechanical work and devote themselves to the noblest vocations that life affords—namely, motherhood, reform work, and philanthropy." Women would return to these areas of life through a sort of "specific gravity."[40] This vision is one of women's invasion writ large. It also adds a dimension to the old debate about the WCTU's relationship to the feminists on the one hand and the proponents of traditional domesticity on the other. Willard has generally been understood as straddling the two camps—a reluctant feminist, a cagey traditionalist. Yet, as her statement suggests, she did not understand these two visions as an either/or choice. Rather, she saw the one as leading to the other. She was suggesting that the contemporary era in which lower-class women worked and middle-class women stayed at home would give rise to a period of middle-class women's full entry into the economic sphere. Eventually, women of all classes, having established a more just economic order, would return voluntarily to the domestic sphere.

Temperance reformers had to proceed with care. They wanted to put enough muscle behind women's "influence" to make it competitive with alcoholic coercion. Nevertheless, the vast majority of temperance reformers did not want to dramatically change traditional family structures or gender relations. They decidedly did not want to bring about on a large scale the sort of role reversal so common in drunkards' households—indeed, they wished to undo such reversal where it had occurred. Temperance reformers, as they never ceased insisting, above all were engaged in a project of restoring the drinking man to his lost manhood. They wanted him to resume both his full humanity and his proper position as head of the family. It was toward this end that they formulated female invasion, a tactic of intervention in which women exerted a brief coercive power, freed men from alcohol's grasp, and then immediately retreated to their traditional domestic sphere.

One way to appreciate how organic temperance reformers' relative conservatism was to their ideas is to contrast the drunkard narratives that were so central to the movement to another contemporary body of stories that attacked gender inequality much more directly. Just as temperance reformers used the drunkard narrative to express the threats posed by drinking men, so those who believed that men's dominance over the family and society was chiefly to blame for a host of problems and injustices told their own type of story. While these stories shared some elements with drunkard narratives, the two also differed tellingly from one another. The most memorable of the stories of patriarchy-gone-amok —such as Charlotte Perkins Gilman's "The Yellow Wallpaper" (1899), Kate Chopin's *The Awakening* (1899), Colette's *Claudine and Annie* (1903), and Henrik Ibsen's *A Doll's House* (1889)—fit into a consistent pattern. The heroines in all of these stories are oppressed by strong husbands. Competent, self-assured, controlling, these husbands are sure of their mastery within their families. Like the "perverse patriarchs" in woman-authored Gothic plots examined by Kari Winter, these husbands are "perverse not because they deviate from normative social roles but because they fill their roles so exactly that their behavior calls attention to the injustice embedded in patriarchal ideology."[41] They meticulously fulfil their socially determined responsibilities and expect their wives to do the same. Perhaps more out of blindness and conformity than cruelty, these husbands leave their wives with such a limited space of autonomy that they resort to extraordinary measures—flight, madness, suicide—to escape. These husbands embody patriarchy, graphically illustrating exactly what the authors believed was wrong with socially endorsed gender relations.

The drunkard at the center of the drunkard narrative bore some resemblance to the "perverse patriarch." He was certainly a powerful symbol of abusive patriarchy. In many ways, the drunkard stood for all that reformers hated about male power. He was violent, irrational, and irresponsible, yet the law recognized him, in preference to his sober, intelligent wife, as the head of his household. David Reynolds has referred to the drunkard's wife as "the pitiable victim of male bestiality, a victim who became a particularly vivid emblem of women's wrongs and at the same time a kind of walking advertisement for the need for women's rights."[42] Many other historians of the temperance movement have shown how reformers wove their temperance and suffrage agendas around this powerful image.

Many reform-minded women must have latched on to the drunkard as a symbol of corrupt patriarchy precisely because he was such a weak link in the patriarchal chain. It is important to remember that many important leaders of the mainstream woman suffrage movement—and many of their less-famous followers—also participated in the temperance movement. Such was the case for Amelia Bloomer, Susan B. Anthony, Elizabeth Cady Stanton, and countless others.[43] By repeatedly evoking the image of the drunkard, these women's rights advocates reminded their opponents that all men did not fit the idealistic image of husbands and fathers, and that society should not be organized around the assumption that they did. Many of the most radical critics of patriarchy included a condemnation of the drunken husband in their rhetorical arsenals.

However, though the drunkard narrative fulfilled many of the same functions as the story of the perverse patriarch, it also differed from it in many ways. Consider one drunkard's wife's characteristic declaration against her husband in a case heard before the Illinois Supreme Court in 1907: "[He has] wasted and squandered all [our] means and property, and became greatly impoverished, reduced, degraded and wholly ruined as well in his mind and body as in his estate and capability for work, and lost his means of securing work in his said trade, and neglected and ceased to exercise or attend to the duties of his said trade or in any manner to provide a proper livelihood for [his] children."[44]

Bankrupt, unemployed, degraded, incompetent—drunkards had "neglected and ceased to exercise or attend to" not only their trades but also all of their responsibilities to society and family. Through their own choice or otherwise, they had failed to be patriarchs. Drink, in drunkard narratives, inspired drunkards to violence, but it also incapacitated them and distracted them from providing leadership to their families. Drunkards spent their money at the saloon rather than bringing it home to their needy families, forcing their wives to step out of the domestic sphere to make up for that missing money. The wives' moral authority in the home increased, as their husbands awoke the morning after—sick, ashamed, and repentant. Neighbors, both in fictional and actual drunkard narratives, often rallied behind drunkards' wives, materially as well as emotionally.

Being a drunkard's wife was an awful fate, but it was awful more because of the drunkard's abdication than because of his abuse of traditional male roles. Gilman's, Chopin's, Colette's, and Ibsen's patriarchs were relentlessly sober; it is precisely their unceasing self-control that makes them so terrifying and destructive toward their wives. If they spent evenings getting soused with their drinking buddies, there would be a host of other domestic tragedies, but perhaps their weakness would give their desperate wives a space in which to develop their own power and autonomy. If not a pleasant alternative, it would at least pose an entirely different set of problems. If the trouble with patriarchy came down to men having too great a share of power, authority, and autonomy and women having too little, the drunkard's relationship with his sober wife on one level seemed to offer as much an alleviation as an illustration.

Although the story of the drunkard could be used by those who demanded an end to patriarchal oppression, it could also be used by those who wanted merely to fix the patriarchal system by making sure their patriarchs were sober. Temperance reformers were often ambiguous about which of these messages they were sending. Barbara Epstein has argued that temperance women were "motivated to a large degree by [their] anger over their subordinate status."[45] Their rhetoric, however, frequently subordinated a critique of unequal power to a demand that those who filled the role of patriarch be compelled to do so properly. Some, certainly, evoked the drunken husband as a rhetorical tool to win empowerment; much more frequently, however, temperance reformers called for empowerment so that they could address the problem of the drunken husband.

A number of scholars have addressed the problem of why temperance reformers' discourse of gender differed so strikingly from that of other women's rights advocates. Some have suggested that temperance reformers, among others, were "pragmatic feminists" rather than fully matured ones. While they objected to abuses of the patriarchal system, they were not ready to attack patriarchy itself. It is also possible to look at the mixed gender messages sent by the temperance movement as largely a problem of available language. Even as reformers pushed for more rights for women, they made their argument largely through the melodramatic language of sentimental fiction, a genre committed to differentiating between men's and women's roles and natures.[46] Perhaps temperance reformers' language had not caught up to the radical potential of their ideas. Other historians have dismissed reformers' frequent argument that they wanted power for fundamentally conservative ends as a disingenuous discursive strategy thinly veiling the women's rights advocacy beneath. None of these explanations, however, is entirely satisfying. As temperance reformers fought for power, the drunkard was constantly at the center of their agenda. In fundamental ways, this group, which banded together against the incompetent drunken husband, differed from more radical women's rights groups of the period who aimed their rhetoric against the all-too-competent sober patriarch.

Nineteenth-century temperance reformers seem at times to have opposed rather than participated in much of the women's rights agenda. When they did work in the same direction as their suffragist associates, they often seem to have done so for what may seem, to twenty-first-century eyes, to be the wrong reasons. The irony is that they ultimately played an indispensable role in the collapse of patriarchal privilege. These women, who aimed ambiguously at the drunken husband, may well have done more to advance women's rights than did those who set their sights, through the sober patriarch, on patriarchy itself. It would be too pat to divide nineteenth-century women's rights advocates into two camps, one that set itself in opposition to the successful patriarch and the other that protested the failed patriarch. Many of the most strident principled opponents of patriarchy shared a passionate dislike for the drunkard. Similarly, many temperance advocates questioned the power relations even in the soberest of marriages, calling for a more egalitarian "White Life for Two." Yet there was a large group of women (and some men) who were indisputably instrumental in the movement toward women's empowerment but who spent more time condemning men for not fulfilling patriarchal responsibilities than they did questioning the patriarchal system.

Temperance women called for some significant changes in relationships between the sexes. They wanted women to be educated enough to converse with their husbands as equals; they wanted women to have more power to resist their husbands' sexual demands; they wanted women to have enough opportunities to support themselves so that they were not forced to fly to an unsavory male for economic protection; by the last decades of the century, they even wanted women to have the vote so that they could pass antivice legislation. They did not, however, hope to usher in a matriarchy to replace the patriarchy. The vast majority of female temperance reformers did not even want to see men and women equally divide rights and responsibilities. What they wanted was to put enough muscle behind their influence to enable them to compete with the baneful influence of corrupt male spaces and institutions.

Nevertheless, even if most temperance women and the drunkards' wives they represented were fundamentally more invested in propping up the patriarch than in dethroning him, male drinkers such as Midwestern saloongoers experienced women's interventions as unmanning. Though many drinkers themselves agreed that alcohol, taken in excess, compromised men's volitional freedom and ability to fulfil their manly duties, the idea that men could maintain their manhood and volition only with the assistance of their wives and other women was profoundly threatening. Drinking men had to navigate a careful course between allowing themselves to be "enslaved" by alcohol and giving way to the influence of the women who aimed to save them from it. Moreover the leaders of the temperance movement, male and female, would not in principle have disagreed with the drinkers' distaste for being under the control of women. What happened to William and Harriet Ferman was something nobody wanted.

In this context, it becomes easier to understand why the drunken and unmanned husband served to mobilize many women into political action much more effectively than the spectacle of the sober and overbearing patriarch. Although temperance women wanted to change and improve the patriarchal system and although they were willing to enter briefly into the realm of men's business in order to do so, most were not interested in moving toward a society in which men no longer had authority over women. The drunken patriarch bothered them more than did the oppressive one because he threatened permanently to undermine the patriarchal system altogether. If the young Frances Willard, like many women in her circle, fantasized about being man—and a "beau" at that—this fantasy had very different implications than if she had fantasized that power relations between men and women were equalized. It was a desire for a different position within a power structure but also a commitment to, and even an eroticization of, the structure itself. In her youth, when Willard was frustrated, her mother frequently advised her, "Keep quiet child; we were not born to reign but to wrestle."[47] Most temperance women did not envision a future in which women reigned or even one in which they permanently exercised equal authority with men. They imagined a future in which they would periodically intervene in men's business only to improve and stabilize it.

That women could exercise certain forms of power and enter certain spaces that had been seen previously as inappropriate had broader political implications. Take the case of the Wisconsin legislature. Toward the end of a report by a committee of Wisconsin assemblymen advocating a civil damage act in February 1872, the authors mused that "If anything could reconcile us to woman suffrage it would be that upon moral issues . . . her voice would be on the right always."[48] Wisconsin's civil damage law, like those of many other states, preceded legislation giving women the right to go to court in their own names. The civil damage law included provisions giving women special permission to bring civil damage suits in their own names and without their husbands' consent.[49] In the case of Wisconsin, though, more general broadening of women's legal rights followed hard on the heels of civil damage legislation. Indeed, Wisconsin gave married women property rights and the right to sue and be sued exactly a week after it implemented its civil damage law.[50]

Temperance women's commitment to the circular pattern of entering unwomanly spaces only to retreat to their (now safer) homes extended to the world of politics. Nineteenth-century opponents of women's suffrage repeatedly described the offices of political leaders, political conventions, voting booths, and other spaces of politics as smoke-filled, oppressive, vile, and impure. They argued that bringing women into politics would not make politics more pure; it would only make women less so.[51] Temperance reformers believed, to the contrary, that women's entry into the political process could permanently transform it for the better without transforming them for the worse. As one 1869 article in the *Iowa Temperance Standard* put it, woman should "take her sphere with her" into corrupt male spaces.[52] If they remained grounded in their own morally safe domestic world, women could make brief forays into the space of politics without losing their purity and volitional strength.

As radical as it was for women to demand the vote, female invasions of the polls, like other female invasions, could ultimately have some conservative implications. Indeed, a popular argument among temperance reformers calling for woman suffrage was that they could vote and still be home to make their husbands dinner. In the presidential elections of November 1872, southern temperance reformer Elizabeth Avery Meriwether cast a vote.[53] Although she both registered and voted, she was never arrested for having done so. Somewhat ironically, it was almost certainly the clash between recently enfranchised African Americans and their Republican allies, and violent conservative white groups like the Ku Klux Klan that made her vote possible. Meriwether, for all her reformist credentials, had become a passionate Confederate once the war began. Allowing such right-thinking white women to vote, and thus to challenge enfranchised freedmen, suddenly seemed less odious than it otherwise would have to many conservative white Southerners. Just as the heroine of Meriwether's temperance play had bound her drinking husband hand and foot in order to restore him to his position as head of the household, so Meriwether, when she voted, no doubt voted Conservative.

In casting her vote, Meriwether was participating in a national woman suffrage strategy. Indeed, the year after her vote, she spoke at the National Woman Suffrage Association (NWSA) meeting.[54] Under the NWSA plan, women's rights advocates interpreted the Fourteenth and Fifteenth Amendments as conferring voting rights on them, and a small number of women throughout the country first attempted to register and then entered the polls on election day, demanding their ballot.[55] Susan B. Anthony's participation in this strategy has received the most historical attention, but other noted women's rights advocates, including Victoria Woodhull and the Grimké sisters, also took part.[56] Virginia Minor, a temperance reformer in St. Louis and later a friend of Elizabeth Meriwether's, inspired—and lost—an important lawsuit with her participation in the same strategy.[57] This collective female invasion of polling places preceded the women's crusades by a bit more than a year and no doubt contributed to temperance reformers' choice of tactics. Some suffragists directly participated in temperance efforts. Susan B. Anthony, for instance, became involved in the women's crusades when they reached Rochester in the spring of 1874. While the Rochester group never actually invaded saloons, Anthony encouraged them to move in a more militant direction.[58]

Through the narrative of feminine invasion reformers ultimately addressed the problem of the individual as posed by the drunkard narrative. Women reformers imagined that they could step outside of their protected domestic confines to construct a virtuous and stable society. Once they had done so, there would be no further call for them to leave the home, for the home would no longer be threatened. Without drink and the saloon—and this is important to realize—there would be no further call for "home protection."

In the meantime, however, the act of entering into, or simply learning about, such forbidden spaces was fraught with consequence. When crusades leader Mother Stewart entered her first saloon, she "felt buoyed as if [she] was treading on the air."[59] The way civil damage act plaintiff Mary Fox talked about her experience outside a saloon doorway gives some impression of the weighty significance of the barrier. She followed her husband from their home to the saloon. "He went around to 10th street and opened the side door. It was left ajar. I was behind him. I touched the door and opened it a little wider, so that I could see everybody in the room and what was going on."[60] The pacing and language of Fox's testimony evokes a gothic novel or ghost story. What would be behind the door? As it turns out, of course, it was her husband purchasing liquor from the defendant. Yet such spaces were so terrifying and taboo for women like Fox that even standing in the doorway was a moment of dramatic tension. In temperance novels, virginal young girls who entered saloons in search of fathers died almost as frequently as young girls who were seduced in sentimental fiction. The saloon, like other improper spaces, posed a real threat to the integrity of those who entered it.

If men who had lost their volitional integrity were said to have lost their manhood, so women, once they had moved out of their domestic sphere and into impure male spaces, could be charged with having lost their womanhood. Accusing temperance women of being "manly" was a common rhetorical device of saloon defenders. Edgar Watson Howe's Atchison, Kansas newspaper characterized reformers as "Women with Whiskers and Bass Voices." An 1890 antitemperance novel depicted a prohibition dystopia in which temperance women, after succeeding in banning all alcohol, stepped into men's roles and took over their town, as their subdued husbands wore aprons and took care of the children. Rhetoric of this sort was frequent, and temperance women took it very seriously.[61] That they pursued their invasion strategy in the face of such critiques and insults points to the extreme value they placed in it.

Why did invading women think that they could get away with violating male roles and male spaces without making themselves vulnerable to the same forces that had undermined men's manhood? When Mother Stewart first became active in the struggle, she had "misgivings about getting the ladies" to rally behind the civil damage laws. She correctly suspected that they would avoid involvement in anything so tawdry. She "knew better than a gentleman could, what the effect upon woman's mind had been of the all-time teaching that they must not seem to know anything about the saloon or men's drinking, it was not lady-like."[62] Despite the initial lack of support from the "ladies," of course, Stewart did involve herself in the civil damage suits, beginning in January 1872.[63] One saloonkeeper's lawyer lambasted Stewart for her role, suggesting that "she had much better have been at home attending to her legitimate duties."[64] In fact, however, Stewart went much further than this into improper spaces: at one point, she dressed as an Irish washerwoman, purchased liquor in a saloon that was illegally selling on Sunday, bolted out, and kept the liquor as evidence and as a sort of trophy (fig. 7). If proper women could not hear about the insides of saloons (and the same held true for other impure spaces), even for a good cause, they certainly could not enter them with impunity. Just as men who entered the saloon were thought to compromise their volitional independence, women who did so were perceived as inviting challenges to their own purity.

Some, like Elizabeth Meriwether, answered this question by arguing that because of their fundamentally domestic nature reforming women lacked the unsettling "desires," the lack of stable contentment, that endangered men.[65] As she had "King Alcohol" lament in *A Devils Dance,* "The sex which for five thousand years has followed where men led, hath broke into rebellion, and now dares itself assume the leadership of human thought. . . . To our seductions, as a sex, they are impervious."[66] Many others agreed that women were sufficiently grounded in the home that brief forays into corrupt spaces would not penetrate their domestic armor. If "he who allows the tendrils of his heart to spread the farthest, and take the deepest, strongest hold of this, is the man who is most secure against all the temptations and evils of a siren world," surely the domestic sex had a distinct advantage over their male relations.[67] Like the middle-class reformers in Charles Sheldon's *In His Steps,* they could make brief entries into the world of fastness, bright lights, and danger, while remaining sufficiently grounded in the home to resist the invasive and seductive forces that awaited them there.

By far the best-known and most fully developed version of the narrative of female invasion was that lived by turn-of-the-century Kansas saloon-smasher

Fig. 7. Mother Stewart, "My First Glass," from Eliza Stewart, *Memories of the Crusade: A Thrilling Account of the Great Uprising of the Women of Ohio in 1873, Against the Liquor Crime* (Columbus, Ohio: William G. Hubbard & Co., 1888) (Photo courtesy of the University of Wisconsin–Oshkosh)

Carry A. Nation.[68] In her career, one can see the roots and the very radical implications of her answer to the problem of alcohol, gender, and influence. Nation's life, as she described it, was a continual series of entries into corrupt and filthy spaces. Though, early in her autobiography, Nation reprinted the popular temperance verse, "Touch not, taste not, handle not," she certainly did not live by this maxim.[69] Even before she had begun her saloon invasions, she served as a prison evangelist, a role she maintained throughout her life. As she explained her work with prostitutes, "There are diamonds in the slush and filth of this world. Happy is he who picks them up and helps to wash the dirt away, that they may shine for God. I am very much drawn to my fallen sisters."[70] She did not stop with merely touching the immoral. In one of her early spectacular attacks against alcohol, Nation tried to persuade a physician of the dangers of prescribing alcohol as medicine by purchasing some herself, bringing it to a temperance meeting, drinking it until she became intoxicated, then having her temperance sisters bring her to the doctor's office as a demonstration of its evils.[71] Later, when her invasions of saloons began in earnest, she often joyfully recounted the extent to which she "touched the impure thing." She recalled in her memoirs that during one of her noted saloon smashings, "I opened the bungs of the beer kegs, and opened the faucets of the barrels, and then the beer flew in every direction and I was completely saturated."[72] She exulted when forced to spend time in filthy jails after her raids. She justified her later career delivering temperance diatribes on the vaudeville stage by claiming that she performed in these morally questionable theaters because it was there that she was most likely to find people who needed her evangelical guidance, but it seems likely that hers was not an unwilling sacrifice.

Carry Nation, at the time of her saloon-smashing activity, was based in Medicine Lodge, Kansas, not far from Charles Sheldon and Edgar Watson Howe. Not surprisingly, both men had strong opinions about her behavior. While Sheldon supported Nation's goals and admired her passion, he questioned the use of private violence against saloons, insisting instead that the police should be made to enforce antiliquor laws.[73] Sheldon probably agreed with the position taken by Topeka's prohibitionist newspaper, *The Capital*, which insisted that "The strongest and most effective missiles women can aim at the saloon business are not brickbats, but moral suasion."[74] Even though the logic of his own argument in *In His Steps* pointed towards the impotence of suasion and the necessity of coercive force, it was one thing to propose force in theory and another to support it in practice.

Howe, of course, also opposed Nation's activities. Although he admitted to a certain level of sympathy for drunkards' wives who smashed the businesses of saloonkeepers who "regularly sell to drunkards, after being warned not to," Carry Nation was an entirely different matter.[75] Howe recognized the difference between a woman who attacked the saloon that had destroyed her husband and a boisterously self-publicizing, articulate, temperance-preaching woman on a mission to enforce the state's prohibitory laws. The latter, whatever her intentions, posed a serious and sustained challenge to male authority. On the same page on which he had expressed sympathy for saloon invasions by drunkards' wives, he stated his confidence that if Carry Nation came to Atchison, local officials would not "permit" her to "run things to suit herself." Perhaps, though, he was not so sure. He ended his article by suggesting that any officer who *did* let Nation get the upper hand "should be called upon by the people to resign."[76] A few months later, Howe reported a rumor that, inspired by Sheldon's week-long stint at running a newspaper "as Jesus would," Nation was planning to run "the municipal affairs" in her Medicine Lodge for a week. Howe assured his readers that the story was false and that if Nation attempted to exercise such political power, even as an experiment, "she will be sent to an asylum."[77]

Nation came to Atchison that spring as Howe had feared, though apparently she was in an unusually pacific mood. She did enter the towns' saloons but limited herself to denouncing the evils of drink. She even "jollied" the saloonkeepers, saying that "she didn't care what business a man was in as long as they have manhood about them."[78] The saloon-smasher and the discontented editor never met face-to-face; Howe, uncharacteristically, laid low during the visit. Nation, according to Howe, attempted to speak against him and his paper, but she was hooted down by the locals.[79] In avoiding violence, Nation did not give the men of Atchison the opportunity to test their mettle against hers. Despite male Atchisonians' bluster, however, it is not at all certain that she would have lost such an encounter. A few months earlier, some men had played a trick on an Atchison saloonkeeper who had been bragging that he would throw Nation into the street if she ever invaded *his* saloon. Unconvinced, one of his patrons dressed up as Nation and entered the saloon with an armful of rocks. The saloonkeeper apparently blanched and ran for cover.[80]

To a great extent, of course, Nation was merely continuing in the tradition of her crusading predecessors; an elderly Mother Stewart, recognizing this, was a great supporter of her "hatchetations." Particularly early on, Nation had enthusiastic and widespread though not universal support among mainline temperance reformers.[81] She was certainly working within a space they had created and enacting a narrative they had told and enacted time and time again. Yet the nineteenth-century reformers who had told the story of the drunkard's decline and answered it with that of the female invasion could never have imagined how powerful their stories would become. Temperance crusaders like Stewart, temperance novelists like Mary Dwinell Chellis, civil damage law plaintiffs like Louise Faivre, and the thousands of women of the nineteenth-century WCTU could hardly have imagined Carry Nation. Nation became a larger-than-life, hatchet-wielding parody of women's castrating power only because the act of female invasion had become much more powerful and much more threatening by the beginning of the twentieth century than it had been in the 1870s. As female political power gradually became more plausible, the political significance that had always been implicit in the narrative of female invasion became increasingly explicit. It should come as no surprise that the masthead to Carry Nation's 1905 newspaper, *The Hatchet,* read "The Ballot is your Hatchet."[82]

Conclusion

The story of the decline of drinking men like Andrew Faivre, and of the attempts of wives like Louise Faivre to save their homes from being destroyed, ultimately had a host of implications. When reformers saw such situations, they first wondered what could be done to alleviate them and set about trying to do it. However, they and many of their less-committed contemporaries did not merely act upon the drunkard narrative; more importantly, they talked about it. In exploring the message of the drunkard narrative and in imaginatively resolving its threats through the narrative of female invasion, temperance reformers confronted and came to terms with two of the most difficult intellectual issues of their period—how to carve out a space for individual autonomy in the face of environmental and hereditary forces, and how to rethink and maintain gender roles that had come to feel unstable in the last decades of the century.

The impressive persistence and pervasiveness of the drunkard narrative throughout a century of profound social, cultural, and intellectual change testifies both to its wide-ranging cultural resonance and to the depth of the issues that it addressed. Of course, it could be argued that the drunkard narrative remained so prominent largely because alcohol consumption remained such a problem. Yet all problems are constructed, and some constructed problems get more cultural attention than others. The drunkard narrative—in its exploration of the consequences of an individual's decision to take a glassful of his environment into his body—became a privileged space in which to contemplate the permeability of the boundaries of the self.

By the later part of the nineteenth century, some reformers interested in increasing women's opportunities recognized that their stories of women's victimization at the hands of their husbands and the narrative of the drunkard's decline could be brought together in politically fruitful ways. In particular, they began to appreciate the extent to which these two stories were the same story. Women were trapped in the home at the mercy of husbands who would not allow them to develop and use their womanly understanding to shape and improve their environment; similarly, drinkers were trapped in the saloon at the mercy of saloonkeepers who prevented them from having a true understanding of, or fruitful interaction with, the world beyond the saloon doors. It was in the intersection of these two stories, in the moment at which the woman marched determinedly out of her confining home and into the saloon to liberate the man trapped there, that many temperance reformers hoped to find a space for true individual volition.

The introduction of the narrative of female invasion, in its particular synthesis of women's rights and the drunkard narrative, was arguably the most important way in which the drink discourse nudged American intellectual life in new directions. Temperance women realized that the slippage between gendered and universal notions of "manhood" could serve not only as a burden but also as an opportunity, and they argued that their moral grounding in the home allowed them to serve as liberators of the saloon. That realization obviously could never fully resolve the problem of individual autonomy posed by the drunkard narrative. Like the rest of their discursive work, their resolution of the moral autonomy problem was fundamentally unstable. Their argument that women had a privileged position from which to restore male autonomy was based precisely in their exclusion from the male power structure. Women, acting out the "invasion" narrative, were not confined to the home, waiting for the return of the family patriarch. Rather, they were bursting through the saloon door, restoring the degraded drunkard to his manhood. Through the very telling of their narratives, through endlessly reciting them and contemplating their implications, reformers created a framework out of which new, more inclusive, ideas of gender and power would grow. Their rhetorical shifting of the problem of autonomy from women to men was an important part of the process through which homosocial male spaces and male political privilege ceased to make sense. The years immediately following the period we have considered saw the closing of some male spaces (most notably the saloon) and the gender integration of others (most notably the polls). The drunkard narrative and the narrative of female invasion were integral to the discursive work that paved the way for these social changes.

Woman suffrage, as much as national prohibition, would be the ultimate end of the female invasions. Carry Nation, Elizabeth Avery Meriwether, Mother Stewart, and their fellow female invaders were at once the apotheosis of temperance discourse and the symbolic opening wedge of a new system of gender relations. Confronted with the instability of gender roles and of the idea of individual autonomy in the nineteenth century, they had responded by imagining how both could be restored. Changing widespread cultural ideas about gender and its relationship to individual volition took many years and much cultural work. When women finally won national suffrage after World War I it was in large part a delayed reaction to the powerful ideas of temperance reformers in the previous century.

Early-nineteenth-century white men justified their monopoly on decision making in a democratic society with the assumption that men's freedom from domestic confinement and their direct interactions with the world of business and commerce gave them a privileged relationship to individual autonomy. Temperance reformers, through the course of the century, had turned this idea on its head, imagining men's forays from domestic spaces as a liability rather than an advantage. Reformers baldly refuted these assumptions and insisted that men's claims to political privilege were fatally flawed, but perhaps more effective than explicit denunciations was the reformers' work with the popular narratives that supported their goals. By appropriating, challenging, and subverting the stories that nineteenth-century Americans liked to tell themselves about gender and volition, they attacked ideas of female inferiority from the inside out. By substituting the drunkard narrative for the narrative of sexual seduction and by answering it with the narrative of female invasion, reformers destabilized and then rebuilt basic cultural assumptions about gender, influence, and power.

Notes

List of Abbreviations

ISA	Illinois State Archives, Springfield, Illinois
ISHS	Iowa State Historical Society, Iowa City, Iowa
ISLL	Iowa State Law Library, Des Moines, Iowa
KSHS	Kansas State Historical Society, Topeka, Kansas
MSLL	Michigan State Law Library, Lansing, Michigan
NMAH	National Museum of American History, Washington, D.C.

Introduction

1. 1880 U.S. Census, Monona County, Iowa.

2. Testimony of Andrew Faivre, *Louise Faivre v. John Mandercheid, John Arensdorf, and E. J. Ressegiu* (1902), Bound Briefs, ISLL, 50.

3. Ibid., 75.

4. Ibid.

5. Ibid., 51.

6. Testimony of Frank Harvey, *Faivre v. Mandercheid*, 130.

7. Appellant's Argument, *Faivre v. Mandercheid*, 58.

8. See George Melville Baker, *A Little More Cider* (Boston: Lee and Sheppard, 1870) and *We're All Teetotalers* (Boston: W. H. Baker, 1876). Also see Edgar Watson Howe, *Story of A Country Town* (Atchison, Kans.: Howe and Company, 1888), 89–90.

9. Harry Gene Levine, "Demon of the Middle Class: Self-Control, Liquor, and the Ideology of Temperance in 19th Century America" (Ph.D. diss., University of California, Berkeley, 1989); Mariana Valverde, *Diseases of the Will: Alcohol and the Dilemma of Freedom* (New York: Cambridge University Press, 1998).

10. John W. Crowley, ed., *Drunkard's Progress: Narratives of Addiction, Despair, and Recovery* (Baltimore, Md.: Johns Hopkins University Press, 1999).

11. John Quist, *Restless Visionaries: The Social Roots of Antebellum Reform in Alabama and Michigan* (Baton Rouge: Louisiana State University Press, 1998); Ian R. Tyrrell, "Drink and Temperance in the Antebellum South: An Overview and Interpretation," *Journal of Southern History* 48 (1982): 485–510, quote at 497.

12. H[enry] An[selm] Scomp, *King Alcohol in the Realm of King Cotton* (n.p.: Blakely Printing Company, 1887), 5.

13. "A Citizen of Teetotalton," *A Treatise: Or, Speculative Philanthropy. The Hot-Corn*

Question Enlarged (Nashville, Tenn.: Printed for the Author, 1859), 202; I. Newton Pierce, *History of the Independent Order of Good Templars* (Philadelphia: Daughaday & Becker, 1869), 232.

14. See Edmund B. O'Reilly, *Sobering Tales: Narratives of Alcoholism and Recovery* (Amherst: University of Massachusetts Press, 1997), 15.

15. Charles Willsie, *The Eye-Opener, or The Evil Fruits of the Prohibitory Law in Kansas* (Wellington, Kans.: n.p., 1890), 5–6 [Kansas State Archives, Topeka, Kansas, Prohibition Pamphlets, vol. 2].

16. Of course, temperance activists were well aware that there were female drunkards, and they worried, talked, and wrote about them a good deal. They very rarely spoke about them in terms of the drunkard narrative, however. The central moment of the drunkard narrative was the dramatic shift from promising young person to hopelessly lost drunkard that was occasioned by a single, quite understandable, slip of the willpower in consuming the fatal first glass. That story does not work well for women, since an upstanding young woman's choice to drink was much more difficult to excuse or empathize with than that of a young man. Most temperance people would have read it as a sign of preexisting immorality.

17. Crowley, *Drunkard's Progress,* is a useful and well-selected collection of antebellum drunkard narratives. For an account of antebellum drunkard narratives told at Washingtonian meetings, see Ian Tyrrell, *Sobering Up: From Temperance to Prohibition in Antebellum America, 1800–1860* (Westport, Conn.: Greenwood Press, 1979), 163–64. For a discussion of drunkard narratives on the antebellum stage, see Judith N. McArthur, "Demon Rum on the Boards: Temperance Melodrama and the Tradition of Antebellum Reform," *Journal of the Early Republic* 9 (1989): 517–40, and John W. Frick, " 'He Drank from the Poisoned Cup': Theatre, Culture, and Temperance in Antebellum America," *Journal of American Drama and Theatre* 4 (1992): 21–41.

18. J. W. Clapp, *Address at Holly Springs, Mississippi July 4, 1848* (Holly Springs, Miss.: Printed at the Office of the *Weekly Jacksonian,* 1848), 7 [Memphis/Shelby County Public Library and Information Center].

19. For an excellent discussion of how nineteenth-century Americans addressed female inebriety, see Catherine Gilbert Murdock, *Domesticating Drink: Women, Men, and Alcohol in America, 1870–1940* (Baltimore, Md.: Johns Hopkins University Press, 1998), 43–52.

20. See, for instance, "The Homestead Scheme," *The National Era,* October 25, 1849, unpaginated: "When we say the earth is man's heritage, we mean that it is the heritage of mankind, and not of men independent of women and children, which latter is the construction that human legislation has put upon this common grant."

21. My appreciation of the allegorical nature of the drunkard narrative comes from the work of Frederic Jameson; *The Political Unconscious: Narrative as a Socially Symbolic Act* (Ithaca, N.Y.: Cornell University Press, 1981) has been particularly helpful.

22. Howard C. Joyce, *The Law Related to Intoxicating Liquors* (Albany, N.Y.: Matthew Bender & Co., 1910), 475–560; G. W. Field, "Civil Damage Liquor Laws," *American Law Review* 43 (1986): 71–83; R. Vashon Rogers Jr., *Drinks, Drinkers and Drinking; or, The Law and History of Intoxicating Liquors* (Albany, N.Y.: Weed, Parsons, and Co., 1881), 184–208; W. W. Woolen and W. W. Thornton, *Intoxicating Liquors: The Law Relating to the Traffic in Intoxicating Liquors and Drunkenness,* vol. 1 (Cincinnati, Ohio: W. H. Anderson Company, 1910), 1837–2013; Jack S. Blocker Jr., *American Temperance Movements: Cycles of Reform*

(Boston: Twayne, 1989), 75, and *Give to the Winds Thy Fears: The Women's Temperance Crusade, 1873–74* (Westport, Conn.: Greenwood Press, 1985), 110, 118, 124–26, 132–33, 220–21. For an interesting description of the operation and effectiveness of the civil damage laws in the United States by an observer sent by the British government, see Evelyn Leighton Fanshawe, *Liquor Legislation in the United States and Canada* (London: Cassell and Company, 1893), 93–94.

23. J. E. Stebbins, *Fifty Years History of the Temperance Cause* (Hartford, Conn.: J. P. Fitch, 1876), 296.

24. J. C. Wells, *An Exposition of the Liquor Laws of the State of Illinois, and of the Decisions of the Supreme Court Thereon with Practical Suggestions for the Enforcement of Such Laws. Prepared in pursuance of the resolution of the Illinois WCTU at their convention, held in Decatur, Oct 1, 2, and 3, 1879* (Springfield: Illinois State Journal Print, 1880). The title page notes that Wells is the "author of *Separate Property for Married Women*, etc."

25. Gov. Horatio Seymour, "Objections to the Bill for the Suppression of Intemperance" (1854) [Wisconsin State Historical Society, Pamphlet 52-4586].

26. Ambiguous temperance novelists Metta Victoria Fuller and Walt Whitman and temperance farce playwright George Melville Baker were also prominent among linecrossers. Nicholas Warner's treatment of the theme of drink in the work of major nineteenth-century American authors uncovers many other such playful or troubled ambiguities. Nicholas Warner, *Spirits of America: Intoxication in Nineteenth-Century American Literature* (Norman: University of Oklahoma Press, 1997).

ONE: Volition

Epigraphs: "The Door of the Heart," *Templar's Magazine; A Monthly Publication Devoted to the Order of the Temple of Honor* (Cincinnati) 5 (1854): 30; J. E. Stebbins, *Fifty Years History of the Temperance Cause* (Hartford, Conn.: J. P. Fitch, 1876), 52.

1. Janet B. Hewett, *The Roster of Union Soldiers 1861–1865*, vol. 3, Illinois (Wilmington, N.C.: Broadfoot Publishing Company, 1999), 96.

2. Testimony of Claudius Richardson, *Rice v. Mapes*, p. 53 [*Rice v. Mapes* is included in the record of ISA Case Files, *People of the State of Illinois v. Frederick Mapes* (1873)].

3. Testimony of Bissell Rice, *Rice v. Mapes*, 39.

4. Testimony of Claudius Richardson, *Rice v. Mapes*, 53.

5. Defendant's proposed instructions to the jury, *Rice v. Mapes*, 77.

6. Brief of defendant in error, *Rice v. Mapes*, 6.

7. *Rice v. Mapes*, 73.

8. Brief of plaintiff in error, *Rice v. Mapes*, 2, 13.

9. Brief of defendant in error, *Rice v. Mapes*, 6.

10. Jack S. Blocker Jr., *American Temperance Movements: Cycles of Reform* (Boston: Twayne, 1989), 16–18; Pertti Alasuutari, *Desire and Craving: A Cultural Theory of Alcoholism* (Albany: State University of New York Press, 1992), 151–56.

11. Catherine Gilbert Murdock, *Domesticating Drink: Women, Men, and Alcohol in America, 1870–1940* (Baltimore, Md.: Johns Hopkins University Press, 1998), 9–10.

12. Thomas Pegram, *Battling Demon Rum: The Struggle for a Dry America, 1800–1933* (Chicago: Ivan R. Dee, 1998), 32.

13. Anonymous, *Female Influence or The Temperance Girl* (Boston: Massachusetts Sabbath School Society, 1837), 84.

14. "Rev. E. H. Chapin," *Templar's Magazine: A Monthly Publication Devoted to the Order of the Temple of Honor* (Cincinnati) 5 (1855): 222.

15. "A Citizen of Teetotalton," *A Treatise; or, Speculative Philanthropy: The Hot-Corn Question Enlarged* (Nashville, Tenn.: Printed for Author, 1859), 62–63.

16. Caleb Ticknor, A.M., M.D., *The Philosophy of Living: The Way to Enjoy Life and Its Comforts* (New York: Harper & Brothers, 1846), 95.

17. *A Treatise; or, Speculative Philanthropy,* 5.

18. Joseph Gusfield, *Symbolic Crusade: Status Politics and the American Temperance Movement* (Urbana: University of Illinois Press, 1963); Blocker, *American Temperance Movements,* 51–60; Ian Tyrrell, *Sobering Up: From Temperance to Prohibition in Antebellum America, 1800–1860* (Westport, Conn.: Greenwood Press, 1979), 199–201, 226–43.

19. Walter Whitman, *Franklin Evans; or, The Inebriate* (New York: Random House, 1929), 147.

20. John W. Crowley, "Slaves to the Bottle: Gough's Autobiography and Douglass' Narrative," in David S. Reynolds and Debra J. Rosenthal, eds., *The Serpent in the Cup: Temperance in American Literature* (Amherst: University of Massachusetts Press, 1997), 115–35.

21. John B. Gough, *Autobiography and Personal Reflections of John B. Gough* (Springfield, Mass.: n.p., n.d.), 15, 18, 28, 35, 36, 38.

22. Ibid., 66, 85, 173–78.

23. John W. Crowley, *Drunkard's Progress: Narratives of Addiction, Despair, and Recovery* (Baltimore, Md.: Johns Hopkins University Press, 1999), 14–15.

24. A. B. Grosh, *Washingtonian Pocket Companion; Containing a Choice Collection of Temperance Hymns, Songs, & Co.* (Utica, N.Y.: B. S. Merrell, 1843), 5.

25. *Templar's Magazine: A Monthly Publication Devoted to the Order of the Temple of Honor* (Cincinnati) 5 (1854): 30.

26. This paralleled the movement of another prominent reformed-inebriate speaker and writer, John Hawkins. See Crowley, *Drunkard's Progress,* 15.

27. Gough, *Autobiography,* 119–21.

28. Ronald G. Walters, *American Reformers, 1815–1860* (New York: Hill and Wang, 1978), 128.

29. Crowley, "Slaves to the Bottle."

30. Mark V. Tushnet, *The American Law of Slavery, 1810–1860* (Princeton, N.J.: Princeton University Press, 1981), 53; Ariela Gross, "Pandora's Box: Slave Character on Trial in the Antebellum Deep South," *Yale Journal of Law and Humanities* 7 (1995): 267–316; Eugene Genovese, *Roll, Jordan, Roll: The World the Slaves Made* (New York: Vintage, 1976), 25–31.

31. Helen Tunnicliff Catterall, *Judicial Cases Concerning American Slavery and the Negro* (Washington, D.C.: Carnegie Institution of Washington, 1926), lists other such cases throughout the antebellum South, including *Redman v. Roberts,* an 1841 North Carolina case (2: 93), and *Delery v. Mornet,* an 1822 Louisiana case (3: 470).

32. *Skinner v. Hughes* 13 Mo. 440, as reported in 97 ALR 3d 528, and *Harrison v. Berkeley* 32 SCL 525, as reported in 97 ALR 3d 528 [emphasis mine].

33. See, for instance, *John S. Godfrey v. Boston Old Colony Insurance Company, et al.* 97-568 (La. App. 4 Cir. 5/27/98), 718 So. 2d 441 (1998); *Douglas Christiansen, Respondent, v. James Campbell and Rosaleen K. Forcier* 285 S.C. 164, 328 S.E. 2d 351 (1985).

34. "The People of Color in Ohio Speak Out," *The North Star,* July 6, 1849.

35. Herman Humphrey, D.D., *Parallel between Intemperance and the Slave-Trade* (n.p.: John B. Haven, n.d.) [Newberry Library].

36. Robert R. Dykstra, *Bright Radical Star: Black Freedom and White Supremacy on the Hawkeye Frontier* (Cambridge, Mass.: Harvard University Press, 1993), has analyzed antebellum Iowan elections and shown a strong correlation between support for prohibition and positions on slavery and equal rights for African Americans. This is a theme throughout the book, but see, in particular, 124–25.

37. *Often Warned* (Richmond, Va.: Presbyterian Committee of Publication, 1861).

38. "A Physician," *Liquor and Lincoln,* undated pamphlet, ISHS, 3. This was written between the first battle of Bull Run and Lincoln's assassination.

39. Richard Hamm, *Shaping the Eighteenth Amendment: Temperance Reform, Legal Culture, and the Polity, 1880–1920* (Chapel Hill: University of North Carolina Press, 1995), 31.

40. "The Analogy of Slavery and Intemperance before the Law," *New Englander and Yale Review* 39 (1880): 374–84, quote at 376.

41. "Analogy of Slavery and Temperance," 379.

42. Grace Strong, *The Worst Foe: A Temperance Novel* (Columbus, Ohio: Wm. G. Hubbard and Co., 1886), 35.

43. Jane S. Collins, *Free At Last* (Pittsburgh: Murdoch, Kerr & Co., 1896), 114 [my emphasis], 163.

44. *Rice v. Mapes,* 77.

45. Appellee's argument, *J. E. Sansom v. James Greenough and Charles Bullock* (1880), Bound Briefs, ISLL, 5; appellee's argument, *Louise Faivre v. John Mandercheid, John Arensdorf, and E.J. Ressegiu* (1902), Bound Briefs, ISLL, 13.

46. Appellant's argument, *A. F. Bissell l, Administrator of Estate of Frank S. Law, Deceased v. Frank Starzinger* (1900), Bound Briefs, ISLL, 6.

47. Cecil E. Greek, *The Religious Roots of American Sociology* (New York: Garland, 1992), 59.

48. Walter Rauschenbusch, *Selected Writing,* ed. Winthrop S. Hudson (New York: Paulist Press, 1984), 178.

49. Washington Gladden, *Ruling Ideas of the Present Age* (Boston: Houghton, Mifflin, 1895), 84.

50. Phillips Brooks, *Perfect Freedom* (Boston: Charles E. Brown & Co., 1893), 107.

51. Henry Woods, "No Man Liveth to Himself," *Union Signal,* July 21, 1892, 5.

52. Thomas Haskell, *The Emergence of Professional Social Science: The American Social Science Association and the Nineteenth-Century Crisis of Authority* (Urbana: University of Illinois Press, 1977). T. J. Jackson Lears, *No Place of Grace: Antimodernism and the Transformation of American Culture, 1880–1920* (1981; reprint Chicago: University of Chicago Press, 1994), 34, takes up this issue as it was addressed by late-nineteenth-century antimodernists.

53. Ian Hacking, *The Taming of Chance* (New York: Cambridge University Press, 1990); Mariana Valverde, *Diseases of the Will: Alcohol and the Dilemmas of Freedom* (Cambridge: Cambridge University Press, 1998), 36–39, contains an interesting discussion of Dewey's and James's work on the relationship between the will, desire, habit, and the environment.

54. Herbert Spencer, *Principles of Psychology,* vol. 1 (New York: D. Appleton and Company, 1897), 500.

55. Franklin Henry Giddings, *Democracy and Empire: With Studies of Their Psychological, Economic, and Moral Foundations* (New York: Macmillan, 1900), 31.

56. Richard T. Ely, "Heredity and Circumstances," *Outlook* 48 (September 16, 1893): 505–6; James T. Kloppenberg, *Uncertain Victory: Social Democracy and Progressivism in European and American Thought* (New York: Oxford University Press, 1986), 227–28.

57. Lester Frank Ward, *Dynamic Sociology; or, Applied Social Science as Based Upon Statical Sociology and the Less Complex Sciences,* vol. 1 (New York: D. Appleton and Co., 1883), 50.

58. Ward, *Dynamic Sociology,* 44.

59. Rauschenbusch, *Selected Writings,* 178; Brooks, *Perfect Freedom,* 107.

60. Josiah Royce, *The World and the Individual* (New York: Macmillan, 1920), 238–39. The speech was delivered in January 1900.

61. Ward, *Dynamic Sociology,* 367.

62. Valverde, *Diseases of the Will,* 54–60.

63. Robert L. Dugdale, *The Jukes: A Study in Crime, Pauperism, Disease, and Heredity,* introduction by Franklin H. Giddings (1877; reprint, New York: Putnam's, 1910), 11.

64. Andrew Wilson, "What is Inheritance?" *Harper's Magazine,* August 1891, 358–60.

65. Nathan Allen, *The Effects of Alcohol on Offspring,* bound with Norman Kerr, M.D., *The Heredity of Alcohol* (New York: Published for the Woman's National Christian Temperance Union by the National Temperance Society and Publication House, 1882), 24.

66. Allen, *Effects of Alcohol,* 24.

67. Mary Zollinger Giele, *Two Paths to Women's Equality: Temperance, Suffrage, and the Origins of Modern Feminism* (New York: Twayne, 1995), argues that WCTU women maintained an abiding faith in individual volition through the progressive era. It is important to remember that there was a good deal of diversity within the movement on that, as every, issue. Still, I would argue that, on the whole, WCTU women had moved radically away from such a faith.

68. Mary Dwinell Chellis, *Wealth and Wine* (New York: National Temperance Society and Publication House, 1874), 48.

69. Julia Colman, *No King in America* (New York: National Temperance Society and Publishing House, 1888); William Hargreaves, M.D., *Lost and Found; or, Who is the Heir?* (Philadelphia: National Temperance Society and Publication House, 1901).

70. "Scrapbook," Meriwether Family Papers, Box 2, Folder 4, Mississippi Valley Collection, University of Memphis, Memphis, Tenn., 7–8.

71. Julia Colman, *Alcohol and Hygiene: An Elementary Lesson Book for Schools* (New York: National Temperance Society and Publication House, 1880), 113.

72. Wm. Hargreaves, M.D., *Alcohol and Science; or Alcohol: What It Is, and What It Does* (New York: National Temperance Society and Publication House, 1884), 76. See also T. D. Crothers, M.D., *Are Inebriates Curable?* (Danbury, Conn.: The Danbury Printing Co., 1892), 26, and George D. Lind, M.D., *Lessons in Physiology For Use in Schools, including Anatomy, Physiology, and Hygiene and The Effects of Alcohol and Other Stimulants on the Human Body and Mind* (Danville: Indiana Publishing Company, 1892), 173.

73. Ward, *Dynamic Sociology,* 69.

74. T[om] P. Taylor, *The Bottle: A Drama in Two Acts* (New York: DeWitt Publishing House, 1847), 38.

75. It is interesting to consider the relationship between fictional accounts of *delirium tremens* and of hysteria. They were both characterized by fits in which the sufferer was perceived to be out of control of his or her own body and out of touch with his or her surroundings. Both were extremely disturbing largely because they challenged ideas of

autonomous selfhood. As Gillian Brown has argued in *Domestic Individualism: Imagining Self in Nineteenth-Century America* (Berkeley: University of California Press, 1990), 63, "Hysteria seems, then, to exemplify the pathological potential in work, the negative effects of the dissociation between self and body that makes housekeeping the transcendent activity Beecher celebrates. The dynamic of disembodiment the hysteric displays, however, reduces her to nothing but a body."

76. Isaac Ray, *Treatise on the Medical Jurisprudence of Insanity* (1871; reprint, New York: Arno Press, 1976), 557–58.

77. George B. Cutten, *The Psychology of Alcoholism* (1907; reprint, New York: Arno Press, 1981), 55.

78. Martha E. Whitten, *The Drunkard's Wife* (Austin, Tex.: Hutchins Printing House, 1887); *The Itinerant's Daughter: A Temperance Story compositely written by members of Burlingame W. C. T. U., each taking a chapter* (Burlingame, Kans.: 1908), 2 [Kansas State Historical Society].

79. William J. Rorabaugh, *The Alcoholic Republic: An American Tradition* (New York: Oxford University Press, 1979), 151, explores drinkers' experience of autonomy. "While drinking in a group made the participants equals, it also gave them a feeling of independence and liberty. Drinking to the point of intoxication was done by choice, an act of self-will by which a man altered his feelings, escaped from his burdens, and sought perfection in his surroundings. Because drinking was a matter of choice, it increased a man's sense of autonomy. To be drunk was to be free. The freedom that intoxication symbolized led Americans to feel that imbibing lustily was a fitting way for independent men to celebrate their country's independence."

80. Mary Dwinell Chellis, *All For Money* (New York: National Temperance Society and Publication House, 1876), 142; James M'Closkey, *The Fatal Glass; or, The Curse of Drink: A Drama in Three Acts* (New York: Samuel French and Son, 1872), 25.

81. Rev. Emma Pow (Smith) Bauder, *Anarchy: Its Cause and Cure Told in Story* (Oakland, Calif.: Occidental Publishing Co., 1902), 179.

82. Mary Dwinell Chellis, *From Father to Son* (New York: National Temperance Society and Publication House, 1879), 404, 405.

83. Chellis, *From Father to Son*, 412. In the same novel, the father has a discussion with the temperate minister. He confesses that he "can't see why folks are any to blame for the way they are made up. It is the natural disposition of some folks to be cross, and ugly, and stingy. They show it when they ain't much more than babies, and they certainly don't know any better, do they?" (133).

84. Ian Tyrrell, *Sobering Up*, 252–89; Thomas Pegram, *Battling Demon Rum*, 25–42.

85. "Civil Damage Laws," *Standard Encyclopedia of the Alcohol Problem*, vol. 2 (Westerville, Ohio: American Issue Publishing Company, 1924), 617–18.

86. Ibid.

87. *Journal of Proceedings of the Twenty-Fifth Annual Session of the Wisconsin Legislature: Assembly* (Madison, Wis.: Atwood & Culver, 1872), 226–36.

88. For the fascinating minority report, which drew invidious comparisons between New England and Germany, see ibid., 772–75.

89. *Journal of Proceedings of the Twenty-Fifth Annual Session of the Wisconsin Legislature: Senate* (Madison, Wis.: Atwood & Culver, 1872), 385.

90. Ibid., 387–91.

91. Ibid., 442–44.

92. "An Act to Provide against the Evils Resulting from the Sale of Intoxicating Liquors," chapter 127 of *General Laws Passed by the Legislature of Wisconsin in the Year 1872* (Madison, Wis.: Atwood & Culver, 1872), 171–74.

93. *King v. Henkie* (1886) WL 85 (Ala.).

94. Instructions to jury, *Joseph Meyer v. Sophia Butterbrodt* (1891), ISA, 79.

95. See, for instance, discussion of *King v. Henkie* (1886) 80 (Ala.) 505, 60 Am. Rep. 119, in 54 ALR 2d, 1156: "Whatever wrong or negligence might be attributable to the defendant was not an approximate or efficient cause of death, because the defendant merely sold the liquor, and that in and of itself would not have produced the fatal result had not the decedent of his own volition, or as a result of his voluntarily having destroyed his senses, drunk the liquor." See also 97 ALR 3d 528: "At common law, it was not a tort to either sell or give intoxicating liquor to ordinary able-bodied men, and no cause of action existed in favor of these injured but the intoxication of the person so furnished, the reason usually given for the rule being that the drinking of the liquor, not the furnishing of it, was the proximate cause of the injury."

96. *Nolan v. Morelli* (1967) 154 Conn. 432, 437.

97. See Timothy Lytton, "Responsibility for Human Suffering: Awareness, Participation, and the Frontiers of Tort Law," *Cornell Law Review* 78 (1993): 492–95.

98. W. W. Woollen and W. W. Thornton, *Intoxicating Liquors: The Law Relating to the Traffic in Intoxicating Liquors and Drunkenness* (Cincinnati, Ohio: The W. H. Anderson Company, 1910), 1864.

99. Appellant's brief, *Carrie Kearney v. James Fitzgerald* (1876), Bound Briefs, ISLL, 37.

100. *Kearney v. Fitzgerald*, Bound Briefs, ISLL, 586. Notice, in this quote, the seeming elision of "influence" and compulsion. The judge is arguing that to be influenced by others is to lack volition. This is particularly interesting in connection with the early temperance opponents discussed at the beginning of this chapter who felt that moral societies threatened individual volition.

101. Testimony of Dr. Robert Boal, *William Roth v. Mary Eppy* (1874), Case Files, ISA, 225.

102. *Bissell v. Starzinger*, 10.

103. Instructions to jury, *Martha Lafler v. Edward L. Fisher, Henry Kirchgessner, and Enos Plumadore* (1899), Bound Briefs, MSLL, 127.

104. Appellant's argument, *E. M. Calloway, Appellee, v. James Laydon, Appellant* (1875), Bound Briefs, ISLL, 10.

105. *Bissell v. Starzinger*, 5.

106. Testimony of Elizabeth Engleken, *Elizabeth Engleken v. Hubert Webber and John Weston* (1877), Bound Briefs, ISLL, 13.

107. Testimony of Wiley Sanderson, *John Siegle v. Emma Rush* (1898), Case Files, ISA, 48.

108. Testimony of John Funk, *The People of Illinois for the Use of Anna Williamson v. James M. Smith et al.* (1890), Case Files, ISA, 112.

109. There is a good deal of recent scholarship on the question of the relationship between legal and fictional narratives. See, for instance, Richard A. Posner, *Law and Literature: A Misunderstood Relation* (Cambridge, Mass.: Harvard University Press, 1988); Natalie Zemon Davis, *Fiction in the Archives: Pardon Tales and Their Tellers in Sixteenth-Century France* (Stanford, Calif.: Stanford University Press, 1987); and Alan Hyde, *Bodies of Law* (Princeton, N.J.: Princeton University Press, 1997).

110. Argument for appellee, *Mary J. Judge v. John Jordan and Patrick O' Connor* (1890), Bound Briefs, ISLL, 1.

111. Appellee's brief, *John Meidel v. Mariah Anthis* (1873), Case Files, ISA, 4–5.

112. *Friend v. Danks* 37 Mich. 31, quoted in appellee's brief, *Samantha Rosecrants v. William Shoemaker and Charles Cole* (1886), Bound Briefs, MSLL, 10.

113. Argument for appellee, *Elizabeth Engleken v. Michael Hilger* (1877), Bound Briefs, ISLL, 2.

114. Testimony of Amanda Parker, *John W. Stringam v. Amanda J. Parker* (1896), Case Files, ISA, 47.

115. Argument for appellee, *Elizabeth Engleken v. Hubert Webber and John Weston,* Bound Briefs, ISLL, 4.

116. Argument for appellee, *Nancy Jewett v. Lorenz Wanshura* (1876), Bound Briefs, ISLL, 5.

117. Testimony of Amanda Woolheather, *Amanda Woolheather v. Frank Risley* (1874), Bound Briefs, ISLL, 13.

118. Argument for appellee, *Louise Faivre v. John Mandercheid* (1902), Bound Briefs, ISLL, 36.

119. G[allus] Thomann, *Real and Imaginary Effects of Intemperance: A Statistical Sketch,* (New York: United States Brewers' Association, 1884), 4.

120. Appellant's brief, *Woolheather v. Risley,* 54.

121. Appellant's brief, *Peter Ewen v. Ellen Wertz* (1878), Bound Briefs, ISLL, 5.

122. Argument for appellant, *Regina Bellison v. A. Apland & Co., Anfin Apland, and Arthur Gandrup* (1900), Bound Briefs, ISLL, 23–24.

123. Appellant's reply, *Louise Faivre v. John Mandercheid* (1902), Bound Briefs, ISLL, 2.

124. "A Very Daniel Come to Judgment," *Harper's Weekly,* June 28, 1873, 560.

125. David S. Reynolds, "Black Cats and Delirium Tremens: Temperance and the American Renaissance," in David S. Reynolds and Debra J. Rosenthal, eds., *The Serpent in the Cup: Temperance in American Literature* (Amherst: University of Massachusetts Press, 1997), 22–59, quote at 31.

126. Edgar Watson Howe, *The Story of a Country Town* (Atchison, Kans.: Howe and Co., 1888), 98.

127. John W. Crowley, "Paradigms of Addiction in Howells' Novels," *American Literary Realism* 25 (1993): 3–17.

128. Testimony of John Hable, *Douglas D. Lowry v. Sylvia L. Coster* (1877), Case Files, ISA, 49.

129. Defendant's response, *Jennie E. Woody v. John Coenen* (1876), Bound Briefs, ISLL, 4.

130. Argument for appellee, *Bissell v. Starzinger,* 5.

131. *George E. Jewell v. Patrick Welch, Herbert Babcock, and Andrew Haberstumpf* (1898), Bound Briefs, MSLL, 14.

132. Charge to the jury, *Harriet Dennison v. Charles W. Van Wormer, Myer Ephraim, and Thomas Doyle* (1896), Bound Briefs, MSLL, 35.

133. "From Scott County," *Iowa Temperance Standard,* June 10, 1869, 2.

134. Thomann, *Real and Imaginary Effects,* 66.

135. Starkloff, "To the Committee on Course of Study," a report to the public schools of St. Louis, Jan. 29, 1886, Elizabeth Avery Meriwether Scrapbook, Meriwether Family Papers, Box 2, Folder 4, Mississippi Valley Collection, University of Memphis, Memphis, Tenn., 7.

136. B[enajah] H[arvey] Carroll, " 'Personal Liberty': A Lecture by Rev. B. H. Carroll, D.D., Delivered at Waco, Texas, January 18th, 1887" (n.p.: n.d.) [Texas State Library]; Almer M. Collins, *Prohibition v. Personal Liberty, or, The Liquor Traffic Critically Examined in the Light of Science, Theology, and Civil Government* (St. Louis, Mo.: J. Burns, 1882). Herbert Asbury, *The Great Illusion: An Informal History of Prohibition* (New York: Doubleday, 1950), 106, describes the founding of the Milwaukee personal liberty league in 1882. See also Hamm, *Shaping of the Eighteenth Amendment*, 49–50. Perry Duis, *The Saloon: Public Drinking in Chicago and Boston 1880–1920* (Urbana: University of Illinois Press, 1983), 81, discusses the founding of Chicago's Liberty League in 1875.

137. Rorabaugh, *Alcoholic Republic*, 37.

138. George Maskoff, *Last Follies: A Drama in Five Acts* (n.p., 1890), 15.

139. E. N. Chapin, *Iowa Cranks, or The Beauties of Prohibition, A Political Novel*, 2 ed. (Marshalltown, Iowa: Hartwell Brothers, 1893), 12.

140. Starkloff, "To the Committee."

141. T. D. Crothers, M.D., *Are Inebriates Curable?* (Danbury, Conn.: The Danbury Printing Co., 1892), 26.

142. Instructions to the jury, *Augusta Thomas v. William H. Dansby, Amos Deming, and James Bennett* (1889), Bound Briefs, MSLL, 9: "The word 'intoxication' is plain English and easily understood and needs no definition."

143. Testimony of Clay Smith, *Rachel Huff v. Aulman & Schuster, William Aulman and John B. Schuster* (1886), Bound Briefs, ISLL, 8: "When he was drunk he used the word 'galvanize' a great deal. I don't know what in reference to." Testimony of Henry Young, *Joseph Meyer v. Sophia Butterbrodt* (1891), Case Files, ISA, 75; testimony of Edgar M. Beeman, deputy sheriff, *Elizabeth Doty v. Wellington Postal, Frank Postal, and Orville M. Bush* (1891), Bound Briefs, MSLL, 50; testimony of James Cascarden, *Harriet Dennison v. Charles W. Van Wormer, Myer Ephraim, and Thomas Doyle* (1894), Bound Briefs, MSLL, 32; testimony of Rose Ann Sankey, *Daniel McMahon and John Powers v. Rose Ann Sankey* (1890), Case Files, ISA, 106; testimony of Charles Mead, *Lafler v. Fisher* (1899), MSLL, 44.

144. Testimony of Martin Olson, *Andra Gullikson v. Otto Gjorund* (1890), Bound Briefs, MSLL, 19: "I thought I was not full, but I might have been full for all that I know"; testimony of J. Carmichael, *Nancy Jewett v. Lorenz Wanshura* (1876), Bound Briefs, ISLL, 45: "No, sir. It is a hard matter to tell whether he is drunk. Have seen him when he acted as if he was"; testimony of Marcel Dumas, *Catherine McMahon v. Marcel Dumas* (1893), Bound Briefs, MSLL, 19: "People don't act all the same when they are drunk, some sing and some dance and some holler. Some can walk straight and others cannot walk; some are noisy and some are very quiet" and testimony of Samuel Gimlet (bartender), 21; testimony of Louis Preitz, *Joseph Meyer v. Sophia Butterbrodt* (1893), Case Files, ISA, 60.

145. Testimony of Michael Kerns, *McMahon v. Sankey* (1890), ISA, 160: "Q. When do you consider a man the worse of liquor . . . A. You are getting too deep on that for me you know, I am not a physician"; testimony of William Edelmann, *Charles Hanewacker v. Harriet Ferman* (1894), Case Files, ISA, 451: "And as to the drunk part, I never saw it because I don't know that that means, drunk"; testimony of W.C. Holt [a manufacturer], *Agnes McIntyre, by Josephine McIntyre, her next friend, and Josephine McIntyre v. Bernard H. Anderly and James Triggs* (1905), Case Files, ISA, 67: "A. I would like to have a definition of intoxication . . . I do not hardly understand the rule as to where you draw the line of intoxication."

146. Testimony of Dr. Linton, *Maria Moreland v. Leon Durocher, Adam Hemmeter and*

John G. Schemm (1899), Bound Briefs, MSLL, 50: "A. I am 34 years of age; I have not had much practical experience in the drinking of lager beer . . . I have no personal knowledge of how many glasses of beer it would take to intoxicate"; testimony of Dr. Isaac Levere, *Marilla Van Alstine v. Phillip Kaniecki* (1896), Bound Briefs, MSLL, 24, "testified that . . . he is not in [the] saloon very often; that he don't drink; takes a glass of beer once in a while."

147. Argument and brief for plaintiff in error, *People of the State of Illinois v. Jacob Albrecht* (1874), Case Files, ISA, 5; testimony of Mr. Roach, *Robert McCann v. Rachel Roach* (1876), Case Files, ISA, 65; testimony of saloonkeeper and co-defendant "Jock" Reddick, *Baker & Reddick v. Emma Summers* (1903), Case Files, ISA, 299 and 311.

148. *Catherine Nagle v. John Keller and Peter T. McCarthy* (1907), Case Files, ISA, 183–84.

149. Testimony of Peter McCarthy, *Nagle v. Keller* (1907), ISA, 206.

150. Testimony of Daniel McMahon, *McMahon v. Sankey* (1890), ISA, 266.

151. Testimony of Dr. Linton, *Moreland v. Durocher* (1899), MSLL, 52.

152. Testimony of Mrs. Olive A. Tatt, *Jewett v. Wanshura* (1876), ISLL, 14.

153. Testimony of Eugenia Peacock, *Eugenia Peacock v. Daniel Oaks* (1891), Bound Briefs, MSLL, 36.

154. *Elizabeth H. Edwards v. Howard C. Woodbury* (1890), Law and Equity File Papers, File 2776, Massachusetts Trial Court Record Center, 6–7.

155. Testimony of Frances Cox, *Frances A. Cox v. W. B. Newkirk* (1886), Bound Briefs, ISLL, 3.

156. *Quarterly Journal of Inebriety* 12 (1890): 61.

157. A. B. Richmond, *Leaves from the Diary of an Old Lawyer; Intemperance, The Great Source of Crime* (New York: American Book Exchange, 1880), 122.

158. Rev. J. T. Crane, D.D., *Arts of Intoxication: The Air, and the Results* (New York: Carlton & Lanahan, 1870). Incidentally, the Rev. J. T. was the father of Stephen Crane; see George Moneiro, *Stephen Crane's Blue Badge of Courage* (Baton Rouge: Louisiana State University Press, 2000), 8.

159. George D. Lind, M.D., *Lessons in Physiology for Use in Schools including Anatomy, Physiology, and Hygiene and The Effects of Alcohol and Other Stimulants on the Human Body and Mind* (Danville: Indiana Publishing Company, 1892), 167.

160. George B. Cutten, *Psychology of Alcoholism* (1907; reprint, New York: Arno Press, 1981).

161. Ian R. Tyrrell, *Woman's World/Woman's Empire: The Woman's Christian Temperance Union in International Perspective, 1880–1930* (Chapel Hill: University of North Carolina Press, 1991), 123; James Timberlake, *Prohibition and the Progressive Movement, 1900–1920* (Cambridge, Mass.: Harvard University Press, 1963), 6.

162. For references to Sheldon's role in the broader context of Kansas reform and politics, see Robert Smith Bader, *Prohibition in Kansas: A History* (Lawrence: University Press of Kansas, 1986), 129, 136.

163. Charles M. Sheldon, *In His Steps: "What Would Jesus Do?"* (1896; reprint, New York: Grosset and Dunlap, 1935). The popularity of Sheldon's novel has persisted to the present in U.S. evangelical Christian circles. Not only is the book still in print with a number of presses, but there was, in the late 1990s, a large national marketing of "WWJD" (What Would Jesus Do?) T-shirts, belt buckles, bumper stickers, etc.

164. Ibid., 87; 96.

165. Ibid., 59; 60; 64; 66; 78–79; 80; 61, 64; 99; 101; 117.

166. Ibid., 111.

167. Ibid., 86.
168. Ibid., 197.

TWO: Manhood

1. Testimony of Henry "Chicken" Johnson, *Baker and Reddick v. Emma Summers* (1903), Case Files, ISA, 51; 1900 U.S. Census, Ill., DeWitt County, Nixon Township, Weldon Village. S. D. 7, E. D. 41.

2. Testimony of Zeke Lane, *Baker v. Summers* (1903), ISA, 259.

3. Testimony of Dick Greenwood, *Baker v. Summers* (1903), ISA, 76.

4. Testimony of C. C. Murdock, *Baker v. Summers* (1903), ISA, 98.

5. Record of *People v. Dock Marcum* decision, *Baker v. Summers.* For a discussion of nineteenth-century theories about self-defense, see Richard Maxwell Brown, *No Duty to Retreat: Violence and Values in American History and Society* (New York: Oxford University Press, 1991).

6. *Baker and Reddick v. Emma Summers* 201 Ill 52; 66 N.E. 302; 1903 Ill LEXIS 2680. 1900 U.S. Census, Ill., DeWitt County, Nixon Township, Weldon Village. S. D. 7, E. D. 41.

7. Eve Kosofsky Sedgwick, *The Coherence of Gothic Conventions* (New York: Methuen, 1986); Gillian Brown, *Domestic Individualism: Imagining Self in Nineteenth-Century America* (Berkeley: University of California Press, 1990).

8. Shawn Michelle Smith, *American Archives: Gender, Race, and Class in Visual Culture* (Princeton, N.J.: Princeton University Press, 1999), 11.

9. Ruth M. Alexander, " 'We Are Engaged As a Band of Sisters': Class and Domesticity in the Washingtonian Temperance Movement, 1840–1850," *Journal of American History* 75 (1988), 782.

10. Louise Michele Newman, *White Women's Rights: The Racial Origins of Feminism in the United States* (New York: Oxford University Press, 1999), 56. For another excellent treatment of the significance of "influence" in late-nineteenth-century reform thought, see Beryl Satter, *Each Mind a Kingdom: American Women, Sexual Purity, and the New Thought Movement, 1875–1920* (Berkeley: University of California Press, 1999). Gillian Brown, "Getting in the Kitchen with Dinah: Domestic Politics in Uncle Tom's Cabin," *American Quarterly* 36 (1984): 503–23.

11. Karen Sánchez-Eppler, "Temperance in the Bed of a Child: Incest and Social Order in Nineteenth-Century America," in David S. Reynolds and Debra Rosenthal, eds., *The Serpent in the Cup: Temperance in American Literature* (Amherst: University of Massachusetts Press, 1997), 79–80, argues that children were preferred to adult women as agents of reform in temperance fiction because they posed less of a challenge to adult male authority.

12. "A Clergyman" [Rev. C. Reed], *Reasons for Not Joining the Temperance Society* (Richmond, Va.: n.p., 1836).

13. "A Protestant" [Mrs. A. E. Bray?], *Protestant Jesuitism* (New York: Harper Brothers, 1836), 69. Ralph Waldo Emerson had the same objection to pledge-signing. See Nicholas O. Warner, *Spirits of America: Intoxication in Nineteenth-Century American Literature* (Norman: University of Oklahoma Press, 1997), 35. See also a discussion of nineteenth-century literary representations of the threats to volition posed by prohibitory legislation in David Reynolds, "Black Cats and Delirium Tremens," in Reynolds and Rosenthal, *Serpent in the Cup,* 30. This free will issue may well explain why, as Ian Tyrrell has pointed out, some southern churches actually excommunicated members of antebellum temper-

ance societies. Ian Tyrrell, *Sobering Up: From Temperance to Prohibition in Antebellum America, 1800–1860* (Westport, Conn.: Greenwood Press, 1979), 56.

14. "A Protestant," *Protestant Jesuitism*, 69–70.

15. Ibid., 29. The author discusses Maria Monk's *Awful Disclosures*, though she rejects its truthfulness.

16. Of course, women occasionally made appearances in these "all male" saloons, whether they were immigrant women picking up a bucket of beer to bring home for dinner, members of the saloonkeeper's family helping him with the business, or prostitutes plying their trade. Even in the face of these exceptions, however, contemporaries perceived saloons to be, and they more or less were, "thoroughly male institutions," as Jon M. Kingsdale has described urban saloons. See Jon M. Kingsdale, "The 'Poor Man's Club': Social Functions of the Working-Class Saloon," *American Quarterly* 25 (1973), 485.

17. These images parallel the "two competing mythic dramas" of the "frail and endangered adolescent male" whose bad habits led to uncontrollable instincts potentially "culminating in death" and the "autonomous young man of the frontier" discussed in Caroll Smith-Rosenberg, "Davy Crockett as Trickster: Pornography, Liminality, and Symbolic Inversion in Victorian America," in *Disorderly Conduct: Visions of Gender in Victorian America* (New York: Knopf, 1985), 91–92. Both E. Anthony Rotundo, *American Manhood: Transformations in Masculinity from the Revolution to the Modern Era* (New York: Basic Books, 1993), 180, and Catherine Gilbert Murdock, *Domesticating Drink: Women, Men, and Alcohol in America, 1870–1940* (Baltimore, Md.: Johns Hopkins University Press, 1998), 15, point out this seeming contradiction.

18. Rotundo, *American Manhood;* Gail Bederman, *Manliness and Civilization: A Cultural History of Gender and Race in the United States, 1880–1917* (Chicago: University of Chicago Press, 1995), 17; Kim Townsend, *Manhood at Harvard: William James and Others* (Cambridge, Mass.: Harvard University Press, 1996), Elliott Gorn, *The Manly Art: Bare-Knuckle Prize Fighting in America* (Ithaca, N.Y.: Cornell University Press, 1986), 192–93.

19. For a discussion of manly identity among late-nineteenth-century railroad men, see John Williams-Searle, "Courting Risk: Disability, Masculinity, and Liability on Iowa's Railroads, 1868–1900," *Annals of Iowa* 58 (1999), 27–77.

20. Of course, even those saloongoers who were self-employed probably did feel threatened by "the octopus." They were in a perilous economic position, aware that their prosperity depended on distant forces such as railroad directors and commodities brokers. For a discussion of the crisis of manhood as experienced by Kansans in the Gilded Age, for instance, see Michael Lewis Goldberg, *An Army of Women: Gender and Politics in Gilded Age Kansas* (Baltimore, Md.: Johns Hopkins University Press, 1997), 148–71. As shown in Perry Duis, *The Saloon: Public Drinking in Chicago and Boston 1880–1920* (Urbana: University of Illinois Press, 1983), 15–47, late-nineteenth-century saloons were increasingly owned or controlled by national brewing companies.

21. Duis, *The Saloon*, 274–303; Madelon Powers, "Decay from Within: The Inevitable Doom of the American Saloon," in Susanna Barrows and Robin Room, eds., *Drinking: Behavior and Belief in Modern History* (Berkeley: University of California Press, 1991), 112–31. Murdock, *Domesticating Drink*, 83, explores the same question.

22. In some states, "civil damage laws" were known as "dramshop laws." Ernest Hurst Cherrington, ed., "Civil Damage Laws," in *Standard Encyclopedia of the Alcohol Problem* (Westerville, Ohio: National Issues Publishing House, 1925–30), 617. Colorado, Connecticut, Delaware, Illinois, Indiana, Iowa, Kansas, Maine, Massachusetts, Michigan, Ne-

braska, New Hampshire, New Mexico, New York, North Carolina, Ohio, Pennsylvania, Rhode Island, Vermont, West Virginia, and Wisconsin passed these laws between the 1840s and the 1890s. Jack Blocker cites this information in *"Give to the Winds Thy Fears": The Women's Temperance Crusade, 1873–1874* (Westport, Conn.: Greenwood Press, 1985), 115. See Duis, *The Saloon*, 98.

23. Testimony of Peter Ewen, *Peter Ewen v. Ellen Wertz* (1878), Bound Briefs, ISLL, 32: "He would come in from the country at ten or eleven o'clock, as farmers do, and call for bologna and boiled eggs, and sometimes would ask for a glass of beer to drink with it." On urination troughs, see Madelon Powers, *Faces along the Bar: Lore and Order in the Working-man's Saloon: 1870–1920* (Chicago: University of Chicago Press, 1998), 30–31. On the nature of saloon camaraderie see Kingsdale, "Poor Man's Club," 472–89; Powers, *Faces along the Bar;* Roy Rosenzweig, *Eight Hours for What We Will: Workers and Leisure in an Industrial City, 1870–1920* (New York: Cambridge University Press, 1983); Thomas Noel, *The City and the Saloon: Denver 1858–1916* (Lincoln: University of Nebraska Press, 1982); Duis, *The Saloon;* and George Ade, *The Old-Time Saloon: Not Wet—Not Dry Just History* (New York: Ray Long & Richard R. Smith, Inc., 1931).

24. Albert J. Bellows, M.D., *The Philosophy of Eating* (New York: Hurd and Houghton, 1868), 222; Joel Dorman Steele, *Hygienic Physiology, with Special Reference to the Use of Alcoholic Drinks and Narcotics, Being a Revised Edition of the Fourteen Weeks in Human Physiology* (New York: A. S. Barnes & Co., 1888), 140; Rev. J. T. Crane, *Arts of Intoxication: The Air, and the Results* (New York: Carlton & Lanahan, 1870). John B. Gough, "Risky Business," in *Tipton (Iowa) Advertiser,* March 20, 1862: "It is a risky business to touch the brain, and it is the business of alcohol to do it."

25. Lee Edelman, in his *Homographies: Essays in Gay Literary and Cultural Theory* (New York: Routledge, 1994), 50–51, uses the phrase "enacting manhood" in a different context. Dana D. Nelson, *National Manhood Capitalist Citizenship and the Imagined Fraternity of White Men* (Durham, N.C.: Duke University Press, 1998), 81–82, appropriates the phrase. Testimony of Robert Connelly, *C. S. McVey v. William Manatt* (1884), Bound Briefs, ISLL, 14. Connelly, a fifty-nine-year-old laborer, claimed to have kicked a "Johnny Reb" and his son out of the saloon. Testimony of Richard Setchfield, *Augusta Thomas v. William H. Dansby, Amos Deming, and James Bennett* (1889), Bound Briefs, MSLL, 61.

26. Gorn, *Manly Art,* gives full emphasis to the competitive nature of saloon interactions. Testimony of G. H. Crawford and Gideon Cooper, *Hugh M. Shorb v. Keturah Webber* (1900), Case Files, ISA, 124, 130; Testimony of Henry Spiegel, *Nancy Jewett v. Lorenz Wanshura* (1874), Bound Briefs, ISLL, 41; Noel, *City and the Saloon,* 91; Testimony of Louis Haussler, *Nancy Jewett v. Lorenz Wanshura* (1876), Bound Briefs, ISLL, 43: "Q. Is it not a fact that he can drink any six men in Monticello drunk? A. He never tried me."

27. Declaration of plaintiff, *Augusta Thomas v. William H. Dansby, Amos Deming, and James Bennett* (1889), Bound Briefs, MSLL, 3. For A. A. Free's teary confession, see testimony of Margaret Wells, *Thomas v. Dansby;* testimony of Harry Lott, *Winnifred Woodring, a minor, by Mary Woodring, Guardian ad Litem v. P. Jacobino* (1908), Case #7653, Washington State Archives, Olympia, Wash., 83, and testimony of Garfield Hamilton, *Woodring v. Jacobino,* 88.

28. Testimony of John Kyle, *People of the State of Illinois v. Jacob Albrecht* (1874), Case Files, ISA, 14.

29. Deposition of William Reneer, *Ruth Reneer v. Rosina Zibold and Emma Haegelin, partners in the firm doing business under the firm name . . . of Zibold and Haegelin* (1901), Case

#8738, Atchison County Court House, Atchison, Kans., 3. The defendants, female saloon-owners, were the widows of the original partners.

30. *Ambrose Betting et al. v. Tarjon O. Hobbett* (1890), Case Files, ISA. Andrew Larson, who was boarding with the Hobbetts, and Ole Hobbett were run over by a train on their way back from a saloon. Defense attorneys argued that they were run over not because they were too intoxicated to move off the tracks but because they were fighting over Tarjon. According to a defense witness, they had begun quarreling over Tarjon in the saloon. Tarjon's attorneys denied this, and they prevailed, but the transcript suggests that, whether or not it led to their deaths, they had been quarreling over Tarjon in the barroom.

31. Testimony of James Powell, *Elizabeth Doty v. Wellington Postal, Frank Postal, and Orville M. Bush* (1889), Bound Briefs, MSLL, 27.

32. Testimony of William Baldridge, *Woodring v. Jacobino*, 28.

33. Edw. Carswell, *John Swig: The Effect of Jones' Argument* (n.p.: 1871) [Oshkosh Public Museum].

34. "Self Respect," *(Marshalltown) Iowa Temperance Standard,* June 10, 1869, 4. Abby Eldridge, *Norman Brill's Life-Work* (New York: National Temperance Society and Publishing House, 1875), 62; Grace Strong, *The Worst Foe: A Temperance Novel* (Columbus, Ohio: n.p., 1885); *The Itinerant's Daughter: A Temperance Story compositely written by members of Burlingame W. C. T. U., each taking a chapter* (Burlingame, Kans.: 1908) [Kansas State Historical Society].

35. Arthur West, "Night Owls," (New York, 1894); "Rollicking Rams," in *Emma Grattan's Favorite Songs* (Boston, 1869); "Rollicking Rams," in *Elise Holt's Celebrated Songs* (Boston, 1869); "Hi! Waiter," as sung by Miss Ella Wesner, composed for Zitella and Flynn, (New York, 1888). All of these songs are located in the Lester Levy Sheet Music collection of the Johns Hopkins University, Box 98–99. On drinkers not interested in their wives, see "Hi! Waiter," which contains the line, "There's my wife I've not seen for a year / and she has not seen me for a week."

36. Testimony of William Ferman, *Charles Hanewacker v. Harriet Ferman* (1894), Case Files, ISA, 339.

37. Testimony of W. H. Parker, *Maria Smith v. John J. Mayers, Harry H. Miller, Chris Haker and Charles Lowentrout* (1885), Case Files, ISA, 86. Similarly, see testimony of Mr. Roach, *Rachel Roach v. Robert McCann* (1876), Case Files, ISA, 81: "I call a man intoxicated when he can't attend to his business"; testimony of Rose Anne Sankey, *Daniel McMahon and John Powers v. Rose Ann Sankey* (1890), Case Files, ISA, 106: "Q. Do you make any distinction between drunkenness and intoxication? When do you consider a man drunk? A. I consider a man drunk when he is not able to attend to his duty and to his business."

38. Testimony of Charles McRoberts, *Olive Bell v. August Zelmer, Jacob Schmoltz, and Bartholomew Kennedy* (1886), Bound Briefs, MSLL, 40; summary of testimony of Bernard Worth, *Marilla Van Alstine, Appellant v. Phillip Kaniecki, et al.* (1895), Bound Briefs, MSLL, 18: "On cross-examination witness testified that when a man is drunk he will lie down; as long as he stands up and does his own business, walking around and doing his own business and talking, he don't consider him drunk." Of course there was some slippage in this identification between intoxication and the inability to do one's business. In the testimony of William Courney, *Nettie Wood v. Joseph Lentz* (1898), Bound Briefs, MSLL, 24, for instance, Courney testified that he had "never saw Wood so drunk but that he could attend to his business all right," which seems to suggest that one could be drunk without being too drunk to take care of one's business.

39. Testimony of William Horner, *Eugenia Peacock v. Daniel Oaks* (1891), Bound Briefs, MSLL, 58.

40. Testimony of Frank Wietke, *Clara Cramer v. Charles W. Danielson* (1894), Bound Briefs, MSLL, 15.

41. Testimony of William Loomer, *Hugh M. Shorb v. Keturah Webber* (1899), Case Files, ISA, 135.

42. See, for instance, John H. Allen, *The Fruits of the Wine Cup: A Drama, in Three Acts* (New York: Happy Hours Company, 1858), 12, 15; George M. Baker, *The Tempter; or, The Sailor's Return* (1866; reprint, Boston: W. H. Baker, 1894), 75; William Comstock, *Rum; or, The First Glass: A Drama in Three Acts* (New York: Robert M. DeWitt, 1875), 4.

43. Testimony of Frank Harvey, *Louise Faivre v. John Mandercheid, John Arensdorf, and E. J. Ressegiu* (1902), Bound Briefs, ISLL, 130; testimony of William Blakesley, *Rachel Huff v. Aulman & Schuster* (1886), Bound Briefs, ISLL, 35, and testimony of Warren Harris, 12; testimony of W. W. Buell, *Mary J. Judge v. John Jordan and Patrick O' Connor* (1889), Bound Briefs, ISLL, 22.

44. Testimony of C. C. Murdock, *Baker v. Summers,* Case Files, ISA, 98. When asked why he thought Doc Marcum had been intoxicated, Murdock replied, "Well, on account of [his] putting in there where he had no business, I thought: interfering." The idea of minding one's own business, of course, was not restricted to saloongoers. Intriguingly, one of Harriet Beecher Stowe's temperance stories, about an intemperate wealthy man and his family who descend into poverty as neighbors fail to intervene, is ironically entitled "Let Every Man Mind His Own Business," *Betty's Bright Idea* (New York: Ford, 1875).

45. In the civil damage courtroom, attorneys frequently accused those who had witnessed or attempted to assist the drunkard in question of having been intoxicated themselves. See, for instance, testimony of Andrew Grover, *Betting v. Hobbett,* 88; testimony of John MacAlvory, *William Roth v. Mary Eppy* (1875), Case Files, ISA, 157.

46. For a discussion of the threat of voyeurism to identity in nineteenth-century fiction, see Gillian Brown, *Domestic Individualism: Imagining Self in Nineteenth-Century America* (Berkeley: University of California Press, 1990), 115. Testimony of Fred Slater, *Nettie Wood v. Joseph Lentz* (1898), MSLL, 23: "I never paid any attention to it. I thought it was none of my business." In *Roth v. Eppy,* the drinker at issue was the twenty-six-year-old German-immigrant plaintiff, Mary Eppy. In a German community, during a party in the room above the saloon, some women sat in the barroom. Witness Robert Jeffry insisted, "I can't recollect what she drank, I did not consider it my business to see what the lady drank" (310). Another witness in the same case, Moses Ayers, similarly avoided noticing Mary Eppy's husband's comportment, "Him getting tight was none of my business. I did not bear it in mind nor take any account of it" (333). In the same case, Patrick Cartin, a fireman, testified that he had not noticed whether Eppy's husband had become a drunkard, "I cannot tell. I had my own business to attend to." For a similar argument, see testimony of Henry Hammers, *Vertura Miller v. Henry Hammers* (1895), ISLL, 15. In contrast, consider the testimony of William H. Hammond from *McMahon v. Sankey.* Hammond, a former tugboat captain currently running a pop-wagon, was more brazen than many witnesses. He had observed Sankey dangerously attempting to board a moving streetcar with his pipe hanging upside-down, and had assisted him. After his detailed testimony about Sankey's intoxication, defense attorneys insinuated that he had been inappropriately interested in the affairs of another. "Q. Do you mean to say you were

watching through the window all the time? A. Yes, sir. Just watching that man. Q. That was your sole business at that time? A. Yes sir, all that time" (118). Shortly thereafter, the defense attempted to portray Hammond as a drunkard.

47. Testimony of Joseph Williams, *John W. Stringam v. Amanda J. Parker* (1896), Case Files, ISA, 72.

48. Testimony of Mr. Lode, *Ambrose Betting v. Tarjon O. Hobbett* (1890), Case Files, ISA, 295.

49. Testimony of H. A. Schofell, *Ewen v. Wertz*, 30; testimony of Andrew J. Ridnour, *The People of the State of Illinois for the use of Anna Williamson v. James M. Smith et al.* (1890), Case Files, ISA, 110; testimony of Elmer Knutson, *Betting v. Hobbett*, 310: "A. I say he would have to be down before I would call a man drunk." Testimony of John Woods, *Joseph Meyer v. Sophia Butterbrodt* (1893), Case Files, ISA, 40.

50. Testimony of David Livingstone, *Jewett v. Wanshura*, 39.

51. Testimony of Harvey Gibson (railway engineer), *William Roth v. Mary Eppy* (1875), Case Files, ISA, 96, and testimony of John Gross (gas fitter and plumber), 184–85.

52. Testimony of Bernard Worth, *Marilla Van Alstine v. Phillip Kaniecki* (1896), Bound Briefs, MSLL, 18.

53. Elliott J. Gorn, " 'Gouge and Bite, Pull Hair and Scratch': The Social Significance of Fighting in the Southern Backcountry," *American Historical Review* 90 (1985): 18–43, quote at 41; Gunther Peck, "Manly Gambles: The Politics of Risk on the Comstock Lode, 1860–1880," *Journal of Social History* 26 (1993): 701–23. Pertti Alasuutari, *Desire and Craving: A Cultural Theory of Alcoholism* (Albany: State University of New York Press, 1992), 77–79, contains an interesting discussion of twentieth-century Finnish bar-goers, who apparently saw delegating self-control to others as a way of achieving personal freedom.

54. Testimony of Joseph Hermes, *Charles Hanewacker v. Harriet Ferman* (1894), Case Files, ISA, 423.

55. Testimony of George Webber, *Louisa B. Weiser v. Patrick Welch, Herbert Babcock and Andrew Haberstumpf* (1897), Bound Briefs, MSLL, 14.

56. Testimony of G. B. Duckworth, *Martha J. Duckworth v. Floyd Stalnaker* (1908), Case #1285, Supreme Court of Appeals of West Virginia, 43 and 46. West Virginia, of course, was culturally rather different from the Midwestern states from which most of my material comes.

57. Declaration, *Duckworth v. Stalnaker,* 8.

58. Testimony of G. B. Duckworth, *Duckworth v. Stalnaker.* Testimony of John Roach, *Robert McCann v. Rachel Roach* (1876), Case Files, ISA, 77–78.

59. Testimony of James Powell, *Elizabeth Doty v. Wellington Postal, Frank Postal, and Orville M. Bush* (1891), Bound Briefs, MSLL, 29. For a similar situation, see testimony of nineteen-year-old Charles Girard, *Baker v. Summers*, 159. "Q. Now it seemed to you that Marcum didn't walk exactly straight? A. Yes sir. Q. Did it seem to you that [sic] sidewalk kept still? A. Yes, sir. Q. Didn't it seem to you that the building went around? A. No, sir."

60. Argument for defense, *Hester Worley v. L. D. S. Spurgeon* (1874), Bound Briefs, ISLL, 18; brief of O. B. Ficklin, attorney for the defendant, *John Kellerman v. Phoebe Arnold* (1873), Case Files, ISA, 3; argument of appellant, *Frances L. Applegate v. John C. Winebrenner* (1885), Bound Briefs, ISLL, 13. All of these examples are from written briefs to superior courts, which one would presume would be more temperate than any oral comments in local courtrooms.

61. In the testimony of Thomas Heavener, *John Siegle v. Emma Rush* (1897), Case Files, ISA, 81, for instance, a witness appeared reluctant to testify to his saloongoing because his father was a juror. In other cases, witnesses and lawyers occasionally addressed one another by first names or exchanged inside jokes. A few briefs and case files include partial transcripts of jury selection, and from those it becomes apparent that, except in population centers like Dubuque or Detroit, many potential jurors knew the parties involved in the cases.

62. Testimony of Joseph Williams, *John W. Stringam v. Amanda Parker* (1896), Case Files, ISA, 71; testimony of Jerome Couture, *Maria Moreland v. Leon Durocher, Adam Hemmeter and John G. Schemm* (1899), Bound Briefs, MSLL, 24.

63. Testimony of Harry Miller, *Maria Smith v. John J. Mayers, Harry H. Miller, Chris Haker and Charles Lowentrout* (1887), Case Files, ISA, 151.

64. Testimony of William Ferman, *Hanewacker v. Ferman*, 338: "Q. What did you go there for? A. Why, I go into stores lots of times when I don't buy anything." Testimony of Walter Kohler, *Lafler v. Fisher*, 50: "I just went into the saloon on an errand; to see a man about working for me the next day; went right out again; did not stay over three or four minutes." Testimony of H. C. McLachlin, *Lafler v. Fisher*, 83–84: "I did not remain in there to exceed five minutes . . . did not stop to get a drink . . . I don't know what I happened to be in Kirchegessener's saloon for that night unless it was to get a glass of lager, and when I got it I went out. I did not go for a drink and I did not take a drink: I think it was simple curiosity; I had no purpose in going in there." "Q. Are you in the habit of going into saloons at nine o' clock to see who is in there?" Testimony of Ivan Lovelace, *Hugh M. Shorb v. Keturah Webber* (1900), Case Files, ISA, 121: "Q. Where were you? A. I was outside . . . There was a young man opened the door and hollered out and said Mr. Webber is drunk. I looked in and saw him." Testimony of Fred Lindsley, *Wood v. Lentz*, 23. Testimony of Thomas Caummy, *Ambrose Betting v. Tarjon O. Hobbett* (1891), Case Files, ISA, 273: "Q. But you don't drink? A. No, sir. Q. What do you go in for?" Testimony of William Edelman, *Charles Hanewacker v. Harriet Ferman* (1894), Case Files, ISA, 454–55: "Q. Do you drink in there? A. I drink soda water. Q. You drink soda water entirely? A. Yes sir. . . . Q. You like soda water, don't you?"

65. Amendment to motion for new trial, *Vertura Miller v. Henry Hammers* (1895), Bound Briefs, ISLL, 30; testimony of Jerome Couture, *Moreland v. Durocher*, 24; testimony of [Mr.] Whitney, a day laborer, *Douglas D. Lowry v. Sylvia L. Coster* (1877), Case Files, ISA, 32.

66. For accounts of the many social functions saloons fulfilled, see Kingsdale, "Poor Man's Club"; Duis, *The Saloon*; Rosenzweig, *Eight Hours*; and Powers, *Faces Along the Bar*.

67. Edmund B. O' Reilly, *Sobering Tales: Narratives of Alcoholism and Recovery* (Amherst: University of Massachusetts Press, 1997), 65–76; John W. Crowley, *The White Logic: Alcoholism and Gender in American Modernist Fiction* (Amherst: University of Massachusetts Press, 1994), 19–42.

68. Jack London, *John Barleycorn* (New York: The Century Co., 1913), 9.

69. Crowley, *White Logic*, 28.

70. London, *John Barleycorn*, 49.

71. Ibid., 7.

72. Ibid.

73. Ibid., 6.

74. Ibid., 338.

75. Ibid., 4.

THREE: Contentment

Epigraphs: J. E. Stebbins, *Fifty Years History of the Temperance Cause* (Hartford, Conn.: J. P. Fitch, 1876), 53; Samuel W. Small, "Deliverance From Bondage: A Temperance Sermon," in Rev. Sam P. Jones, *Quit Your Meanness: Sermons and Sayings of Rev. Sam P. Jones of Georgia with an Introduction by W. M. Leftwich, D.D.* (Cincinnati, Ohio: Cranston and Stowe, 1890), 504.

1. Testimony of Frank Wietke, *Clara Cramer v. Charles W. Danielson* (1894), Bound Briefs, MSLL, 15.

2. Testimony of Clara Cramer, *Cramer v. Danielson,* 5.

3. Ibid., 12.

4. Ibid., 8.

5. Clarence Tinker's exchange with judge, *Cramer v. Danielson,* 11.

6. Statement from the bench, *Cramer v. Danielson,* 22.

7. *Cramer v. Danielson,* 99 Mich 531; 58 N.W. 476; 1894 Mich LEXIS 739.

8. Karen Sánchez-Eppler, "Temperance in the Bed of a Child," in David S. Reynolds and Debra J. Rosenthal, eds., *The Serpent in the Cup: Temperance in American Literature* (Amherst: University of Massachusetts Press, 1997), 60–92, reads stories of the redemption of drunkards through daughters' love as accounts of the domestication of desire.

9. Harry Seymour, *Aunt Dinah's Pledge* (New York: Happy Hours Co., n.d. [late 19th c.]), 17.

10. See, for instance, "Always Look on the Bright Side," *(Marshalltown) Iowa Temperance Standard,* June 3, 1869, 6. This article criticizes "a discontented person" and advises, "It is true we cannot arrive at perfect happiness in this world; but let us not think because we have me with some trouble there is nothing worth living for."

11. This evokes the central argument in Robert H. Wiebe, *The Search for Order 1877–1920* (New York: Hill and Wang, 1967), applied to drink and temperance by Norman Clark, *Deliver Us from Evil: An Interpretation of American Prohibition* (New York: Norton, 1976), 29–30, 120.

12. Judy A. Hilkey, *Character Is Capital: Success Manuals and Manhood in Gilded Age America* (Chapel Hill: University of North Carolina Press, 1997), 102, 133. The story is still being recycled in Protestant sermons to this day.

13. Eric Foner, *Free Soil, Free Labor, Free Men: The Ideology of the Republican Party Before the Civil War* (Oxford: Oxford University Press, 1995), 13, explores a similar dynamic in his discussion of the tensions within the Protestant work ethic.

14. For a discussion of temperance reformers' concerns about the relationship among imagination, fiction, and social instability, see Alison M. Parker, *Purifying America: Women, Cultural Reform, and Pro-Censorship Activism, 1873–1933* (Urbana: University of Illinois Press, 1997), 52–53.

15. See J. G. A. Pocock, *The Machiavellian Moment: Florentine Political Thought and the Atlantic Republican Tradition* (Princeton, N.J.: Princeton University Press, 1975), and the enormous literature on republican political thought that has followed it.

16. For a discussion of the persistence of republican thought into nineteenth-century

culture, see Michael Denning, *Mechanic Accents: Dime Novels and Working-Class Culture in America* (London: Verso, 1987), 73; Sean Wilentz, *Chants Democratic: New York City and the Rise of the American Working Class, 1788–1850* (New York: Oxford University Press, 1984); and Ann Fabian, *Card Sharps, Dream Books, and Bucket Shops: Gambling in Nineteenth-Century America* (Ithaca, N.Y.: Cornell University Press, 1990), 165–68.

17. *Iowa Messenger,* April 7, 1887, 8.

18. For a discussion of the idea of desire as a fundamentally male characteristic in mid-nineteenth-century American literature, see Gillian Brown, "Getting in the Kitchen with Dinah: Domestic Politics in Uncle Tom's Cabin," *American Quarterly* 36 (1984): 503–23.

19. Kristie Hamilton, "An Assault on the Will: Republican Virtue and the City in Hannah Webster Foster's *The Coquette,*" *Early American Literature* 24 (1989): 135–51.

20. "A Lady" [Sarah J. Hale], *My Cousin Mary; or, The Inebriate* (Boston: Whipple and Damrell, 1839); M. F. Carey, *Adela Lincoln: A Tale of the Wine Cup* (Philadelphia: See, Peters & Co., 1854).

21. For a parallel, see Hamilton, "Assault on the Will," 142.

22. Hilkey, *Character Is Capital,* 133.

23. See, for instance Julia Colman, *Alcohol and Hygiene: An Elementary Lesson Book for Schools* (New York: The National Temperance Society and Publication House, 1880), 106: "Many a student has been sent home from college in disgrace, because he indulged in drink, while his sober, manly classmates whom he may have laughed at as 'slow coaches,' have remained and graduated with honor."

24. Jack London, *John Barleycorn* (New York: Macmillan, 1913), 228.

25. Rev. J. T. Crane, *Arts of Intoxication: The Air, and the Results* (New York: Carlton & Lanahan, 1870), 37.

26. R. Vashon Rogers Jr., *Drinks, Drinkers, and Drinking, or The Law and History of Intoxicating Liquors* (1881; reprint, Littleton, Col.: Fred B. Rothman & Co., 1985), 58.

27. Lucius Manlius Sargent, *My Mother's Gold Ring* (Boston: Ford and Damrell, 1833), 6.

28. "A Cloud of Witnesses who Testify to the Efficacy of the D. Leslie E. Keeley Double Chloride of Gold Remedies for Drunkenness" (Leslie E. Keeley Co., 1895), 21, 38, 61, "Whiskey," Box 5, Folder 7, Warshaw Collection, NMAH.

29. "A New England Journalist," *The Ramrod Broken; or, The Bible, History, and Common Sense in Favor of the Moderate Use of Good Spirituous Liquors: Showing the Advantage of a License System in Preference to Prohibition, and "Moral" in Preference to "Legal Suasion"* (Boston: Albert Colby and Company, 1859), 22.

30. Pabst Brewery, "Ominous Secrets" (1896), 36, "Beer," Box 3, Folder 16, Warshaw Collection, NMAH.

31. G[allus] Thomann, *Real and Imaginary Effects of Intemperance: A Statistical Sketch* (New York: United States Brewers' Association, 1884), 11.

32. E. N. Chapin, *Iowa Cranks; or, The Beauties of Prohibition: A Political Novel* (Marshalltown, Iowa: Hartwell Brothers, 1893), 19.

33. Pabst Brewery, "Ominous Secrets."

34. For a discussion of antebellum temperance as a path to social mobility, see Ronald G. Walters, *American Reformers, 1815–1960* (New York: Hill and Wang, 1978), 141, and Ian Tyrrell, *Sobering Up: From Temperance to Prohibition in Antebellum America, 1800–1860* (Westport, Conn.: Greenwood Press, 1979), 141–45.

35. In George Melville Baker, *The Last Loaf* (Boston: Walter H. Baker and Co., 1870), for instance, Mark Ashton, who is seduced into drink by a villain, wears "neat modern

dress" in Act 1 and a "rusty-black suit without collar, seedy appearance" in Act 2. The only other character described as wearing "modern" clothing is the villain himself, who wears "modern suits." In Nellie H. Bradley, *The Young Teetotaler; or, Saved at Last!* (Rockland, Maine: Z. Pope Vose, 1868), 2, the young villain, "a fast clerk," is "attired in flashy clothing."

36. *Samantha Rosecrants v. William Shoemaker and Charles Cole* (1886), Bound Briefs, MSLL, 2.

37. Plaintiff's declaration, *Olive Bell v. August Zelmer, Jacob Schmoltz, and Bartholomew Kennedy* (1889), Bound Briefs, MSLL, 2.

38. Plaintiff's declaration, *Nettie Brockway v. Robert Patterson* (1888), MSLL, Bound Briefs, 4.

39. Testimony of Mrs. S. S. Tingley, *Winnifred Woodring, a minor, by Mary Woodring, guardian v. P. Jacobino* (1908), Case 5168, Washington Superior Court, 47.

40. Lower court decision paraphrased in appellant's argument, *Regina Bellison v. A. Apland & Co., Anfin Apland, and Arthur Gandrup* (1902), Bound Briefs, ISLL, 7.

41. Both the wording and the interpretation of the acts differed from state to state and over time. In some states, and at some times, judges specifically denied that previously wealthy plaintiffs should be awarded enough damages to restore them to their former luxury.

42. *Female Influence; or, The Temperance Girl*, written for the Massachusetts Sabbath School Society and revised by the committee for publication (Boston: Massachusetts Sabbath School Society, 1837), 5; G. M. Baker, *Little Brown Jug* (1871; reprint, Boston: W. H. Baker, 1876), 7. Ian Watt, *The Rise of the Novel: Studies in Defoe, Richardson, and Fielding* (Berkeley: University of California Press, 1957), 65, argues that the "original sin" of Robinson Crusoe, the protagonist of what was arguably the first novel, was "Leaving home, improving on the lot one was born to . . . the economic and social embodiment of the 'uneasiness' which Locke had made the center of his system of motivation."

43. Walter Whitman, *Franklin Evans; or, The Inebriate* (New York: Random House, 1929), 45.

44. William Comstock, *Rum; or, The First Glass: A Drama in Three Acts* (New York: Robert M. DeWitt, 1875), 12.

45. Isaac Ray, *Treatise on the Medical Jurisprudence of Insanity* (1871; reprint, New York: Arno Press, 1976), 554–55. For a similar story, this time involving a man who received an $80,000 inheritance, see "A Convict in the Maryland Penitentiary," *Iowa Temperance Standard*, September 23, 1869, 8.

46. Steward Paton, M.D., *Psychiatry: A Textbook for Students and Physicians* (Philadelphia: J. B. Lippincott, 1905), 310.

47. For a discussion of the relationship of neurasthenia and drink, see Catherine Gilbert Murdock, *Domesticating Drink: Women, Men, and Alcohol in America, 1870–1940* (Baltimore, Md.: Johns Hopkins University Press, 1998), 15–16.

48. Mary Dwinell Chellis, *From Father to Son* (New York: National Temperance Society and Publication House, 1879), 46.

49. Thomann, *Real and Imaginary Effects*, 31.

50. Testimony of Dick Flynn, *John Siegle v. Emma Rush* (1897), Case Files, ISA, 132, and testimony of Emma Rush, 40.

51. Michael Warner, "Whitman Drunk," in Betsy Erkkila and Jay Grossman, eds., *Breaking Bounds: Whitman and American Cultural Studies* (New York: Oxford University

Press, 1996), 36. Warner argues that alcohol itself is not so much literally as symbolically important in Whitman's *Franklin Evans*.

52. Louisa May Alcott, "Fair Rosamond," ms. Am. 1130.13 (19) 73–147, Houghton Library, Harvard University, Cambridge, Mass., 7.

53. Metta V. Fuller, *Fashionable Dissipation* (Philadelphia: See, Peters & Co., 1854), 8. Metta Fuller's temperance writing is quite idiosyncratic, and was written before the temperance genre was well developed. Actually, Rosa ends up being saved from a union with a drunkard by handsome young mesmerist Pierre who, having won his own battle with alcoholic temptation, had the unique power of "diffusing a look of contentment wherever he went" (135).

54. Mary Dwinell Chellis, *Wealth and Wine* (New York: National Temperance Society and Publication House, 1874), 18.

55. Brief of appellant, *John Kellerman v. Phoebe Arnold* (1873), Case Files, ISA, 3, 5.

56. It is important to bear in mind that this is exactly what temperance reformers were accusing saloonkeepers of doing: entering into spurious "contracts" with drinkers in which they receive money but give drinkers nothing of value. As an 1849 article, "The Homestead Scheme," *The National Era*, October 25, 1849 (n.p.) put it, " 'the value received' by [the drinker's family] was a thousand fold worse than nothing[.] The father took, in exchange for his property, a broken constitution and a drunkard's fate. The wife was forced to trade a tender husband for a besotted beast."

57. Appellant's brief, *Carrie Kearney v. James Fitzgerald* (1875), Bound Briefs, ISLL, 46–47 [emphasis in original].

58. Appellant's brief, *Frances L. Applegate v. John C. Winebrenner and A. C. Sharp* (1885), Bound Briefs, ISLL, 5–6.

59. Defendant's response, *Jennie E. Woody v. John Coenen* (1876), Bound Briefs, ISLL, 4.

60. Gillian Brown, *Domestic Individualism: Imagining Self in Nineteenth-Century America* (Berkeley: University of California Press, 1990), 5, argues that whereas in earlier fiction, such as Rip Van Winkle, "the paradigm of the dreamer's flight from the shrew defined the domestic as a pole from which the individual must escape in order to establish and preserve his identity," later nineteenth-century domestic fiction strove to ground selfhood in domesticity.

61. "Prospect Brewing Company" (Philadelphia, Pa.) Advertising Card (n.d.) "Beer": Box 3, Folder 22; and "Stroh Brewing Company" Advertising Card (1908) "Beer": Box 3, Folder 32, Warshaw Collection, NMAH.

62. "Bartolomy Beer" [n.d.], "Beer": Box 2, Folder 8; "Dole Brothers Company" [n.d.], "Beer": Box 2, Folder 31; and "Quandt Brewing Company," "Beer": Box 3, Folder 23, Warshaw Collection, NMAH.

63. "Beer": Box 2, Folder 26, Warshaw Collection, NMAH.

64. "Wine": Box 4, Folder "Zimmerman, Peter" (n.d.), Warshaw Collection, NMAH.

65. Murdock, *Domesticating Drink*.

66. Testimony of Regina Bellison, *Bellison v. A. Apland & Co.*, 4.

67. In fact, more than being hypocritical, it sometimes invalidated the plaintiff's claim to recover by making her complicit in the very harm for which she sought damages. If a plaintiff was asking for compensation for her husband's having become a drunkard, rather than for a discreet instance of becoming intoxicated and being killed or maimed, and if the jury believed the defense's claims that she served alcohol in the home or

consumed alcohol with her husband, and if she could not convince the jury that her husband coerced her into doing so, she would generally not be eligible for damages.

68. Chapin, *Iowa Cranks*, 12, 46.

69. *An Address to the Citizens of New Orleans on the Subject of Temperance. Published by the order of the New Orleans Temperance Society* (New Orleans: Toy, Printer, Office of the Lafayette City Advertiser, 1841), 18 [Historic New Orleans Collection].

70. A. B. Grosh, *Washingtonian Pocket Companion; Containing a Choice Collection of Temperance Hymns, Songs, & Co.* (Utica, N.Y.: B. S. Merrell, 1843), 82–83.

71. T. P. Taylor, *The Bottle: A Drama in Two Acts* (New York: DeWitt Publishing House, 1847). This play may well have been written in London, but it was both published and preformed in New York.

72. F. L. Cutler, *Lost! Or The Fruits of the Glass: A Temperance Drama in Three Acts* (Clyde, Ohio: A. D. Ames, 1882), 9.

73. Clara B. Drake, *The Doom of King Alcohol* (Chicago: Workmen's Temperance Publishing Association, 1903), 11.

74. Testimony of Martha Johnson, *Martha Johnson v. Julius Schultz* (1889), Bound Briefs, MSLL, 46.

75. Plaintiff's brief, *Ann J. Wilson v. Frank Booth* (1885), Bound Briefs, MSLL, 2–3.

76. Testimony of Anna Peters, *Bridget Peters v. Henry Kehrig* (1879), Bound Briefs, MSLL, 7, and testimony of Margaret Peters, 10.

77. Testimony of Hester Worley, *Hester Worley v. L. D. S. Spurgeon* (1874), Bound Briefs, ISLL, 7. Plaintiff alleged that Robert Worley "had run them out of the house; they would go away and sit awhile till he had gone to bed."

78. Mother Stewart, *Memories of the Crusade: A Thrilling Account of the Great Uprising of the Women of Ohio in 1873, against the Liquor Crime* (Columbus, Ohio: William G. Hubbard, 1888), 35.

79. Appellee's brief, *Bellison v. A. Apland & Co.* (1902), 7.

80. Sarah Josepha Hale, *My Cousin Mary; or, The Inebriate* (Boston: Whipple and Damrell, 1839), 52.

81. See, for instance, Lizzie May Elwyn, *Dot: The Miner's Daughter; or, One Glass of Wine* (Clyde, Ohio: Ames' Publishing Co., 1888).

82. John H. Allen, *The Fruits of the Wine Cup: A Drama, in Three Acts* (New York: Happy Hours Company, n.d.). This edition lists the cast from performance at the Old Bowery in 1858.

83. Charles W. Babcock, M.D., *Adrift: A Temperance Drama in Three Acts* (Clyde, Ohio: A. D. Ames, 1880); S. N. Cook, *Out in the Streets: A Temperance Play in Three Acts* (New York: Dick and Fitzgerald, 1870).

84. Chas. Edward Prior (music) and A. C. (words), "Redeemed: A Temperance Song," (Boston, Mass.: C. D. Russell & Co., 1876) [Lester Levy Sheet Music Collection, Johns Hopkins University, Baltimore, Md.].

85. Plaintiff's declaration, *Jennie Franklin v. Henry Frey, Maria Frey, Gottfried Grau, Robert Mahrle, James Taylor, and James Hudler* (1895), Bound Briefs, MSLL, 8.

86. Plaintiff's declaration, *Eugenia Peacock v. Daniel Oaks* (1891), Bound Briefs, MSLL, 16.

87. John K. Cornyn, *Dick Wilson, the Rumseller's Victim; or, Humanity Pleading for the "Maine Law": A Temperance Story Founded on Fact with an introduction by Thurlow W. Brown* (Auburn, N.Y.: Miller, Orton, and Mulligan, 1854), 33–34.

88. A. B. Richmond, Esq., *Leaves from the Diary of an Old Lawyer; Intemperance: The Great Source of Crime* (New York: American Book Exchange, 1880), 31.

89. *Narinah Ennis v. George Shiley and Henry Shiley* (1877), Bound Briefs, ISLL, 308.

90. Plaintiff's declaration, *Martha Johnson v. Julius Schultz* (1889), Bound Briefs, MSLL, 4.

91. Plaintiff's declaration, *Louise Faivre v. John Mandercheid, John Arensdorf, and E .J. Ressegiu* (1902), Bound Briefs, ISLL, 3.

92. Robert H. Wiebe, *The Search for Order 1877–1920* (New York: Hill and Wang, 1967).

93. Grace Strong, *The Worst Foe: A Temperance Novel* (Columbus, Ohio: Wm. G. Hubbard and Co, 1886), 6.

94. Appellant's brief, *Elizabeth Engleken v. Hubert Webber and John Weston* (1876), Bound Briefs, ISLL, 11.

95. Appellant's brief, *Polly Jackson v. J. W. Noble* (1880), Bound Briefs, ISLL, 5.

96. Edgar Watson Howe, *Plain People* (New York: Dodd, Mead & Co., 1929), 80.

97. *Atchison Daily Globe*, Feb. 7, 1901, 2.

98. *Atchison Daily Globe*, Oct. 14, 1903, 4.

99. *Atchison Daily Globe*, Aug. 19, 1899, 4. For a discussion of Howe's attitude toward drink, see Calder M. Pickett, *Ed Howe: Country Town Philosopher* (Lawrence: University Press of Kansas, 1968), 151–57.

100. "Sunday Afternoon's Tragedy," *Atchison Daily Globe*, June 4, 1900, 4.

101. *Atchison Daily Globe*, Oct. 18, 1904.

102. *Atchison Daily Globe*, May 3, 1901, 4; Oct. 28, 1903, 2; Oct. 31, 1903, 1; Nov. 2, 1903, 2; Nov. 14, 1904, 2.

103. Pickett, *Ed Howe*, 172–80.

104. *Atchison Daily Globe*, Dec. 6, 1900, 2.

105. Edgar Watson Howe, *The Story of a Country Town* (Atchison, Kans.: Howe and Co., 1888), *A Man Story* (Boston: Ticknor, 1889), *A Moonlight Boy* (Boston: Ticknor, 1886), and *The Mystery of the Locks* (Boston: James R. Osgood, 1885).

106. Howe, *Plain People*, 62–63.

107. Ibid., 65.

108. Howe, *Moonlight Boy*, 276.

109. Howe, *Man Story*, 83.

110. Ibid., 266, 332. For a discussion of the relationship between drink and sexuality in William Dean Howell's fiction, see John Crowley, *The White Logic: Alcoholism and Gender in American Modernist Fiction* (Amherst: University of Massachusetts Press, 1994), 11–18.

111. *Atchison Daily Globe*, July 25, 1900, 2; Dec. 6, 1900, 2; Jan. 22, 1901, 2.

112. Pickett, *Ed Howe*, 148–51.

FOUR: Seduction

Epigraphs: Julia Colman, *Alcohol and Hygiene: An Elementary Lesson Book for Schools* (New York: National Temperance Society and Publication House, 1880), 168; Mary Dwinell Chellis, *Wealth and Wine* (New York: National Temperance Society and Publication House, 1874), 88.

1. 1880 U.S. Census, Osceola County, Mich.

2. Declaration of plaintiff, *Eugenia Peacock v. Daniel Oaks* (1891), Bound Briefs, MSLL, 2.

3. Ibid., 3.

4. Ibid., 10.

5. Ibid., 13.

6. Daniel Oaks' name is alternately spelled Oaks and Oakes. He shows up as Dan Oaks on the 1880 U.S. Census, Osceola County, Mich. In the official name of the case, however, his name is spelled without the "e."

7. Declaration of Plaintiff, *Peacock v. Oaks*, 3.

8. Ibid., 4.

9. Ibid., 9, and testimony of Eugenia Peacock, 21.

10. Testimony of Eugenia Peacock, *Peacock v. Oaks*, 26.

11. Declaration of Plaintiff, *Peacock v. Oaks*, 9.

12. Testimony of Burt Peacock, *Peacock v. Oaks*, 39.

13. Karen Sánchez-Eppler, *Touching Liberty: Abolition, Feminism, and the Politics of the Body* (Berkeley: University of California Press, 1993), 17.

14. "Amicus Justitiae," *The Utility of Ardent Spirits: An Address for an Anti-Temperance Society* (Boston: Light and Horton, 1835). Despite the title, this is actually a temperance tract.

15. Jonathan Zimmerman, *Distilling Democracy: Alcohol Education in America's Public Schools, 1880–1925* (Lawrence: University Press of Kansas, 1999).

16. "Beer": Box 2, Folder 36, Warshaw Collection, NMAH.

17. Ibid.

18. "Beer": Box 3, Folder 26, Warshaw Collection, NMAH.

19. "Beer": Box 2, Folder 6, Warshaw Collection, NMAH.

20. N. S. Davis, M.D., *Influence of Alcohol on the Human System, Especially As Used in Beer and Wine. Viewed from a Scientific Stand-Point* (New York: National Temperance Society and Publication House, 1890), 7.

21. E. A. Meriwether, *Black and White: A Novel* (New York: E. J. Hale and Son, 1883), 6; Rev. John Marsh, *Hannah Hawkins, the Reformed Drunkard's Daughter* (New York: American Temperance Union, 1844), 16.

22. Perttii Alasuutari, *Desire and Craving: A Cultural Theory of Alcoholism* (Albany: State University of New York Press, 1992).

23. A. D. Milne, *Uncle Sam's Farm Fence* (New York: C. Shepard and Co., 1854), 69: "is there nothing of the man left in your polluted heart?"

24. John K. Cornyn, *Dick Wilson, the Rumseller's Victim; or, Humanity Pleading for the "Maine Law": A Temperance Story Founded on Fact with an introduction by Thurlow W. Brown* (Auburn, N.Y.: Miller, Orton, and Mulligan, 1854), x: "The very heart of human society has been poisoned, until along every artery of health and strength, the hot currents have swept their blighting power." T. P. Taylor, *The Bottle: A Drama in Two Acts* (New York: Dewitt Publishing House, 1847), 4, "Ruth: It is that which causes me sorrow [points to bottle]. Its progress is slow, but sure; it is the pest of the humble home; it is the withering curse of the happy circle the deadly poison that corrupts and withers, changing the good to the bad; it fascinates but to destroy. . . ."

25. The influx of liquor, in this last version, robbed the metaphorical body of legitimate moisture. Mary Dwinell Chellis, *All For Money* (New York: National Temperance Society and Publication House, 1876), 158: "It is draining the resources of the country," it

"sucks out the juices of prosperity, leaving everywhere only dryness and putrefaction!" "The Rum Traffic," *(Des Moines) Iowa Messenger,* March 31, 1887: "It is a leech upon the body politic, drawing the life blood from all kinds of legitimate business." "Editorial Notes," *Iowa Messenger,* April 7, 1887: the liquor business is "a vampire on the public." Rev. T. Dewitt Talmage, "Always in Imminent Peril," *The Morning and Day of Reform: A National Journal of Prohibition, Gospel Temperance, and Family Reading* (Washington, Kans.) Vol. 6, No. 9, September 1884, 1: "The lion of our nation's strength is covered all over with green bottle flies that are sucking the life-blood out of its neck and flanks." A prize essay by Rev. Richard Wake, written for the United Kingdom Alliance in Manchester, England, but found in a Kansas temperance pamphlet collection, suggests that "the liquor trade [is] nothing more or less than a leech absorbing the life-blood of the nation." *The Problem of the Nineteenth Century or Reasons For the Suppression of the Liquor Trade* (1896), 6; John Harvey Kellogg, *Practical Manual of Health and Temperance Embracing the Treatment of Common Diseases, Accidents, and Emergencies, the Alcohol and Tobacco Habits, Useful Hints and Recipes* (Battle Creek, Mich.: Health Publishing Co., 1886), 10: "Alcohol is a Desiccant." T. S. Arthur, *Woman to the Rescue: A Story of the New Crusade* (Philadelphia: J. M. Stoddart & Co., 1874), 194.

26. Meriwether, *Black and White,* 9.

27. Jean Baudrillard, *Seduction,* trans. Brian Singer (New York: St. Martin's, 1990).

28. Though temperance opponents rarely used the language of seduction in criticizing reformers, temperance reformers often portrayed them as doing so in their fiction. In Cornyn, *Dick Wilson,* 184, the author portrays rumsellers calling temperance advocates "constitutional vampyres."

29. Alexander S. Davis, *A Loud Call, to the Citizens of this Nation. Universal Virtue, Liberty and Independence Defended: A True, Honest, and Impartial Investigation of the Present Temperance Question* (Hanover, Penn.: Joseph S. Gitt, Printer, 1842).

30. See, for instance, David Sutherland, *A Caution against Seduction: The Substance of a Sermon Delivered at the Funeral of a Young Woman of Lyman, N.H., Feb. 22, 1812* (Hanover, N.H.: Charles Spear, 1812); *The Victim of Seduction: An Affecting Narrative of the Tragical Death of Miss Fanny Salisbury, A Native of New Jersey, Who, Having Been Enticed from Her Widowed Parent, and Basely Seduced by a Young Man of the City of New York, after Enduring Incredible Hardships in That City, Terminated Her Own Existence by Hanging Herself in a Forest Near Newark, on the 23d of January Last* (Boston: Artemus Belcree, 1820); James Penn, *The Life of Miss Davis, the Farmer's Daughter of Essex: Who Was Seduced by Her Lover, under a Promise of Marriage* (Philadelphia: Freeman Scott, 1827); Edward Seaman, *Report of the Trial of Ann Saffen versus Edward Seaman, for Seduction* (New York: Grattan & Banks, 1818); Regina Maria Roche, *Melinda; or, the Victim of Seduction: A Moral Tale* (Danbury, Conn.: "Printed for the Booksellers," 1804).

31. Katherine Cummings, *Telling Tales: The Hysteric's Seduction in Fiction and Theory* (Stanford, Calif.: Stanford University Press, 1991), 3: "It is difficult to disentangle the seduced from the seducer, to attribute power to a single subject, or to say who has finally been taken by whom . . . the boundaries are blurred between seduced and seducing subjects."

32. Julia A. Stern, *The Plight of Feeling: Sympathy and Dissent in the Early American Novel* (Chicago: University of Chicago Press, 1997).

33. William E. Gienapp, *The Origins of the Republican Party, 1852–1856* (New York: Oxford University Press, 1987); John Higham, *Strangers in the Land: Patterns of American*

Nativism, 1860–1925 (1955; reprint, New Brunswick, N.J.: Rutgers University Press, 1992), 5–7; Jenny Franchot, *Roads to Rome: The Antebellum Protestant Encounter with Catholicism* (Berkeley: University of California Press, 1994).

34. Franchot, *Roads to Rome*, 394–95, n.

35. "From Clinton," *Iowa Temperance Standard,* July 1, 1869, 6.

36. Nina Baym, *Woman's Fiction: A Guide to Novels by and about Women in America, 1820–1870* (Ithaca, N.Y.: Cornell University Press, 1978), 26.

37. Elizabeth Barnes, *States of Sympathy: Seduction and Democracy in the American Novel* (New York: Columbia University Press, 1997), 15.

38. See, for instance, "The Late Nunnery Investigation," *Boston Herald,* April 3, 1855.

39. John W. Crowley, "Paradigms of Addiction in Howells' Novels," *American Literary Realism* 25 (1993): 3–17.

40. M. F. Carey, *Adela Lincoln: A Tale of the Wine Cup* (Philadelphia: See, Peters & Co., 1854), 200.

41. Nellie H. (Stella) Bradley, *The First Glass; or, the Power of Woman's Influence* (Washington, D.C.: n.p., 1867), 6–7; Rev. Emma Pow (Smith) Bauder, *Anarchy: Its Cause and Cure Told in Story* (Oakland, Calif.: Occidental Publishing Co., 1902), 57: "Exultantly she laughed, while with her jeweled hand she pressed the cup to his lips"; S. N. Cook, *Broken Promises* (New York: Happy Hours Co., 1879), 14; Metta V. Fuller, *Fashionable Dissipation* (Philadelphia: See, Peters & Co., 1854), 122; Abby Eldridge, *Norman Brill's Life-Work* (New York: National Temperance Society, 1875), 36.

42. Charles W. Babcock, M.D., *Adrift: A Temperance Drama in Three Acts* (Clyde, Ohio: A. D. Ames, 1880), 12; George Melville Baker, *The Last Loaf* (Boston: Walter H. Baker and Co., 1870); George Melville Baker, *The Tempter; or, The Sailor's Return* (Boston: W. H. Baker, 1894 [1866]); William Comstock, *Rum; or, The First Glass: A Drama in Three Acts* (New York: Robert M. DeWitt, 1875), 8–17. For a slight variation on this theme, see Fuller, *Fashionable Dissipation,* 43: "your rhetoric was so specious, the pictures you drew of the bewitching Lotos; the bewildering opium; the cheering social glass, were so alluring to his long stifled passion, that with his soul on fire, he hastened from the hall to drown it in the forbidden flood"; Mrs. L. D. Shears, *The Wife's Appeal: A Temperance Drama in Six Acts* (New York: n.p., 1878), 6, 30: "Why he exerts such an influence over me, I cannot divine. Would to God I could break the fascinating spell his presence ever casts about me"; and *Female Influence; or, The Temperance Girl,* written for the Massachusetts Sabbath School Society and revised by the committee for publication (Boston, Mass.: Massachusetts Sabbath School Society, 1837): "[T]houghtless and unprincipled associates allured him to places of public amusements." See also *The Itinerant's Daughter: A Temperance Story compositely written by members of Burlingame W. C. T. U., each taking a chapter* (Burlingame, Kans.: 1908), n.p., [KSHS]: "soon [Harry] fell in with that young scape-grace Turner Hubbel; the vice and mischief he can think of is only equal to his Santanic [sic] Majesty. Together they planned to get Al drunk"; Harriet Beecher Stowe, *Betty's Bright Idea* (New York: National Temperance Society and Publication House, 1875), 18; and William Carleton, *Art Maguire; or, The Broken Pledge: A Narrative* (New York: D. and J. Sadler and Co., 1846), 51: "Art had, unfortunately, contracted an intimacy with one of the class I speak of, an adroit fellow with an oily tongue, vast powers of flattery, and still greater powers of bearing liquor."

43. John H. Allen, *The Fruits of the Wine Cup: A Drama, in Three Acts* (New York: Happy Hours Company, 1858), 15.

44. T. P. Taylor, *The Bottle: A Drama in Two Acts* (New York: J. Douglas, 1847).

45. E[lmer] C[harles] Whalen, *Under the Spell: A Temperance Play in Four Acts* (Chicago: T. S. Denison, 1890), 21; T. S. Arthur, *Three Years in a Mantrap* (Philadelphia: J. M. Stoddard and Company, 1872), 64, 78, 87, 96; C. H. Rutledge, *Flashes from the Furnace* (n.p.: C. H. Rutledge, 1912), 70; Harry Seymour, *The Temperance Doctor* (New York: Samuel French, n.d.), dramatized from the story "The Temperance Doctor."

46. Arthur, *Three Years in a Mantrap*, 78.

47. This description of saloonkeepers as profit-oriented, amoral seducers, as Nicola Beisel points out in *Imperiled Innocents: Anthony Comstock and Family Reproduction in Victorian America* (Princeton, N.J.: Princeton University Press, 1997), 63, mirrors antipornography language of the same period.

48. "A Citizen of Teetotalton," *A Treatise; or, Speculative Philanthropy: The Hot Corn Question Enlarged* (Nashville, Tenn.: Printed for the Author, 1859), 61.

49. Rev. Robert W. Bigham, *Wine and Blood* (Nashville, Tenn.: Southern Methodist Publishing House, 1879), 61–62.

50. Elizabeth Avery Meriwether, *The Devil's Dance: A Play for the Time* (St. Louis, Mo.: Hailman Brothers, 1886), 1–24.

51. R. Vashon Rogers Jr., *Drinks, Drinkers, and Drinking; or, The Law and History of Intoxicating Liquors* (1881; reprint, Littleton, Col.: Fred B. Rothman & Co., 1985), 199, cited from *John Kellerman v. Phoebe Arnold, 74 Ill 69.*

52. Declaration, *Margaret Dunlavey v. I. C. Watson* (1874), Bound Briefs, ISLL, 2.

53. Declaration, *Peacock v. Oaks* (1891), 11–12.

54. Norman Kerr, M.D., "Study of Inebriety and Its Relations to the Temperance Movement," *Quarterly Journal of Inebriety* 12 (1890): 127.

55. Jan Lewis, "The Republican Wife: Virtue and Seduction in the Early Republic," *William and Mary Quarterly* 44 (1987), 717; Lewis A. Erenberg, *Steppin' Out: New York Nightlife and the Transformation of American Culture, 1890–1930* (Westport, Conn.: Greenwood Press, 1981), 79, 84; Jed Dannenbaum, *Drink and Disorder: Temperance Reform in Cincinnati from the Washingtonian Revival to the W.C.T.U.* (Urbana: University of Illinois Press, 1984), 81–83, also notes that late-nineteenth-century temperance advocates tended to place the blame for inebriety on the shoulders of the saloon keepers and drink manufacturers rather than on those of the drinker. Also see Epstein, *Politics of Domesticity,* 104.

56. Grace Strong, *The Worst Foe* (Columbus, Ohio: W. G. Hubbard, 1885), 150.

57. For an interesting discussion of accounts of sexual seduction, see Beisel, *Imperiled Innocents,* 27.

58. Colman, *Alcohol and Hygiene,* 168. Edgar Watson Howe, *Story of a Country Town* (Atchison, Kans.: Howe and Co., 1888), 97, mobilized temperance seduction language against them, and placed them in the role of seducers, when he suggested that their exaggerated descriptions of saloons "caus[e] young men and boys who would otherwise never have thought of it to be seized with an uncontrollable desire to try the experiment for themselves."

59. Mary Dwinell Chellis, *From Father to Son* (New York: National Temperance Society and Publication House, 1879), 352.

60. David Reynolds, *Beneath the American Renaissance: The Subversive Imagination in the Age of Emerson and Melville* (New York: Knopf, 1988), 47.

61. T. J. Jackson Lears, *No Place of Grace: Antimodernism and the Transformation of American Culture, 1880–1920* (Chicago: University of Chicago Press, 1994).

62. For more on this process, see Reynolds, *Beneath the American Renaissance.*

63. Howe, *Story of a Country Town,* 98.

64. Edgar Watson Howe, *A Moonlight Boy* (Boston: Ticknor, 1886), 182, and *Story of a Country Town,* 30, 111. Nicholas O. Warner, in his *Spirits of America: Intoxication in Nineteenth-Century American Literature* (Norman: University of Oklahoma Press, 1997), suggests that such glorifications of alcohol were uncommon in popular temperance fiction, though more common in the more sophisticated works of major literary figures such as Hawthorne.

65. Chellis, *Wealth and Wine,* 88.

66. Chellis, *Father to Son,* 44.

67. Martha E. Whitten, *The Drunkard's Wife* (Austin, Tex.: Hutchins Printing House, 1887).

68. In Arthur, *Three Years in a Mantrap,* 87, 96, the narrator's saloon is described as "shiny as a new pin" and as "done . . . up elegantly." In Emma Pow Bauder, *Ruth and Marie: A Fascinating Story of the Nineteenth Century* (n.p.: L. W. Walter, 1895), 57, Marie entices her future husband to drink "with jeweled hand"; in Bradley, *The First Glass,* 7, before Frank West succumbs to the seductions of Mollie Mason, "Often ha[d] the ruby wine been proffered by the hand of beauty only to be refused."

69. Mary T. Lathrap, *The Poems and Written Addresses of Mary T. Lathrap, President of the Michigan Woman's Christian Temperance Union for Fourteen Years with a Short Sketch of Her Life* ("Published in the Interest of the W. C. T. U. of Michigan," 1895), 101.

70. George M. Beard, *Sexual Neurasthenia: Its Hygiene, Causes, Symptoms, and Treatment* (New York: Arno Press, 1972); Kerr, "Study of Inebriety," 137.

71. William Hargreaves, M.D., *Alcohol and Science; or, Alcohol: What It Is, and What It Does* (New York: National Temperance Society and Publication House, 1884), 199; L. D. Mason, M.D., "A Study of the Social Statistics of 4,663 Cases of Alcoholic Inebriety," *Quarterly Journal of Inebriety* 12 (1890), 247.

72. Harry Gene Levine, "Demon of the Middle Class: Self-Control, Liquor, and the Ideology of Temperance in Nineteenth-Century America" (Ph.D. diss., University of California, Berkeley, 1978), 36–37.

73. Howe, *Story of a Country Town,* 97.

74. Fuller, *Fashionable Dissipation,* 67.

75. Gough quoted in *(Iowa City) Iowa State Journal,* February 1, 1854, 1.

76. Strong, *The Worst Foe: A Temperance Novel,* 13; see also the description in Nellie H. Bradley, *Reclaimed; or, The Danger of Moderate Drinking* (Rockland, Maine: Z. Pope Vose, 1868), 4, of drunkard George Stanley, "so proud and ambitions, possessing a cultivated mind and more than ordinary talent." According to one character, "a firmer, stronger, nobler mind and clearer intellect than George Stanley's was never given to man" (6). In Nellie Bradley, *The Stumbling Block; or, Why a Deacon Gave up His Wine* (Rockland, Maine: Z. Pope Vose, 1871), 8, a young Irish maid described her suitor in similar terms: "Barrin' his longin' for sthrong drink, there's not a braver, kinder, thruer lad than Barney McCarthy"; George S. Vautrot, Esq., *At Last* (Clyde, Ohio: A. D. Ames, 1879), 9: "Frank is too noble, too generous to suspect anyone."

77. Chellis, *Father to Son,* 124: "Somebody thought the books before they were made, and somebody saw the pictures before a single line had been traced. How? Where? Why? There were the questions which perplexed Caspar Manning."

78. B. G. McFall, *Among the Moonshiners; or, A Drunkard's Legacy: A Temperance Drama,*

in Three Acts (Clyde, Ohio: Ames Pub. Co., 1897), 3, 21–22; A. D. Milne, *Uncle Sam's Farm Fence* (New York: C. Shepard & Co., 1854), 50; Mary Dwinell Chellis, *Out of the Fire* (New York: National Temperance Society and Publishing House, 1869), 236.

79. Meriwether, *Devil's Dance*, 51; Robert M. Peace, *A Drunkard's Wife: A Drama in Four Acts* (Plainview, Tex.: Robert M. Peace, 1911), 15–17; T. Trask Woodward, *Social Glass, or, the Victims of the Bottle, The Great Sensational Temperance Drama in Five Acts* (New York: S. French, 1887), 14; Cornyn, *Dick Wilson*, 186.

80. Nellie H. Bradley, *Wine as a Medicine; or, Abbie's Experience* (Rockland, Maine: Z. Pope Vose, 1873); Chellis, *Wealth and Wine*, and, *All For Money*, 297. There are some exceptions to this generalization, of course. In Bauder, *Ruth and Marie*, Polly Hopkins is brought into a peripheral role in the story as a public drunkard. She had been made to drink her first glass by the heroine's father and was eventually discharged. Whereas the story required the redemption of the heroine's husband, to whom she had given the first glass, the end of the story found Hopkins, the female drunkard, still out on the streets.

81. Chellis, *Wealth and Wine*, 88.

82. Chellis, *Father to Son*, 45.

83. Arthur, *Three Years in a Mantrap*.

84. Chellis, *Out of the Fire*, 75.

85. Testimony of William Ross, *Della Welch v. William Jugenheimer and William Jugenheimer, Jr.* (1881), Bound Briefs, ISLL, 28.

86. See, for instance, *The Affective History of Fair Rosamond, Only Daughter of the Earl of Clifford, Who Was Seduced from the Protection of Her Parents by King Henry II . . . And during His Absence in the Holy War Met an Untimely Death through the Jealousy of His Queen Eleanor* (London: Printed For the Booksellers and For T. Deichler, n.d.).

87. Louisa May Alcott, "Fair Rosamond," ms. Am. 1130.13 (19) 73–147, Houghton Library, Harvard University, Cambridge, Mass., 7. This part does hearken back to some versions of "Fair Rosamond" in which Rosamond was faulted for her "ambitious spirit" in being attracted by the king's attentions; see *Affective History*, 15.

88. Alcott, "Fair Rosamond," 22–24.

89. Ibid., 44.

90. Whereas, in the traditional Fair Rosamond stories, Rosamond was killed by the king's jealous wife, in Alcott's story, Rosamond flees to Tempest's real wife for protection from him, on the theory that that would be the last place he would look. They establish an idyllic matriarchal household interrupted only by Rosamond's need to collect her inheritance from her grandfather.

91. Warner, *Spirits of America*, 204–8.

92. Louisa May Alcott, "The Marble Woman," in Madeleine Stern, ed., *Louisa May Alcott Unmasked* (Boston: Northeastern University Press, 1995), 215. The young woman had been reading *Confessions of an Opium Eater;* Louisa May Alcott, *Silver Pitchers, and Independence, A Centennial Love Story* (Boston: Roberts Brothers, 1876), and *Rose in Bloom* (Boston, Roberts Brothers, 1876). Warner, *Spirits of America*, 204–8.

FIVE: Invasion

Epigraphs: "A New England Journalist," *The Ramrod Broken; or, The Bible, History, and Common Sense in Favor of the Moderate Use of Good Spirituous Liquors: Showing the Advantage of a License System in Preference to Prohibition, and "Moral" in Preference to "Legal Suasion"*

(Boston: Albert Colby and Company, 1859), 142; Norman Kerr, *The Heredity of Alcohol* (New York: Published for the Woman's National Christian Temperance Union by the National Temperance Society and Publication House, 1882), 8.

1. Testimony of Rose Ann Sankey, *Daniel McMahon v. Rose Ann Sankey* (1890), Case Files, ISA, 71.

2. Ibid., 59.

3. Statement of appellants, *McMahon v. Sankey*, 1.

4. Testimony of Rose Ann Sankey, *McMahon v. Sankey*, 59.

5. Ibid., 11.

6. Testimony of Michael Kerns, *McMahon v. Sankey*, 161, 164.

7. Illinois State Supreme Court Opinion, *McMahon v. Sankey*, 133 Ill 636; 24 N.E. 1027; 1890 Ill Lexis 1140.

8. Testimony of Rose Ann Sankey, *McMahon v. Sankey*, 7.

9. Testimony of Daniel Lavin, *McMahon v. Sankey*, 293.

10. Testimony of Frank Dasso, *McMahon v. Sankey*, 284.

11. Ibid., 288.

12. Testimony of Rose Ann Sankey, *McMahon v. Sankey*, 45.

13. Testimony of Jerry C. Ryves [streetcar conductor], *McMahon v. Sankey*, 131; testimony of William H. Hammond [soda pop vendor], 110–21.

14. Testimony of Rose Ann Sankey, *McMahon v. Sankey*, 65.

15. Ruth Bordin, *Woman and Temperance: The Quest for Power and Liberty, 1873–1900* (Philadelphia: Temple University Press, 1981), 85–88.

16. In some rare cases, temperance reformers imagine immigrants as "dupes" of the trusts, as in W. H. Boles, *A Voice from a Distiller, Two Millionaires, and Bob Ingersoll* (Anthony, Kans.: Mathis' Book and Job Print, 1898), 15–16: " 'Do you think that your church [Catholic], the whiskey power and the money power are in league with each other?' '. . . I do believe that the leaders and members of my church are being used by the money and liquor powers for base purposes.' "

17. Andrew Sinclair, *Age of Excess: A Social History of the Prohibition Movement* (1962; reprint, New York: Harper and Row, 1964), 5; Joseph Gusfield, *Symbolic Crusade: Status Politics and the American Temperance Movement* (Urbana: University of Illinois Press, 1963). Ian Tyrrell, *Sobering Up: From Temperance to Prohibition in Antebellum America, 1800–1860* (Westport, Conn.: Greenwood Press, 1979), 264–69, on the other hand, has pointed out that nativism and temperance did not always go hand in hand.

18. A. D. Milne, *Uncle Sam's Farm Fence* (New York: C. Shepard and Co., 1854), 44, 170.

19. Jed Dannenbaum, *Drink and Disorder: Temperance Reform in Cincinnati from the Washingtonian Revival to the W.C.T.U.* (Urbana: University of Illinois Press, 1984), 22; Jack S. Blocker Jr., *American Temperance Movements: Cycles of Reform* (Boston: Twayne Publishers, 1989), 22. Tyrrell, *Sobering Up*, 126–31, discusses perfectionist social optimism in antebellum temperance thought.

20. Alison Parker, *Purifying America: Women, Cultural Reform, and Pro-Censorship Activism, 1873–1933* (Urbana: University of Illinois Press, 1997), focuses on the issue of purity. Ian Tyrrell, *Woman's World / Woman's Empire: The Woman's Christian Temperance Union in International Perspective, 1880–1930* (Chapel Hill: University of North Carolina Press, 1991), 191–220, devotes a chapter to the WCTU's social purity movement.

21. Karen Halttunen, *Confidence Men and Painted Women: A Study of Middle-Class Culture in America, 1830–1870* (New Haven, Conn.: Yale University Press, 1982).

22. See, for instance, Mary Dwinell Chellis, *All for Money* (New York: National Temperance Society and Publication House, 1876), 211.

23. For examples of counterfeiters and forgers in temperance fiction, see Daphne S. Giles, *East and West* (New York: R. Craighead, 1853), 49; S. N. Cook, *Out in the Streets: A Temperance Play in Three Acts* (New York: Dick and Fitzgerald, n.d.); and T[om] P. Taylor, *The Bottle: A Drama in Two Acts* (New York: J. Douglas, 1847), 2.

24. Richard Hofstadter, *Age of Reform* (1955; reprint, New York: Vintage Books, 1960), 17.

25. Bernard Bailyn, *Ideological Origins of the American Revolution* (Cambridge, Mass.: Belknap Press of Harvard University Press, 1967); J. G. A. Pocock, *The Machiavellian Moment: Florentine Political Thought and the Atlantic Republican Tradition* (Princeton, N.J.: Princeton University Press, 1975), 506–52.

26. "To the Friends of Temperance in Iowa," *Iowa State Journal*, June 29, 1854, 146–47.

27. Giles, *East and West*, 29.

28. *Ramrod Broken*, 22.

29. A. B. Grosh, *Washingtonian Pocket Companion; Containing a Choice Collection of Temperance Hymns, Songs, & Co.* (Utica, N.Y.: B. S. Merrell, 1843), 33, 142–43.

30. *An Address to the Citizens of New Orleans on the Subject of Temperance. Published by the Order of the New Orleans Temperance Society* (New Orleans: Toy, Printer, Office of the Lafayette City Advertiser, 1841) [Historic New Orleans Collection].

31. Rev. Frederick A. Ross, *A Sermon, on Intemperance* (Rogersville, Tenn.: "Calvinistic Magazine" Office, 1830), 4. The sermon was delivered in the First Presbyterian Church in Knoxville, October 12, 1829.

32. Ben Sawtelle to Mary Porter, July 23, 1847, Porter Family Papers, Box 1, Folder 3, Mississippi Valley Collection, University of Memphis, Memphis, Tenn. Also see J. W. Clapp, *Address at Holly Springs, Mississippi July 4, 1848* (Holly Springs, Miss.: Printed at the Office of the *Weekly Jacksonian*, 1848), 9. Clapp offers his audience an opportunity of "enlisting in this glorious war" against intemperance.

33. "A Member of the Order," *An Authentic Exposition of the K.G.C. Knights of the Golden Circle; or, A History of Secession from 1834 to 1861* (Indianapolis, Ind.: Asher & Co., 1861), 40.

34. Ibid., 49.

35. Herman Humphrey, D.D., *Parallel between Intemperance and the Slave-Trade* (n.p.: John B. Haven, n.d.) [Newberry Library].

36. Richard W. Leeman, *Do Everything Reform: The Oratory of Frances E. Willard* (New York: Greenwood Press, 1992), 26–31.

37. Good Templars [New London, Conn.], *Great Slaughter* (New London, Conn.: Union Lodge No. 7, 1865) [Connecticut Historical Society]; American Temperance Union, *Mustered Out—Now Look Out* (New York: American Temperance Union, n.d.).

38. Albert J. Bellows, M.D., *The Philosophy of Eating* (New York: Hurd and Houghton, 1868). Similarly, see Joel Dorman Steele, *Hygienic Physiology, with Special Reference to the Use of Alcoholic Drinks and Narcotics, Being a Revised Edition of the Fourteen Weeks in Human Physiology* (1872; reprint, New York: A. S. Barnes & Co., 1888), 177: "If . . . you take into your stomach a little alcohol, it receives no such welcome. Nature treats it as a poison, and seeks to rid herself of the intruder as soon as possible. The juices of the system will from every pore to dilute and weaken it, and to prevent its shriveling up the delicate membranes with which it comes in contact"; also, A. B. Richmond, *Leaves from the Diary*

of an Old Lawyer: Intemperance, the Great Source of Crime (New York: American Book Exchange, 1880), 238–39: "It goes into the stomach as alcohol, is taken up by the secretory organs as alcohol, passes into the blood as alcohol, and, preserving its identity, careers through the veins and arteries . . . it is discharged as it was received—as alcohol. . . . All through its inglorious career it remains alcohol, first and last, until it is cast out as an unwelcome guest, dangerous to the health of the body."

39. Elizabeth Young, *Disarming the Nation: Women's Writing and the American Civil War* (Chicago: University of Chicago Press, 1999), 88; "Strike for Temperance," *Iowa Temperance Standard,* July 29, 1869, 2. For a discussion of Civil War references in temperance rhetoric, see Carol Mattingly, *Well-Tempered Women: Nineteenth-Century Temperance Rhetoric* (Carbondale: Southern Illinois University Press, 1998), 54–57. Richard Hamm, *Shaping the Eighteenth Amendment: Temperance Reform, Legal Culture, and the Polity, 1880–1920* (Chapel Hill: University of North Carolina Press, 1995), 31.

40. Samuel W. Small, "Deliverance from Bondage: A Temperance Sermon," in Rev. Sam P. Jones, *Quit Your Meanness: Sermons and Saying of Rev. Sam P. Jones of Georgia* (Cincinnati, Ohio: Cranston and Stowe, 1890), 501.

41. C. H. Fowler, *Impeachment and Conviction of King Alcohol under the New Temperance Law of Illinois together with the New Temperance Laws of Illinois and Wisconsin* (Chicago: Carpenter & Sheldon, Publishers, 1872), 4.

42. "Senator Blair's New Book," *Iowa Messenger,* December 1887, 7, singles out the map for praise: "Perhaps the most unique feature of the illustration, however, is a folding map of New York City, showing the location and the extent of the drinking-places in the metropolis." The author goes on to refer to the map as "startling."

43. Henry William Blair, *The Temperance Movement, or the Conflict between Man and Alcohol* (Boston: William E. Smythe Co., 1888). Blair was a senator from New Hampshire.

44. John Wooley, "New Declaration of Independence," *Union Signal,* July 7, 1892, 3.

45. C. H. Rutledge, *Flashes from the Furnace* (n.p.: C. H. Rutledge, 1912), 70; Nellie H. Bradley, *The Young Teetotaler or Saved at Last!* (1867; reprint, Rockland, Maine: Z. Pope Vose, 1868), 2; Rev. H. W. Hampe, "The Purple Rose of the Law," *A Bouquet of Flowers in Rhyme on the Liquor Trade* (Topeka, Kans.: 1890) [KSHS].

46. Hamm, *Shaping the Eighteenth Amendment,* 175–202.

47. See K. Austin Kerr, *Organized for Prohibition: A New History of the Anti-Saloon League* (New Haven, Conn.: Yale University Press, 1985), especially the first chapter on image and actuality of Liquor Trust.

48. Perry Duis, *The Saloon: Public Drinking in Chicago and Boston 1880–1920* (Urbana: University of Illinois Press, 1983), 15, argues that these tied houses "came to resemble the prototype of the modern chain store operation."

49. H. C. Bradbury, *"Sweet William," A Story About the "Joints"* (Lincoln, Kans.: Sentinel Book and Job Print, 1898), 1. Though this stranger appears to be independent (and though many temperance fiction saloonkeepers were), at the end of the story, Sweet William's saloonkeeper confesses that "Twenty-three years ago I escaped from the Colorado state penitentiary, and when seeking a job to make money without work, I was offered by one of the agents of a foreign syndicate that owns over 200 breweries and distilleries in the United States, a position as a missionary of Satan to start a joint in Sweet William" (15).

50. T. S. Arthur, *Woman to the Rescue: A Story of the New Crusade* (Philadelphia: J. M. Stoddart & Co., 1874), 53, 65, 67–68: "Luke Sterling, Frank Gordon and a score or more

besides of Delhi's best men were fast retracing the steps by which they had risen since early manhood to the rank of useful and prosperous citizenship, other men were gathering in, as they and hundreds like them scattered and wasted, a harvest of this world's goods. None of these men had greater thrift than Jimmy Hanlan . . . he was the owner of the fastest and most valuable horses in the own. He wore a diamond pin worth at least two thousand dollars, the admiration or envy of all the fast young men . . . a massive gold chain decorated his flashy vest, and he might often be seen drawing forth his three-hundred-dollar gold watch."

51. Ibid., 91: "There was found no man of strength and influence courageous enough to lift a standard and call for an army to set itself in battle array against an enemy [the saloon] that was ravaging the town . . ."; E[lmer] C[harles] Whalen, *Under the Spell: A Temperance Play in Four Acts* (Chicago: T. S. Denison, 1890), 50: "No man has ever crossed the threshold of this place without being corrupted; and the stream of pollution that flows from these doors has poisoned all the moral atmosphere of this community."

52. See, for instance, Effie W. Merriman, *The Drunkard's Family* (Chicago: The Dramatic Publishing Company, 1898).

53. Testimony of Hester Worley and testimony of Robert Worley, *Hester Worley v. L. D. S. Spurgeon* (1874), Bound Briefs, ISLL, 8; testimony of S. E. Vane, *John Kellerman v. Phoebe Arnold* (1873), Case Files, ISA.

54. Ida M. Buxton, *On to Victory: A Temperance Cantata* (Clyde, Ohio: A. D. Ames, 1886), unpaginated: "Captain Prohibition: . . . we need everyone in this struggle of the home against the saloon. It is a godly contest, and we hope you will join us."

55. Abby Eldridge, *Norman Brill's Life-Work* (New York: National Temperance Society, 1875), 180.

56. H. W. Adams, "Facts for Temperance Voters," *The Morning and Day of Reform: A National Journal of Prohibition, Gospel Temperance, and Family Reading* (Washington, Kans.), vol. 6, September 1884.

57. Metta Victoria Fuller, *The Senator's Son; or, The Maine Law: A Last Refuge* (Cleveland, Ohio: Tooker and Gatchel, 1858), 74; "How Arkansas People Drink," *Meriwether's Weekly* (Memphis, Tenn.), June 9, 1883, 445. Nicholas O. Warner, *Spirits of America: Intoxication in Nineteenth-Century American Literature* (Norman: University of Oklahoma Press, 1997), 77, mentions scenes of forced drinking in Edgar Allan Poe stories.

58. A. D. Milne, *Uncle Sam's Farm Fence* (New York: C. Shepard and Co., 1854), 62; T. Trask Woodward, *The Social Glass; or, Victims of the Bottle: The Great Sensational Temperance Drama in Five Acts* (New York: S. French, 1887), 9; S. N. Cook, *Broken Promises* (New York: Happy Hours Co., 1879), 31; John K. Cornyn, *Dick Wilson, the Rumseller's Victim; or, Humanity Pleading for the "Maine Law": A Temperance Story Founded on Fact with an introduction by Thurlow W. Brown* (Auburn, N.Y.: Miller, Orton, and Mulligan, 1854), 227; C. H. Rutledge, *Flashes from the Furnace* (n.p.: C. H. Rutledge, 1912), 20; James M'Closkey, *The Fatal Glass; or, The Curse of Drink: A Drama in Three Acts* (London: Samuel French and New York: Samuel French and Son, n.d.); George S. Vautrot, Esq., *At Last* (Clyde, Ohio: A. D. Ames, 1879), 13, 19.

59. B. G. McFall, *Among the Moon-Shiners; or, A Drunkard's Legacy: A Temperance Drama in Three Acts* (Clyde, Ohio: Ames Publishing Company, 1897), 17; W. S. (Ivy) Blackburn, *In the Toils of Slavery* (Chicago: American Baptist Publishing Society, 1903).

60. Kerr, *Heredity of Alcohol*, 8.

61. Chellis, *All for Money*, 142; M'Closkey, *Fatal Glass*, 25.

62. J. E. Stebbins, ed., *Fifty Years History of the Temperance Cause* (Hartford, Conn.: J. P.

Fitch, 1876), 108. Of course, the faces of frequent drinkers are in fact often characterized by redness. I do not want to lean too heavily on the interpretation of this one picture, but the spots on the last face do in fact appear quite unnatural; to scale, it is as if the drinker's face is covered with bright red dimes. Similarly, see the description of the drinker's stomach in "Children's Corner: Building the Temple," *Iowa Messenger*, March 17, 1887, 7: "I told you that the natural color was a light red or rosy color. Now, it has become a dark red . . . and the little fine blood vessels are enlarged and look angry."

63. Julia Colman, *Alcohol and Hygiene: An Elementary Lesson Book for Schools* (New York: National Temperance Society and Publication House, 1880), 69.

64. "The Homestead Scheme," *The National Era*, October 25, 1849.

65. C. H. Hoyt, *A Temperance Town* (n.d., n.p.: N.Y. City Museum Readex, 19th c American Drama [microfilm]), 24: "Parson, I'll tell you how to get your heart and your judgment together. Taint your job or any man's to separate the sheep from the goats. Be satisfied to make mankind as one flock and to believe that the best of us ain't perfect, the worst of us have some good streaks, even the town rumseller."

66. Albert Griffin, *An Earnest Appeal for the Substitution of Christian for Pagan Methods in All Moral Reform Work* (Topeka, Kans.: Albert Griffin, 1901), 6.

67. Metta V. Fuller, *Fashionable Dissipation* (Philadelphia: See, Peters & Co., 1854), 19. This ambiguous temperance novel contains an antitemperance speech by one of the main characters.

68. Edgar Watson Howe, *The Story of a Country Town* (Atchison, Kans.: Howe and Co., 1888); for other examples of hypocritical reformers, see the plays of G. M. Baker, especially *A Little More Cider* (Boston: Lee and Shepard, 1870) and *We're All Teetotalers* (Boston: Walter H. Baker, 1876).

69. Laura Sagolla Croley, "The Rhetoric of Reform in Stoker's *Dracula*: Depravity, Decline, and the Fin-de-Siècle 'Residuum,'" *Criticism* 37 (1995), 104–5, discusses the ambiguity of volition in *Dracula*.

70. Joel Dorman Steele, *Hygienic Physiology, with Special Reference to the Use of Alcoholic Drinks and Narcotics, Being a Revised Edition of the Fourteen Weeks in Human Physiology* (1872; reprint, New York: A. S. Barnes & Co., 1888), 140.

71. Not all agreed that the liquor trust was native. See Julia Colman, *No King in America* (New York: National Temperance Society and Publishing House, 1888), in which "Liberty" orates: "The vigilance which has always been the price of my very existence too often reveals to me not only the delusion of German beer and the blarney of Hibernian whiskey, but the trickery of your own brothers and sisters to the manner [*sic*] born. They set up King Cotton and King Corn and the Almighty Dollar and even their own labor itself, and fall down and worship" (23). Also see Bradbury, *"Sweet William,"* 15.

72. Colman, *No King*, 12; also see Elizabeth Avery Meriwether, *The Devil's Dance: A Play for the Time* (St. Louis, Mo.: Hailman Brothers, 1886), 9, in which "Wine," (a European nobleman) conspires with King Alcohol and with his fellow alcoholic beverages, declaring, "To us it doth appear our empire gaineth ground each day."

73. Tyrrell, *Woman's World*, 5.

74. J. Fowler Willing, "Prayer for Our Country," *Union Signal*, June 30, 1892, 5. See also the discussion of Native Americans and drink in James Fennimore Cooper's writings in Warner, *Spirits of America*, 100–105. For a discussion of the earlier history of Native Americans and alcohol, see Peter C. Mancall, *Deadly Medicine: Indians and Alcohol in Early America* (Ithaca, N.Y.: Cornell University Press, 1995).

75. "Indians (North America)," in *The Cyclopedia of Temperance and Prohibition: A*

Reference Book of Facts, Statistics, and General Information on all Phases of the Drink Question, the Temperance Movement, and the Prohibition Agitation (London: Funk & Wagnalls, 1891), 247. Also see the *(Iowa City) Iowa State Journal,* April 13, 1854, 66.

76. Pearl Campbell, "What the Poplar Tree Told Bessie," in "Aunt Jane's Cozy Corner," *Union Signal,* September 29, 1892, 14.

77. J. C. Furnas, *The Life and Times of the Late Demon Rum* (New York: Putnam's, 1965), 33.

78. Clara B. Drake, *The Doom of King Alcohol* (Chicago: Workmen's Temperance Publishing Association, 1903), 13.

79. This is a very strained allegory. The fermentation of fruits and grains is a natural process rather than the result of an intervention by an external force. Reformers occasionally, evoking this, liked to equate fermentation, corruption, and death. Their attempt, in this bizarre allegory and elsewhere, to make "alcohol" the agent of death fits in nicely with their larger commitment to the republican quest for a sort of political immortality.

80. Tyrrell, *Woman's World,* 81–114, 146–69. Hampe, "The Dark Purple Rose of Africa," *Bouquet,* 28; Joseph Cullen, "Stepping Back" (n.p.: n.d) [Boston Public Library].

81. See, for instance, Henry William Blair, *The Temperance Movement; or, The Conflict Between Man and Alcohol* (Boston: William E. Smythe Co., 1888), 256, and William T. Hornaday, *Free Rum on the Congo, and What It Is Doing There* (Chicago: Woman's Temperance Publishing Association, 1887), 98. Rev. Frank S. Dobbins, "The Drink Traffic and Foreign Missions," in J. N. Stearns, ed., *Temperance in All Nations: Papers, Essays, Discussions, Addresses, and Histories of the World Temperance Congress Held by NTS in Chicago, Ill., June 1893* (New York: National Temperance Society and Publishing House, 1893), 320.

82. Blair, *Temperance Movement,* 257.

83. J. H. Fillmore (music) and Ida M. Budd (words), "Bibles and Beer," in Charles M. and J. H. Fillmore, *Fillmore's Prohibition Songs: A Collection of Songs for the Prohibition Campaign, Patriotic Services, and All Meetings in the Interest of Reform* (Cincinnati, Ohio: Fillmore Music House, 1903): "Over the sea in their ignorant blindness, / Dwell the poor heathen 'mid darkness and night. / We in the homeland with brotherly kindness, / Reach out with longing to send them the light. / So o'er the ocean our good ships are speeding / Gladly to bear them the tidings of cheer / But side by side with the word of God—think of it! / Travels its foe—our American beer."

84. Belle M. Brain, *Weapons for Temperance Warfare* (Boston: Publishing Department of the United Society of Christian Endeavor, 1897). Note also that the topos of the red-colored alcoholic invader may be applied to the cartographic and physiognomic maps mentioned above.

85. Drake, *Doom of King Alcohol,* refers to Africa as well. King Alcohol's minions gloat that "The wheels of commerce swift revolving bear / His liquid drafts to earth's remotest shores / Heathens and savage share the Christian's drink" (15).

86. "Africa," *Cyclopedia of Temperance and Prohibition,* 15.

87. Isaac Naylor, *The Stars and Stripes of America Insulted and the Union Jack of Britain Dragged in the Dust: A Trumpet Call to Action* (Philadelphia: The R. E. Lynch Printing House, 1894), 12–13. For the language of permeation, see Richmond, *Diary of an Old Lawyer,* 306.

88. Blair, *Temperance Movement,* 255.

89. Ibid., 274.

90. Naylor, *Stars and Stripes.*
91. See, for instance, Bradbury, *"Sweet William,"* 1.
92. Charles W. Babcock, M.D., *Adrift: A Temperance Drama in Three Acts* (Clyde, Ohio: A. D. Ames, 1880), 18. This was also a common defense employed by saloonkeepers in civil damage suits. For examples of parents disrupting their home through providing drink to their son, see G. M. Baker, *Little Brown Jug* (1871; reprint, Boston: W.H. Baker, 1876); Mrs. L. D. Shears, *The Wife's Appeal: A Temperance Drama in Six Acts* (New York: n.p., 1878), 34: " 'twas you who placed the fatal cup to his lisping lips before he knew the danger."
93. Grace Strong, *The Worst Foe: A Temperance Novel* (Columbus, Ohio: Wm. G. Hubbard and Co., 1886); Emma Pow (Smith) Bauder, *Anarchy: Its Cause and Cure* (Oakland, Calif.: Occidental Publishing Co., 1902), 57; Nellie H. Bradley, *The First Glass; or, The Power of Woman's Influence* (Washington, D.C.: n.p., 1867), 6; Fuller, *Fashionable Dissipation.*
94. Rev. J. T. Crane, *Arts of Intoxication: The Air, and the Results* (New York: Carlton & Lanahan, 1870), 164. Also see George D. Lind, M.D., *Lessons in Physiology for Use in Schools, Including Anatomy, Physiology, and Hygiene, and the Effects of Alcohol and Other Stimulants on the Human Body and Mind* (Danville, Ind.: Indiana Publishing Company, 1892), 173; James Miller, "Alcohol: Its Place and Power," in *Alcohol and Tobacco* (Philadelphia: Lindsay & Blakiston, 1860), 28. Examples of this in temperance fiction are found in Mary Dwinell Chellis, *From Father to Son* (New York: National Temperance Society and Publication House, 1879), 352: "It may be that a single glass might arouse a demon in my breast which would not down at my bidding." At least by 1912, some were suggesting that the beast released from the control of the reason was the "true self." Chellis, *Wealth and Wine* (New York: National Temperance Society and Publication House, 1874), 185. H. Newell Martin, *The Human Body: An Account of Its Structure and Activities and the Conditions of its Healthy Working* (New York: Henry Holt and Co., 1912), 393.
95. Crane, *Arts of Intoxication,* 187, goes on to describe the drinking man as turning "traitor to his own nobler nature . . . He seizes upon the body, and by its abuse fills the mind with dreams and surrounds it with false lights and shadows"; or, see J. W. J. Todd, *Arthur Eustace; or, A Mother's Love: A Temperance Drama in Five Acts* (Clyde, Ohio: Ames Publishing Co., 1891), 19, in which a drunkard refers to "a monster within us that some men call 'habit.' "
96. Steele, *Hygienic Physiology,* 209. Here, Steele is approvingly citing "Dr. Richardson."
97. Ibid., 131, 132.
98. Cornyn, *Dick Wilson,* 94.
99. Lind, *Lessons in Physiology,* 240; Dobbins, "Drink Traffic in Foreign Missions," 319. One temperance poem, Hampe, "A Yellow City Tulip of the Kansas Prairies," *Bouquet,* 15, goes so far as to suggest that "When hops are scarce, brewers burn old shoe leather to use instead of it." A fictional account of adulteration is found in Baker, *A Little More Cider,* in which the self-righteous temperance advocate/cider producer is discovered to be spiking his cider with whiskey.
100. *Ramrod Broken,* 33.
101. Duis, *The Saloon,* 233.
102. C. H. Fowler, "The Sack under the Viper's Fang," *Iowa Temperance Standard,* July 15, 1869, 6.
103. This impressionistic assessment in based on the advertisements for alcoholic beverages in the Warshaw Collection of the NMAH.

104. John Lavens, "The Subscriber Would Announce to the Public" (Philadelphia, 1864), "Whiskey": Box 5, Folder 2, Warshaw Collection, NMAH.

105. "Whiskey": Box 4, Folder "Meadville, Pa. Distilling Co.," Warshaw Collection, NMAH.

106. "Whiskey": Box 8 [unprocessed], Warshaw Collection, NMAH.

107. Ibid.

108. "Wine": Box 4, Folder "Tilforo and Company," Warshaw Collection, NMAH.

109. "Beer": Box 3, Folder 24, Warshaw Collection, NMAH.

110. "Beer": Box 3, Folder 27, Warshaw Collection, NMAH.

111. Prospect Brewing Company Advertising Card (Philadelphia, n.d.), "Beer": Box 3, Folder 22; Hinkle Brewing Company Advertising Card, (Albany, N.Y., n.d.), "Beer": Box 2, Folder 44; Escapernong Wine (1890), "Wine": Box 1, Folder 38, Warshaw Collection, NMAH.

112. "Self-Respect," *Iowa Temperance Standard,* June 10, 1869, 4.

113. Milne, *Uncle Sam's Farm Fence,* 115.

114. Daphne Giles, *East and West* (New York: R. Craighead, 1853), 243; Milne, *Uncle Sam's Farm Fence,* 206.

115. Jane S. Collins, *Free At Last* (n.p.: Press of Murdoch, Kerr & Co., Inc., 1896).

116. Edwin G. Frank, "The Meriwethers of Memphis and St. Louis" (M.A. thesis, University of Memphis, 1999); Kathleen Christine Berkeley, " 'An Advocate for her Sex': Feminism and Conservatism in the Post–Civil War South," *Tennessee Historical Quarterly* 43 (1984): 390–407.

117. Minor Meriwether, *Lineage of the Meriwethers and the Minors from Colonial Times* (St Louis, Mo.: Nixon-Jones Printing Co., 1895), 103, 109.

118. Meriwether, *Lineage,* 101.

119. Elizabeth Avery Meriwether, *The Devil's Dance: A Play for the Time* (St. Louis, Mo.: Hailman Brothers Publishers, 1886).

120. Ibid., preface.

121. Elizabeth Avery Meriwether, *Black and White: A Novel* (New York: E. J. Hale and Son, 1883), 100.

122. Alongside temperance foes' fear that women reformers would merely replace the tyranny of alcohol with their own tyranny was their fear that temperance physicians would do the same. Mariana Valverde, *Diseases of the Will: Alcohol and the Dilemmas of Freedom* (Cambridge: Cambridge University Press, 1998), 47–48.

123. Meriwether, *Black and White,* 101–2.

SIX: Resolution

Epigraphs: Atchison Daily Globe, March 25, 1901, 1; *Atchison Daily Globe,* Nov. 3, 1904.

1. Janet B. Hewett, *The Roster of Union Soldiers 1861–1865* (Wilmington, N.C.: Broadfoot Publishing Company, 1999), Illinois: vol. 1, 366. William Ferman is listed in the Eighty-Ninth Infantry, Company G.

2. Testimony of Harriet Ferman, *Charles Hanewacker v. Harriet Ferman* (1894), Case Files, ISA, 50.

3. Testimony of Thomas Bailey, *Hanewacker v. Ferman.*

4. Testimony of Philena Black, *Hanewacker v. Ferman,* 250.

5. Testimony of Harriet Ferman, *Hanewacker v. Ferman,* 66.

6. Testimony of William Ferman, *Hanewacker v. Ferman,* 368.

7. Testimony of Warren Hunter, *Hanewacker v. Ferman,* 203.

8. Testimony of Henrietta Heagy, *Hanewacker v. Ferman,* 234.

9. Testimony of William Ferman, *Hanewacker v. Ferman,* 362.

10. Ibid., 362–63.

11. Ibid., 371.

12. Ibid., 339.

13. Ibid., 338, 346.

14. Jim Sanderlin, unpublished biographical sketch of William Ferman.

15. "High Carnival," *Memphis Appeal,* Feb. 14, 1872.

16. "It's None of My Business," *Iowa Temperance Standard,* May 1869, 7.

17. Testimony of Ann Wilson, *Ann J. Wilson v. Frank Booth* (1885), Bound Briefs, MSLL, 10; testimony of H. Filloon, *Frances L. Applegate v. John C. Winebrenner* (1885), 14: "Phil. struck his wife. I caught hold of him and pushed her back and they came together again, they both meant fight and both showed fight."

18. Testimony of Emma Rush, *John Siegle v. Emma Rush* (1897), Case Files, ISA, 15.

19. Testimony of Mary Eppy, *William Roth v. Mary Eppy* (1875), Case Files, ISA, 265: appellant's argument, *Jane Rafferty v. Henry Buckman and William Russell* (1877), Bound Briefs, ISLL, 13; testimony of Jane Davis, *Thomas Bates v. Jane Davis* (1873), Case Files, ISA, 33–34: "Q. Well now is it not a fact that you control that farm and have run it for two years? A. When he is sober— Q. But is it not the fact that you are the head man of the house? A. Of course, when he is intoxicated I have to take charge of the place. Q. Drunk or sober. A. No sir, when he is sober I let him take charge of it; but when he is not sober, I take charge of it and do what I can"; testimony of Warren Hunter, *Hanewacker v. Ferman,* Case Files, ISA, 203. Of course, since civil damage cases were brought for loss of support, it was in defense counsel's interest to argue that the female plaintiffs had been supporting themselves and, preferably, the drinker as well.

20. Brief and argument of defendant in error, *Michael Reget v. Caroline Bell* (1874), ISA, 5.

21. Testimony of S. E. Vane, *John Kellerman v. Phoebe Arnold* (1873), Case Files, ISA, n.p.: "He said to me that his wife was trying to drive him off."

22. Testimony of William Young, *John McEvoy v. Louise Humphrey* (1873), Case Files, ISA; testimony of Mittie Hibbard, *Mrs. Mittie Hibbard v. Henry Danley, Joseph Carroll, Edward Argast, Herman Schenk, Peter Schenk, John W. Leisy, and the William J. Lemp Brewing Co.* (1906), Case Files, ISA, 132; testimony of Harriet Ferman, *Hanewacker v. Ferman,* 73–75.

23. Ruth Bordin, *Women and Temperance: The Quest for Power and Liberty, 1873–1900* (Philadelphia: Temple University Press, 1981). Robert Griswold, "Divorce and the Legal Definition of American Manhood," in Mark Carnes and Clyde Griffen, eds., *Meanings for Manhood: Constructions of Masculinity in Victorian America* (Chicago: University of Chicago Press, 1990).

24. *Journal of the Senate of the Twenty-Seventh General Assembly of the State of Illinois* (Springfield, Ill., 1872), 174. The amendment, offered by a young Republican member from Peoria, Lucien Kerr, received eight votes. While it was probably offered in earnest, many of those who supported it went on to vote against the civil damage act, suggesting that they were attempting to derail the act by supporting an extremist amendment.

25. H[enry] An[selm] Scomp, *King Alcohol in the Realm of King Cotton* (n.p.: Blakely Printing Company, 1887), 655.

26. See, for instance, *State of Michigan Laws and Supreme Court Decisions Relating to the Manufacture, Sale, and Use of Spirituous Liquors* (Lansing, Mich., 1900), 33, §5391, Sec 13 [Compiled Laws of 1897]: "It shall not be lawful for any person . . . to sell, furnish, or give any spirituous, malt, brewed, fermented or vinous liquor to any minor, to any intoxicated person, nor to any person in the habit of getting intoxicated, nor to any Indian, nor any person of Indian descent, nor to any person when forbidden in writing to do so by the husband, wife, parent, child, guardian, or employer of such person, or by the supervisor of the township, mayor, or director of the poor, or the superintendent of the poor of the country where such person shall reside or temporarily remain."

27. Samuel W. Small, "Deliverance from Bondage: A Temperance Sermon," in Sam P. Jones, *Quit Your Meanness: Sermons and Sayings of Rev. Sam P. Jones of Georgia* (Cincinnati, Ohio: Cranston and Stowe, 1890), 491.

28. Testimony of Emma Rush, *Siegle v. Rush*, 12.

29. For more detailed descriptions of the crusades, see J. E. Stebbins, *Fifty Years History of the Temperance Cause* (Hartford, Conn.: J. P. Fitch, 1876), 310–500; Eliza Stewart, *Memories of the Crusade: A Thrilling Account of the Great Uprising of the Women of Ohio in 1873, against the Liquor Crime* (Columbus, Ohio: William G. Hubbard & Co., 1888); Jack S. Blocker Jr., *Give to the Winds Thy Fears: The Women's Temperance Crusade, 1873–1874* (Westport, Conn.: Greenwood Press, 1985), 31–51; Thomas Pegram, *Battling Demon Rum: The Struggle for a Dry America, 1800–1933* (Chicago: Ivan R. Dee, 1998), 58–65; Ruth Bordin, *Woman and Temperance: The Quest for Power and Liberty, 1873–1900* (Philadelphia: Temple University Press, 1981), 15–33; and Jed Dannenbaum, *Drink and Disorder: Temperance Reform in Cincinnati from the Washingtonian Revival to the W.C.T.U.* (Urbana: University of Illinois Press, 1984), 212–30.

30. I. Newton Pierce, *History of the Independent Order of Good Templars* (Philadelphia: Daughaday & Becker, 1869), 289, discusses a prewar attack of two hundred women on a saloon in Wisconsin. Rev. T. A. Goodwin, *Seventy-Six Years' Tussle with the Traffic* (Indianapolis, Ind.: Carlon & Hollenbeck, 1883), 9, describes a crusade of fifty hatchet- and axe-wielding girls against saloons in Winchester, Cambridge City, and Centerville, Indiana; Dannenbaum, *Drink and Disorder*, 196.

31. Blocker, *Give to the Winds*, 24, estimates that there were between 57,000 and 143,000 participants in the crusades.

32. Blocker, *Give to the Winds*, 45–46, discusses temperance crusaders' "renunciation of coercion," a formula that cannot be quite correct.

33. "The Temperance Revival in Ohio," *Harper's Weekly*, March 7, 1874, 210.

34. M. R. Lacy to Mattie, April 11, 1874[?],Porter Family Papers, Box 1, Folder 18, Mississippi Valley Collection, University of Memphis, Memphis, Tenn.

35. Stewart, *Memories*, 33, 55.

36. Stebbins, *Fifty Years*, 331.

37. James M'Closkey, *The Fatal Glass; or, The Curse of Drink: A Drama in Three Acts* (New York: Samuel French and Son, 1872).

38. Of course, this pattern of behavior was not limited to the movement against alcohol. Alison Parker, *Purifying America: Women, Cultural Reform, and Pro-Censorship Activism, 1873–1933* (Urbana: University of Illinois Press, 1997); Nicola Beisel, *Imperiled Innocents: Anthony Comstock and Family Reproduction in Victorian America* (Princeton, N.J.: Princeton University Press, 1997); and Ann Fabian, *Card Sharps, Dream Books, and Bucket*

Shops: Gambling in Nineteenth-Century America (Ithaca, N.Y.: Cornell University Press, 1990), among many others, demonstrate other instances of it. This was also one of the central ideas around which the settlement house was conceptualized.

39. Carol Mattingly, *Well-Tempered Women: Nineteenth-Century Temperance Rhetoric* (Carbondale: Southern Illinois University Press), 51–53.

40. Frances E. Willard, *Do Everything: A Handbook for the World's White Ribboners* (Chicago: Miss Ruby I. Gilbert, 1895).

41. Kari J. Winter, *Subjects of Slavery, Agents of Change: Women and Power in Gothic Novels and Slave Narratives, 1790–1865* (Athens: University of Georgia Press, 1992), 22.

42. David Reynolds, *Beneath the American Renaissance: The Subversive Imagination in the Age of Emerson and Melville* (New York: Knopf, 1988), 358.

43. Catherine Gilbert Murdock, *Domesticating Drink: Women, Men, and Alcohol in America, 1870–1940* (Baltimore, Md.: Johns Hopkins University Press, 1998), 26–27.

44. Plaintiff's declaration, *Mary Hedlund, Esther Hedlund, Gurner Hedlund, Waldo Hedlund, and Carl Hedlund, minors, by Caroline Blinn, their next friend v. Oscar Geyer, Edward G. Uihlein, and Joseph Schlitz Brewing Co.* (1907), Case Files, ISA, 5.

45. Barbara Lee Epstein, *The Politics of Domesticity: Women, Evangelism, and Temperance in Nineteenth-Century America* (Middletown, Conn.: Wesleyan University Press, 1981), 4.

46. Mary Poovey, *Uneven Developments: The Ideological Work of Gender in Mid-Victorian England* (Chicago: University of Chicago Press, 1988), 66–70.

47. Quoted in Ruth Bordin, *Frances Willard: A Biography* (Chapel Hill: University of North Carolina Press, 1986), 186.

48. *Journal of Proceedings of the Twenty-Fifth Annual Session of the Wisconsin Legislature: Assembly* (Madison, Wis.: Atwood & Culver, 1872), 236.

49. *General Laws Passed By the Legislature of Wisconsin in the Year 1872* (Madison, Wis.: Atwood & Culver, 1872), 173 (Chapter 127, Section 6).

50. Ibid., 218 (Chapter 155): "An Act to enable married women to transact business, make contracts, and sue and be sued, and to define the liabilities of husband and wife."

51. See, for instance, excerpts from a congressional debate on woman suffrage reprinted in Elizabeth Cady Stanton, Susan B. Anthony, and Matilda Joslyn Gage, eds., *History of Woman Suffrage*, vol. 2 (1881; reprint, New York: Source Book Press, 1970), 99–100, 145–54.

52. Celeste M. A. Winslow, "Over and Over," *(Marshalltown) Iowa Temperance Standard,* May 27, 1869, 2.

53. Elizabeth Avery Meriwether, *Recollections of 92 Years* (Nashville, Tenn.: Tennessee Historical Commission, 1958), 204–5.

54. Anne Firor Scott, *The Southern Lady: From Pedestal to Politics, 1830–1930* (Chicago: University of Chicago Press, 1970), 171.

55. Janet Zollinger Giele, *Two Paths to Women's Equality* (Boston: Twayne Publishers, 1995), 115, has pointed out this connection.

56. Blocker, *Give to the Winds,* 166–67.

57. "Society Events," Elizabeth Avery Meriwether Scrapbook #2, Meriwether Family Papers, Box 2, Folder 4, Mississippi Valley Collection, University of Memphis, Memphis, Tenn., 11.

58. Blocker, *Give to the Winds,* 161.

59. Mother Stewart, *Memories of the Crusade: A Thrilling Account of the Great Uprising of the Women of Ohio in 1873, Against the Liquor Crime* (Columbus, Ohio: William G. Hubbard & Co., 1888), 71.

60. Testimony of Mary Fox, *Mary Fox v. Wunderlich* (1884), Bound Briefs, ISLL, 5.

61. George Maskoff, *Last Follies: A Drama in Five Acts* (Kansas, 1890). For a further discussion of temperance foes' characterization of temperance women as unwomanly, see Mattingly, *Well-Tempered Women,* 96–120.

62. Stewart, *Memories,* 32.

63. Ibid.

64. Ibid., 36. For descriptions of crusaders as "unsexed," see Blocker, *Give to the Winds,* 75–76.

65. Gillian Brown, "Getting in the Kitchen with Dinah: Domestic Politics in *Uncle Tom's Cabin,*" *American Quarterly* 36 (1984): 503–23.

66. Elizabeth Avery Meriwether, *The Devil's Dance: A Play for the Time* (St. Louis, Mo.: Hailman Brothers, 1886), 10. This is in tension with her choice to focus *Black and White: A Novel* (New York: E. J. Hale and Son, 1883), written only three years earlier, around the figure of a female drunkard.

67. Stebbins, *Fifty Years,* 53.

68. For thorough accounts of nation's temperance activism, see Fran Grace, *Carry A. Nation: Retelling the Life* (Bloomington: Indiana University Press, 2001); and Robert Smith Bauder, *Prohibition in Kansas: A History* (Lawrence: University of Kansas Press, 1986), 133–55.

69. Carry A. Nation, *The Use and Need of the Life of Carry A. Nation* (Topeka, Kans.: F. M. Steves and Sons, 1905), 57.

70. Ibid., 60.

71. Ibid., 70.

72. Ibid., 166.

73. *Atchison Daily Globe,* Feb. 12, 1901, 1. Bader, *Prohibition in Kansas,* 144.

74. *Atchison Daily Globe,* Dec. 29, 1900, 2.

75. *Atchison Daily Globe,* Jan. 24, 1901, 4.

76. *Atchison Daily Globe,* Jan. 24, 1901, 4.

77. *Atchison Daily Globe,* Apr. 27, 1901, 4.

78. *Atchison Daily Globe,* Mar. 25, 1901, 2.

79. Ibid.

80. *Atchison Daily Globe,* Jan. 23, 1901, 4.

81. Grace, *Carry A. Nation,* 217. Bader, *Prohibition in Kansas,* 139–40.

82. Grace, *Carry A. Nation,* 246.

Essay on Sources

Because the drink debate was both massive and largely fought in print, there is an abundance of primary sources on the nineteenth-century drink debate. Both saloon supporters and (to a much greater extent) temperance reformers commissioned, wrote, and published newspapers, pamphlets, printed addresses, scientific monographs, statistical studies, histories, poems, novels, plays, sheet music, and advertisements in support of their positions. They generally printed them cheaply and often in vast quantities, so that even the smallest local public library is likely to have a few dusty and crumbling late-nineteenth-century temperance publications. The library I relied on most heavily for my published material was the Library of Congress, though I also made use of others including the Illinois State Library, the Iowa State Historical Society, the Boston Public Library, the Wisconsin State Historical Society, the Kansas State Library and Archives, the Tennessee State Library, the Newberry Library, the Milton S. Eisenhower Library at the Johns Hopkins University, the Houghton Library at Harvard University, and the Oshkosh Public Museum Archives. The Wright American fiction microfilm collection was an invaluable source of temperance fiction, and the English and American drama of the nineteenth century microfilm collection was similarly useful as a source of temperance plays. The temperance and pro-drink sheet music I used primarily came from Johns Hopkins' Lester Levy Sheet Music collection, which is now entirely available on-line. The advertisements I used were from the Warshaw collection at the Smithsonian Institution's National Museum of American History.

I found trial transcripts very useful in exploring the history of the drink debate, and particularly the history of drinking culture. Trial transcripts, including those from drink-related civil trials, have generally been preserved together with other documents relating to a particular lawsuit, in "briefs" or "case files." Too few historians have made use of these extremely valuable resources. Because the vast majority of nineteenth-century case files are housed in dusty basements in our nation's county courthouses and are poorly indexed if at all, it has generally been impractical to find and use more than a handful at a time. In most states, however, briefs of cases that were ultimately appealed to state supreme courts are indexed and housed at state archives or law libraries. I made substantial use of such records at the Illinois State Archives, the Iowa State Law Library, and the Michigan State Library, which occasionally held records from other states as well.

Saloon history and temperance history have largely existed separately. The classic of saloon history is undoubtedly Perry Duis's meticulously researched and comprehensive *The Saloon: Public Drinking in Chicago and Boston 1880–1920* (Urbana: University of Illinois Press, 1983), which deals not only with saloon life but also with the economics of saloonkeeping and with government attempts to regulate saloons. Many other books and articles, most notably Thomas Noel's *The City and the Saloon: Denver, 1858–1916* (Lincoln: University of Nebraska Press, 1982) and Roy Rosenzweig's *Eight Hours for What We Will: Workers and Leisure in an Industrial City, 1870–1920* (New York: Cambridge University Press, 1983) have treated more specific aspects of saloon industry and culture, but Duis's work remains the standard. Madelon Powers' recent book, *Faces Along the Bar: Lore and Order in the Workingman's Saloon: 1870–1920* (Chicago: University of Chicago Press, 1998), takes a more cultural approach, drawing on saloon folklore, oral histories, and literary representations of the saloon. All of these major treatments focus on urban saloons rather than on small-town saloons like those discussed in this book.

The historiography of the temperance movement is substantially larger than that of the saloon. Generally, interpretations of the history of the temperance movement have portrayed it as involved in one of three struggles: middle-class native-born Americans' competition with immigrants and the working class, women's fight for new roles and rights, and individual drinkers' struggles against the increasing regulatory power of the state. Modern scholarship on the temperance movement can best be said to have begun with the publication of sociologist Joseph Gusfield's *Symbolic Crusade: Status Politics and the American Temperance Movement* (Urbana: University of Illinois Press, 1963). *Symbolic Crusade* did more than any other monograph to shape historians' interpretation of the movement through the rest of the century. Gusfield argued that the drink debates were ultimately about participants' desire for prestige, respect, and stability. In his explanation, members of the old middle class spearheaded late-nineteenth-century temperance to allay their anxiety about their declining status. Ronald Walters' treatment of the temperance movement in *American Reformers, 1815–1860* (New York: Hill and Wang, 1978) continued this emphasis on class analysis, though with much richer contextualization.

Versions of this class-based interpretation of the temperance movement have remained important ever since, even as such interpretation has become less fashionable in other subfields. Some of the most notable works since Gusfield which have relied on class analysis are Jack S. Blocker's *Retreat From Reform: The Prohibition Movement in the United States 1890–1913* (Westport, Conn.: Greenwood Press, 1976); Harry Gene Levine's "Demon of the Middle Class: Self-Control, Liquor, and the Ideology of Temperance in 19th-Century America" (Ph.D. dissertation, University of California, Berkeley, 1978); Ian Tyrrell's *Sobering Up: From Temperance to Prohibition in Antebellum America, 1800–1860* (Westport, Conn.: Greenwood Press, 1979); and Roy Rosenzweig's *Eight Hours for What We Will.*

A second common theme in histories of temperance reform has been that of gender conflict. A number of scholars have explored the close, though at times ambiguous, relationship between temperance and woman suffrage. As early as 1944, Mary Earhart Dillon's *Frances Willard: From Prayers to Politics* (Chicago: University of Chicago Press, 1944) anticipated many of the key ideas of this field. In the early 1980s, two important books, Ruth Bordin's *Women and Temperance: The Quest for Power and Liberty, 1873–1900* (Philadelphia: Temple University Press, 1981) and Barbara Epstein's *The Politics of Domesticity: Women, Evangelism, and Temperance in Nineteenth-Century America* (Middletown, Conn.: Wesleyan University Press, 1981) explored how the movement reflected women's growing isolation in the household, how it offered women opportunities to broaden their sphere, and how it served for some as a stepping-stone to the suffrage movement. A few years later, Jack Blocker's *Give to the Winds thy Fears: The Women's Temperance Crusade, 1873–1874* (Westport, Conn.: Greenwood Press, 1985) suggested that the two had overstated gender issues, which, while significant, had to be considered as only one of many factors motivating temperance women. Nancy Hewitt's *Women's Activism and Social Change, Rochester, New York, 1822–1872* (Ithaca, N.Y.: Cornell University Press, 1984) revealed both the networks and divisions among female reformers.

One of the central issues in the gendered analysis of the temperance movement has been the extent to which temperance activism "counts" as feminism. Aileen Kraditor's classic work, *The Ideas of the Woman Suffrage Movement, 1890–1920* (New York: Columbia University Press, 1965) suggested that temperance reformers tended to rely on "expedience" rather than "justice" arguments for suffrage. More recently, Suzanne Marilley's *Woman Suffrage and the Origins of Liberal Feminism in the United States, 1820–1920* (Cambridge, Mass.: Harvard University Press, 1996) has characterized the temperance position as a "feminism of fear" oriented toward protecting women from male threats. This practical feminism was awkwardly sandwiched between earlier and later forms based on more principled grounds, such as the fundamental equality of women and men, and women's rights to have the opportunity to develop their full potentials. While temperance women objected to certain abuses of patriarchy, they were either unable or unwilling to expand their critique into an attack on patriarchy itself. Ian Tyrrell, in *Woman's World / Woman's Empire: The Woman's Christian Temperance Union in International Perspective, 1880–1930* (Chapel Hill: University of North Carolina Press, 1991, 132, 221), agrees that the WCTU "defies the label of an anti-male organization" but he argues that scholars of the temperance movement have overemphasized the distinction between "justice and expediency arguments" for woman suffrage, and that temperance women used both sorts of arguments interchangeably. The most thorough work on the relationship between the suffrage and temperance movements is Janet Zollinger Giele's *Two Paths to Women's Equality: Temperance, Suffrage, and the Origins of Modern Feminism* (New York: Twayne, 1995). More recent gender historians such as Karen Sánchez-Eppler (*Touching Liberty: Abolition, Feminism, and the Politics of the Body* [Berkeley: University of California Press, 1993]) have agreed that the temperance movement importantly shaped women's roles and rights, for better or for worse. Catherine Gilbert Murdock's *Domesticating Drink: Women, Men, and Alcohol in America, 1870–1940* (Baltimore, Md.: Johns Hopkins University Press, 1998) represents an interesting new departure in writings on the relationships among gender, drink, and temperance. Murdock focuses on the extent to which some saw alcohol as compatible with, even integral to, domesticity.

There has been less work on the relationship of the drink debate to male than to female gender roles. Some scholars have considered manhood in the saloon in their treatments of related subjects. Elliott Gorn, in *The Manly Art: Bare-Knuckle Prize Fighting in America* (Ithaca, N.Y.: Cornell University Press, 1986) for instance, often turned to saloon culture in his explorations of manhood and boxing. Only with Madelon Powers' recent *Faces Along the Bar* and, to a lesser extent, Catherine Gilbert Murdock's *Domesticating Drink*, though, has the experience of masculinity in the saloon begun to emerge as a central theme. Powers follows Gorn in seeing the saloon as a space in which urban laborers, lacking manly autonomy in the workplace, regrounded their manhood in "display[ing] an unflinching sense of personal and group honor" in their leisure time (29–30). Murdock generally agrees with Gorn and Powers about the relocation of manly identity into the leisured male sphere, while also pointing out alcohol's potential to "destroy . . . masculinity" by preventing men from fulfilling expectations of "financial success, emotional stability, and restraint" (15–16).

A third group of historians has argued that the drink debate revolved around different interpretations of the appropriate relationship between the individual and society. These historians, who tend to be least sympathetic to the movement, suggest that it was part of a larger impulse toward tighter social control in the form of both intrusive moral pressure and increasing government regulation. Roy Rosenzweig in his *Eight Hours for What We Will,* and Perry Duis in his *The Saloon,* make this argument powerfully. The most developed recent work in this tradition is Richard Hamm's *Shaping of the Eighteenth Amendment: Temperance Reform, Legal Culture, and the Polity, 1880–1920* (Chapel Hill: University of North Carolina Press, 1995).

Closely tied to this theme is the problem of "volition" in temperance and antitemperance thought. Many have argued that temperance reformers, in discussing the drunkard's loss of will, were looking nervously at their own precarious volition. Harry Gene Levine, in his influential unpublished dissertation, *Demon of the Middle Class,* argued that to a great extent temperance reformers looked inward and that "in the drunkard's struggle [they] could find lessons about universal issues of will and resolve" (136, 162). Similar points are made in Jack Blocker's *American Temperance Movements: Cycles of Reform* (Boston, Mass.: Twayne Publishers, 1989), 16; Annette Federico's " 'I Must Have a Drink': Addiction, Angst, and Victorian Realism," *Dionysos* 2 (1990): 11; and John W. Crowley's "Jays and Jags: Gender, Class, and Addiction in Howells' Landlord at Lion Head," *Dionysos* 3 (1992): 36–46.

Other scholarship of the temperance movement has noted and developed the importance of the theme of volition in the drink discourse—from John Kraut's early work, *The Origins of Prohibition* (New York: Alfred A. Knopf, 1925), through literary critic Michael Warner's important essay, "Whitman Drunk," in Betsy Erkkila & Jay Grossman, eds., *Breaking Bounds: Whitman & American Cultural Studies* (New York: Oxford University Press, 1996). Norman Clark, in his *Deliver Us From Evil: An Interpretation of American Prohibition* (New York: W. W. Norton, 1976), also understands temperance advocates to be looking inward when he argues that temperance was a struggle to buttress the "bourgeois interior" against the seemingly chaotic forces of rapid mobility and social change that assailed it. Jed Dannenbaum's *Drink and Disorder: Temperance Reform in Cincinnati from the Washingtonian Revival to the W.C.T.U.* (Urbana: University of Illinois Press, 1984), also suggests that temperance reformers were interested not only in controlling others but also in reinforcing their own self-control. The most thorough and theoretical treatment of the issue has been Mariana Valverde's *Alcohol and the Dilemmas of Freedom* (Cambridge: Cambridge University Press, 1998).

Particularly since the 1980s, a growing number of scholars have turned their attention to representations of alcohol and temperance in literature and oratory. Most, like John Crowley (*The White Logic: Alcoholism and Gender in American Modernist Fiction* [Amherst: University of Massachusetts Press, 1994]), Nicholas Warner (*Spirits of America: Intoxication in Nineteenth-Century American Literature* [Norman: University of Oklahoma Press, 1997]), Michael Warner ("Whitman Drunk"), and, recently, George Monteiro (*Stephen Crane's Blue Badge of Courage* [Baton Rouge: Louisiana State University Press, 2000]) have analyzed the treatment of alcohol by canonical authors such as Jack London, Emily Dickinson, Nathaniel Hawthorne, Walt Whitman, and Stephen Crane. John Crowley's article, "Slaves to the Bottle: Gough's *Autobiography* and Douglass's *Narrative*" in David S. Reynolds and Debra J. Rosenthal, eds., *The Serpent in the Cup: Temperance in American Literature* (Amherst: University of Massachusetts Press, 1997), was particularly influential to my understanding of temperance thought. Fewer scholars have dealt with popular temperance writings. David Reynolds's *Beneath the American Renaissance: The Subversive Imagination in the Age of Emerson and Melville* (New York: Knopf, 1988) situates canonical literature in the context of contemporary popular reformist writings. While I find that he is too dismissive of the genuine motivations and intellectual complexity of reformers, I am indebted to his extensive treatment of the "dark side" of reformist literature. Nicholas Warner's *Spirits of America*, which mainly focuses on major authors, includes a chapter on noncanonical literature. Some of the selections in Debra Rosenthal and David Reynolds's valuable collection of essays, *Serpent in the Cup* (most notably Karen Sánchez-Eppler's "Temperance in the Bed of a Child") analyze popular temperance fiction. Jon Miller's dissertation, "Prohibition and Parties: Temperance in American Literature and Culture, 1784–1855" (Ph.D. dissertation, University of Iowa, 2000), which largely but not exclusively treats canonical authors, is a fascinating study of the relationship of early-republican and antebellum temperance literature to the broader political culture.

In contrast to this wealth of writing on printed temperance literature, there are only two major works on temperance oratory: Richard Leeman's slim volume on Frances Willard, *"Do Everything" Reform: The Oratory of Frances E. Willard* (New York: Greenwood Press, 1992) and Carol Mattingly's more comprehensive monograph on nineteenth-century temperance rhetoric, *Well-Tempered Women: Nineteenth-Century Temperance Rhetoric* (Carbondale: Southern Illinois University Press, 1998). Mattingly also includes in her book a stimulating chapter on popular temperance fiction.

The field of alcohol and temperance history has progressed so substantially in the past few decades that historians of temperance have been able to focus on more specific aspects of the movement, and to use their analysis of the drink debate to make broader arguments about American culture. Jonathan Zimmerman has written a fascinating treatment of temperance pedagogy, *Distilling Democracy: Alcohol Education in America's Public Schools, 1880–1925* (Lawrence: University Press of Kansas, 1999). Alison Parker, in *Purifying America: Women, Cultural Reform, and Pro-Censorship Activism, 1873–1933* (Urbana: University of Illinois Press, 1997), deals with the Woman's Christian Temperance Union's participation in the campaign for "social purity," particularly their drive for censorship, a substantial and problematic part of the movement that has been largely ignored. Ian Tyrrell, with his *Woman's World / Woman's Empire: The Woman's Christian Temperance Union in International Perspective, 1880–1930* (Chapel Hill: University of North Carolina Press, 1991), has published a thorough story of the ambiguous global strategies of the movement, which ends up being largely a study of a woman-led imperialism.

Two topics in temperance history, however, seem strangely neglected given their significance to the movement: religion and the South. Scholars have long been aware of this problem and have made stabs at it in their writings, but few have taken either topic as a central theme. Many years back, Richard Jensen, *The Winning of the Midwest: Social and Political Conflict, 1888–1896* (Chicago: University of Chicago Press, 1971) powerfully argued that various reform movements including temperance had close ties to denominational affiliation. Thus far, no one seems to have followed up on this idea in a substantial way. Ian Tyrrell has given the religious aspects of the movement considerable attention in his work, particularly in his first monograph, *Sobering Up*. The historians who have recently done the most interesting work on religion and temperance before the Civil War are Robert Abzug in *Cosmos Crumbling: American Reform and the Religious Imagination* (New York: Oxford University Press, 1994) and Steven Mintz in *Moralists and Modernizers:*

America's Pre–Civil War Reformers (Baltimore: Johns Hopkins University Press, 1995). Fran Grace's religiously oriented biography of saloon-smasher Carry Nation, *Carry A. Nation, Retelling the Life* (Bloomington: Indiana University Press, 2001), similarly traces the interconnections between piety and reform for the progressive-era Midwest.

The neglect of the quite active Southern wing of the temperance movement may be on its way to being redressed. Ian Tyrrell wrote a review article on the topic in the 1980s ("Drink and Temperance in the Antebellum South: An Overview and Interpretation," *Journal of Southern History* 48 [1982]: 485–510) and generally makes an effort to include it in his writings. John Quist's rather daunting though quite readable monograph on antebellum reform, *Restless Visionaries: The Social Roots of Antebellum Reform in Alabama and Michigan* (Baton Rouge: Louisiana State University Press, 1998), includes a substantial chapter on the temperance movement in Tuscaloosa, Alabama. David Fahey's *Temperance and Racism: John Bull, Johnny Reb, and the Good Templars* (Lexington: University of Kentucky Press, 1996) explores the controversy about black membership in the Good Templars in the reconstruction-era South. As various dissertations on the topic appear to be in process, it seems likely that the next few years will see substantial additions to this literature.

This book is also influenced by a number of writings outside the area of drink and temperance. Most notably, it has benefited from the burgeoning field of manhood studies. Gail Bederman's *Manliness and Civilization: A Cultural History of Gender and Race in the United States, 1880–1917* (Chicago: University of Chicago Press, 1995) is an innovative treatment of the relationship of gender constructions to the rhetoric of civilization. Mary Ryan's *Cradle of the Middle Class: The Family in Oneida County, New York, 1790–1865* (Cambridge, Mass.: Harvard University Press, 1981) considers the female role in developing new meanings for manhood. Others who have written influentially about the volatility of male ideals in the nineteenth century include Anthony Rotundo (*American Manhood: Transformations in Masculinity from the Revolution to the Modern Era* [New York: Basic Books, 1993]), Mark Carnes (*Secret Ritual and Manhood in Victorian America* [New Haven, Conn.: Yale University Press, 1989]), Judy Hilkey (*Character Is Capital: Success Manuals and Manhood in Gilded Age America* [Chapel Hill: University of North Carolina Press, 1997]), Kim Townsend (*Manhood at Harvard: William James and Others* [Cambridge, Mass.: Harvard University Press, 1996]), and Scott Sandage ("Deadbeats, Drunkards, and Dreamers: A Cultural History of Failure in America, 1819–1893" [Ph.D. dissertation, Rutgers University, 1995]).

The chapter on contentment is heavily indebted to the ideas of Walter Michaels, particularly his book, *The Gold Standard and the Logic of Naturalism* (Berkeley: University of California Press, 1987). Michaels explores the economies of desire in major works of progressive-era fiction. Other treatments of the problem of desire and its tension with the ideal of contentment that have influenced this book include Judith Hilkey's work on success manuals, Scott Sandage's much-cited dissertation on failure, and most recently Shawn Michelle Smith's exemplary interdisciplinary treatment of race and visibility in U.S. culture, *American Archives: Gender, Race, and Class in Visual Culture* (Princeton, N.J.: Princeton University Press, 1999). Some scholars of the temperance movement have also treated the problem of desire, most notably Karen Sánchez-Eppler and Michael Warner. Sánchez-Eppler has argued that temperance fiction, through the language of incest, worked to designate the domestic sphere as a space of desire. Similarly, Michael Warner, in his treatment of Walt Whitman's temperance novel *Franklin Evans*, explores how intoxication served as a location for Whitman to "imagine desire no longer as self but rather as the paradigm case of heteronomy." Whereas Sánchez-Eppler focuses on the location of desire, Warner focuses on its ownership.

The literature on the closely related theme of seduction in the nineteenth century is massive. Historians who have written on the subject include Jan Lewis ("The Republican Wife: Virtue and Seduction in the Early Republic," *William and Mary Quarterly* 3rd series 44 [1987]: 689–721) and Carol Smith Rosenberg ("Domesticating 'Virtue': Coquettes and Revolutionaries in Young America," in Elaine Scarry, ed., *Literature and the Body* [Baltimore, Md.: Johns Hopkins University Press, 1988, 160–84]). Literary critics have produced the bulk of writing on the subject, however. Some of the writers whose work has been most useful to me are Katherine Cummings, who, in her *Telling Tales: The Hysteric's Seduction in Fiction and Theory* (Stanford: Stanford University Press, 1991), discusses the ambiguity of subjectivity in nineteenth-century seduction narratives; and Jenny Franchot, who wrote powerfully about the antebellum literature of priestly seduction in *Roads to Rome: The Antebellum Protestant Encounter with Catholicism* (Berkeley: University of California Press, 1994). Also useful were Elizabeth Barnes's *States of Sympathy: Seduction and Democracy in the American Novel* (New York: Columbia University Press, 1997) and Kristie Hamilton's "'An Assault on the Will': Republican Virtue and the City in Hannah Webster Foster's *The Coquette*," *Early American Literature* 24 (1989): 135–51.

The "invasion" chapter was influenced in part by treatments of the fear of losing communal autonomy due to the growth of an increasingly integrated culture in Thomas Haskell's *The Emergence of Professional Social Science: The American Social Science Association and the Nineteenth-Century Crisis of Authority* (Urbana: University of Illinois Press, 1977) and T. J. Jackson Lears's *No Place of Grace: Antimodernism and the Transformation of American Culture, 1880–1920* (Chicago: University of Chicago Press, 1994 [1981]). It is also indebted to both Gillian Brown's *Domestic Individualism: Imagining Self in Nineteenth-Century America* (Berkeley: University of California Press, 1990) and Karen Sánchez-Eppler's *Touching Liberty*. The chapter also draws upon Stephen Araata's analyses of role reversal between invader and invaded in Bram Stoker's *Dracula*, "The Occidental Tourist: Dracula and the Anxiety of Reverse Colonization," *Victorian Studies* 33 (1990): 621–45, and Eve Sedgwick's classic, *The Coherence of Gothic Conventions* (New York: Methuen, 1986).

Index